Paul S. Hirsch

THE SECRET HISTORY OF
COMIC BOOK IMPERIALISM

PULP EMPIRE

The University
of Chicago Press
Chicago and
London

Publication of this book has been aided by a grant from the Meijer
Foundation Fund.

The University of Chicago Press, Chicago 60637
The University of Chicago Press, Ltd., London
© 2021 by The University of Chicago

Published 2021
Paperback edition 2024
Printed in the United States of America

33 32 31 30 29 28 27 26 25 24   1 2 3 4 5

ISBN-13: 978-0-226-35055-4 (cloth)
ISBN-13: 978-0-226-82946-3 (paper)
ISBN-13: 978-0-226-35069-1 (e-book)
DOI: https://doi.org/10.7208/chicago/9780226350691.001.0001

Library of Congress Cataloging-in-Publication Data

Names: Hirsch, Paul S., author.
Title: Pulp empire : the secret history of comic book imperialism
/ Paul S. Hirsch.
Other titles: Secret history of comic book imperialism
Description: Chicago ; London : The University of Chicago Press,
2021. | Includes bibliographical references and index.
Identifiers: LCCN 2020044646 | ISBN 9780226350554 (cloth) |
ISBN 9780226350691 (ebook)
Subjects: LCSH: Comic books, strips, etc.—United States—History
and criticism. | Comic books, strips, etc.—Social aspects—United
States. | Comic books, strips, etc.—Political aspects—United States.
| Propaganda, American. | Literature in propaganda. | United
States—Civilization—1945-
Classification: LCC PN6725 .H57 2021 | DDC 741.5/9730904—dc23
LC record available at https://lccn.loc.gov/2020044646

♾ This paper meets the requirements of ANSI/NISO Z39.48-1992
(Permanence of Paper).

To my families—the one I was born to and the others
formed from friendship and love
And to Laura Lee and Milo—my family, my friends, my more

CONTENTS

INTRODUCTION

MAKING AN AMERICAN MONSTER

IN A DEEPLY TRIBAL SENSE, WE LOVE OUR MONSTERS. —E. O. WILSON

SECRET ORIGINS

When I was ten years old, a comic book shop owner threatened me
with a gun. And it thrilled me.

In the mid-1980s, reading and collecting comic books was deeply
uncool. Interactions with adults made clear that they deemed my interest distinctly antisocial—and they were right. Buying comic books
meant walking two miles from my home to a shop in the next town.
Wedged between a neon-lit audio store packed with off-brand car
stereos and a forlorn florist, it was a narrow, low-ceilinged shop full
of long, white cardboard boxes of old comic books. The store stank of
musty paper, sweat, and wonderful grease from a nearby pizzeria. The
owner, a hostile man whose dark hair hung past a drooping mustache,
always worked alone. He perched on a stool behind a tall counter
that nearly pinned him to an enormous corkboard on the back wall.
On it were mounted rows of expensive, mysterious old comic books
like *Blood Is the Harvest* and *Phantom Lady*. Years later, I would learn
that some of them were Frankensteined forgeries: a cover from one
copy, the interior from another, staples from a third, all meticulously
retouched, repaired, and reattached into a salable whole.

FIGURE I.1 This is the first issue I can remember seeing high up on the wall of my local comic book shop. The Catechetical Guild Educational Society published *Blood Is the Harvest*, an anticommunist propaganda title, in 1950—one of many it created for distribution through religious schools—just six years after issuing a pamphlet called *The Case against the Comics*.

Next to the owner, flat on the counter, invariably lay a briefcase. Once, when I asked if he wanted help running the store, he flipped open the briefcase and pulled out a revolver. He casually pointed the gun at the ceiling tiles, tilted his head, and said, "Nah, I've already got a helper." Then, he returned the weapon to the briefcase and with an easy smile said, "Tell all your friends!" Of course, I didn't tell a soul; I was terrified. But some small, confused bit of my ten-year-old brain was exhilarated too. To me, comic books were primal; they were about pulp, money, funky odors, and violence both on the page and in the world.

Today, the American commercial comic book has been tamed and brought into the light. Comic book culture is beyond mainstream culture—it's *American* culture. The *New York Times* reviews graphic novels, comic-themed shows proliferate on television, and one billion-dollar comic book movie after the next carries bright images of American superheroes around the world. Comic books as objects are of secondary importance, financially and culturally, to the films derived from their contents by entertainment behemoths like Disney and Warner Brothers. Yet these comic books, which initially occupied the dark periphery of the New York publishing world and were often created by poorly paid Jewish American, African American, and Asian American men and women alike, now inform the very heart of that most public, wealthy, and racially oblivious American cultural center: Hollywood. Comic book culture no longer lurks on the periphery; it lies at the very core of our shared visual vocabulary. The comic book, whether in the form of a collectible vintage title, action figure, Halloween costume, graphic novel, or film, is the epitome of American popular media at home and abroad.

It was not always so.

In the years after World War II, comics were seen as a virus: a cultural disease that spread among the young, the poor, and the dim. In America, comic books depicted the darkest, most rudimentary expressions of violence, sex, and xenophobia in the national consciousness—and these traits fueled an anti–comic book campaign, anti–comic book legislation, congressional hearings, and eventually a strict, self-imposed censorship code. Internationally, these same comic books showed the world that American society was racist, gruesomely violent, and soaked in sex. Wherever commercial comic books traveled at midcentury, they tarnished the image of the United States. Titles like *Spectacular Adventures*, *Murder, Inc.*, and *Fight against Crime* depicted a shadowy culture in which criminals thrived, innocents were routinely murdered, and racism, remarkably, was even more grotesque than newspapers reported. Peppered among these stories were advertisements for bogus medicines, cheap weapons, and vibrators. Together, these contents offered global consumers a brutish image of postwar America: a modern society beset by primitive problems and a lack of concern for its young.

Even from a distance of more than sixty years, within a culture shaped and numbed by horrific violence both real and fictional, endless digitized pornography, and unremitting racism, these comic books retain the power to shock. The first panel of a "true crime" story in *Crime Must Pay the Penalty* from 1948 depicts a handsome, well-dressed young man named James Wayburn Hall—"The Red-Headed Monster"—smashing the back of a woman's head with a large wrench. Six panels later, Hall seizes an old-fashioned telephone and uses it to beat an older woman to death before robbing her bloody corpse. When he finds only seventy dollars, the young man mutters, "Seventy lousy bucks for all that trouble. If I'd known that I'd have kicked her ugly pan in." Two pages later, Hall pummels a man to the ground before shooting two gaping, gory holes in his back. Needing transportation, Hall makes his way toward a nearby road, where a truck driver stops to see if Hall needs help. After accepting a ride, Hall shoots the driver in the back, laughing, "I don't need you any longer, sucker!" The next man to offer a ride to Hall dies too, his face beaten in with the butt of a revolver before he is shot in the head. Blood oozes from his shattered face and mouth and the bullet hole in the center of his forehead. Hall burns the corpse, complaining that this victim, too, has caused him too much trouble for too little money.[1]

The cover of a comic book called *The Killers*, published the same year, shows two Middle Eastern men, hairy, shirtless, and simian,

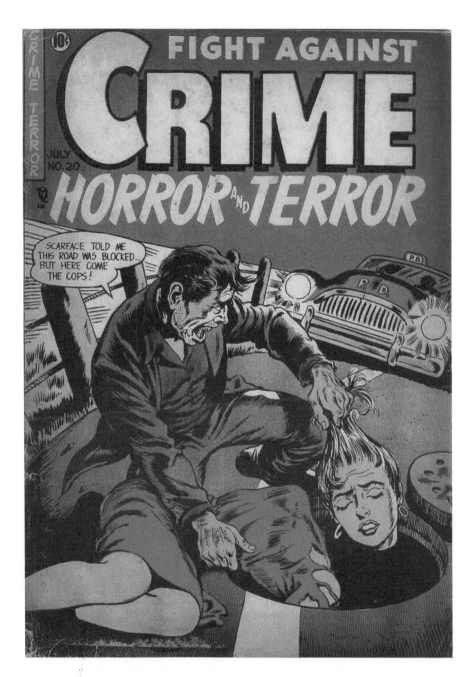

FIGURE I.2 The cover of this 1954 issue of *Fight against Crime* presents postwar America as a dark and vicious place—the very opposite of the national image federal propagandists tried to promote around the world.

inside a bloodred room. On the left is a shadow of a man hanged by his neck. Next to it, in the doorway, one of the killers laughs, a curved sword above his head, about to strike. Before him, on his knees, a lighter-skinned man pleads for his life. In the foreground, the other killer gloats as he chokes to death, with his bare hands, an ashen-faced victim.[2] In a 1952 issue of *T-Man*, US Treasury agent Pete Trask travels to Iran to investigate a communist spy ring. In one scene, a White character calls an Iranian "rag-head." Later, in the process of battling the communist spies, Trask punches a British diplomat, dismisses an Iranian as "fatty," and mocks an angry Iranian official, laughingly telling him to "Take it up with Washington—see how far you get!"[3]

Between World War II and the mid-1960s, American policy makers and propagandists played a vital role in shaping the contents of commercial and propaganda comics. Comic books, particularly violent crime-themed titles, were political media that affected American diplomacy and global perceptions of the United States. Conversely, political events and imperatives influenced the form, content, and distribution of comic books. To really understand this requires grappling with comic books' political and cultural signif-icance, at home and abroad, during the mid-twentieth century. At that time, comic book writers and artists were remarkably free from external supervision. Publishers sold nearly a billion comic books every month, some translated into more than a dozen languages, while American companies, soldiers, tourists, and diplomats trans-mitted many millions globally, distributing comic books wherever the machinery of World War II or the Cold War was found.

The comic book is uniquely powerful. Relatively uncensored, enormously popular around the world, and characterized by the remarkable diversity of its creators and consumers, the American commercial comic book can show us aspects of US policy making during the mid-twentieth century that no other object can. Addition-ally, state-sanctioned propaganda comic books from the same period can tell us much about the cultural Cold War, American imperialism, and how the federal government looked at western Europe and the decolonizing world. This book offers a fresh perspective on the connections between the political and strategic demands for victory in World War II and the Cold War and the appropriation of the comic book medium to achieve these goals, particularly in parts of the world where the United States was seen as racist and culturally oppressive.

The comic book industry burst into existence in the early 1930s; from the beginning, the product was wildly popular. Collectively, publishers sold first tens and then hundreds of millions of comic books every year between 1940 and 1955. They were available to anyone, of any age, at newsstands, drugstores, and markets. Comics were everywhere—in schools, in waiting rooms, in the back seats of cars, beneath children's beds, and wedged between the pages of textbooks. They could be found even in the trenches of the Nevada desert where troops huddled during postwar atomic tests.[4] Yet they were also inseparable from the growth of American activity abroad in this time. Wherever servicemen went during World War II, huge quantities of comic books followed, supplied by the military or sent from home and frequently containing covert, state-sponsored propaganda narratives and images. At the end of the war, servicemen left these comics behind, in local hands. During the high Cold War, members of the military carried comic books throughout the global archipelago of American military outposts. As in World War II, many of these uncensored titles remained at those far-flung locales, read and reread by locals.

During World War II, comic books benefited from the straightforward patriotism and racist imagery within their pages. They were considered harmless—if unsophisticated—pro-American entertainment for soldiers and civilians engaged in a brutal, total, and race-based war against fascism. By 1943, their simplicity even attracted the attention of wartime propaganda agencies like the Writers' War Board (WWB), which saw in the comic book a means of delivering propaganda to a vast and diverse audience. Comic books were entertaining and easy to read, and their lack of censorship meant they could depict extreme violence, racism, and nationalism. Even better, because of their crudity, bold advertisements, and fantastic narratives, comic books also seemed an unlikely vessel for state-sanctioned messages. The WWB capitalized on this perception of comic books as the very opposite of traditional state-sponsored propaganda material. It created stories and characters to shape popular opinions on controversial topics like race relations, then camouflaged them within the comic book's bright colors and simple dialogue. By cooperating with agencies like the WWB and enthusiastically embracing the concept of total war, comic book publishers burnished their patriotic credentials while gaining millions of new readers.

The goodwill built up by the comic book industry during World War II did not survive long, however, in the very different atmosphere of the Cold War. Patriotism was no longer so straightforward an affair; it was difficult to tell heroes from enemies. Accustomed to the safety afforded by the oceans separating them from Europe, Americans now saw dedicated, powerful subversives—both real and imagined—in their midst. They were known by a variety of names—fellow travelers, pinkos, stooges, and useful idiots—and seemed to lurk everywhere, from the roughest union halls to the highest levels of the federal government. Fearful that the entertainment industries were also riddled with communists eager to poison young and impressionable minds, the FBI investigated screenwriters, musicians, actors, and even comic book makers. Soon, ordinary Americans began to think of themselves as participants in a titanic battle between capitalism and a malevolent, resourceful opponent.

By the late 1940s, popular perceptions of the comic book began shifting. What had once been dismissed or even embraced as a harmless, if violent, diversion was now something much more ominous. Communists in the State Department, Soviet spies seeded throughout America's atomic infrastructure, and fellow travelers in the entertainment industries—they all highlighted the vulnerability of Americans. Comic books both reflected and fueled this sensation, as the earnest patriotism of superhero titles became passé, and consumers turned to violent, sexualized, and challenging comics in new genres like true crime and horror. As significant as the imagery itself were the men and women involved. During the war, comics were full of Japanese soldiers and supervillains torturing or killing White American heroes. But this new wave of crime- and horror-themed titles featured White men, women, and even children burning, stabbing, and robbing each other. And at a time when the United States desperately sought allies in the decolonizing world, these comics also offered scenes of vicious racism and cruelty to a global audience.

The contents of commercial comics eventually triggered a series of diplomatic problems for the United States, particularly among its most vital NATO allies. American comics became synonymous with cruelty, violence, and greed. They were a threat to local cultures and young minds. At home, they raised fears that comics led to juvenile delinquency and encouraged a vast and diverse community of anti–comic book crusaders. The comic book, in short, was a domestic and global embarrassment. And yet, government agencies like the Federal Civil Defense Administration, CIA, and State Department recognized the medium's potential for delivering propaganda, both within the United States and around the world. They shipped tens of millions of comic books abroad, and to the nations of the decoloniz-ing world in particular. Policy makers hoped to appropriate the most dangerous traits of the comic book form—its wide appeal, graphic imagery, affordability, and portability—to win allies in the wars against totalitarianism. This was a decision driven overwhelmingly by the matter of race. Non-White populations, it was believed, were eager to read, and susceptible to, American comic books.

What resulted was a pulp empire—a complex and fluid network of interactions among comic books, America's mid-twentieth-century imperialism, and its crusades at home and abroad against fascism and communism. This empire, created by comic books, shows that Cold War diplomacy, culture, and race were a single cultural com-plex; these concepts were all intertwined and blended together, not artificially separated. Within the pulp empire, the power of comic books—and by extension all American popular culture—is real and quantifiable. Here we can see that the comic book is an essential link between numerous events and crises on several continents, across twenty-five critical years of the twentieth century. At its core, in the pulp empire, the comic book is not a collectible or an artistic object: it is a political publication co-opted by government agencies as diverse as the CIA and the New York State Committee on Mental Health. Looking at comic books this way brings us to a new interpretation of American diplomacy during World War II and the high Cold War.

The legacy of the pulp empire was, ironically, created by some of the least influential people in American society: the men and women employed in the comic book industry. Yet the products they created significantly shaped global perceptions of the United States. At the same time, men and women from across the political spectrum in Western Europe and the decolonizing world banded together to reject American commercial comics as particularly grotesque products of American cultural imperialism. They saw these works by relatively powerless Americans as the very embodiment of American cultural authority. Their protests, in turn, influenced domestic and international federal policies toward the comic book.

The pulp empire, as a kind of history, is premised on two ideas: not only that diplomacy and popular culture are connected but also that the American government deliberately used popular culture in its pursuit of victory in World War II and the Cold War. Critics and propagandists alike believed that comic books could create specific meanings, tailored to their audience, and that the process of manufacturing that meaning could be controlled. Policy makers clearly saw the comic book as a significant cultural form and a new kind of weapon—commercial comic books could damage US policy goals, but propaganda comic books could shore them up. Similarly, domestic critics like Dr. Fredric Wertham decried the medium as loathsome and brutalizing ephemera but in the process acknowledged its powerful capability to generate meaning and motivation within the minds of readers.[5] By reading comics, people came to the political or cultural conclusions that writers and artists had embedded in them and made them their own. Or so it was said, despite a remarkable lack of evidence.

Neither the government nor private industry conducted scientific evaluations of how, or even if, consumers produced meaning—let alone the intended meaning—from comic book narratives. Instead, they took the medium's immense popularity to signify that con-

FIGURE I.3   In 1952, one governmental printing office published over one hundred thousand copies of this anticommunist propaganda comic book, *The Korea Story*, in Turkish. It appeared in many other languages as well. Federal propagandists appreciated the ease with which they could translate comic books into a variety of languages for distribution around the world.

sumers either were passively influenced by the images and texts in commercial comic books or actively manufactured meaning from them. The language of comics was so simple, and the pictures so demonstrative, they argued, that even (or especially) a child could absorb the messages embedded by writers and artists and then act on them. In accordance with this understanding of comic book readers as either receptive sponges or highly suggestible actors, critics aimed to save readers from themselves, while propagandists sensed a new cultural weapon in the battle for hearts and minds.

At the outset of the comic book industry, comics were revolution-ary media: they offered new, exciting, and relatively uncensored fantasies of strength, violence, and sexuality. By the mid-1950s, how-ever, they were tamed and controlled. Scholars like Stuart Hall have described the creation and consumption of popular culture as an ongoing battle between containment and resistance. Those in power work to restrain the impulses of the people "outside the walls," the men and women who lack that sort of formal authority.[6] The state thus applies the full weight of inertia and tradition in an effort to retain control over popular expression, while cultural workers try to destroy and reinvent existing, conservative forms of expression.

The American comic book, distinctively, both confirms this model and shatters it. The American government and its supporters—the State Department, local and state officials, members of Congress, public intellectuals, and concerned adults—came to see the uncen-sored commercial comic book as a radical and destructive menace to individual consumers and the American imperial project. Racist, violent, and sexual comic books made a mockery of American claims to cultural supremacy and virtue, both domestically and interna-tionally. They were a dangerous embarrassment at a time when the United States sought to present itself to the world as a kinder, more cultured alternative to totalitarianism.

Within the pulp empire, the struggle between conservation and destruction is blurred. American elites sought to do more than tame the comic book; they wanted to appropriate its power for their own purposes, in what they tended to call "cartoon booklets" or "picture pamphlets." Propagandists valued the comic book as a unique cultural form, one that posed an opportunity for, as well as a challenge to, American cultural hegemony.

TRASH—DON'T PICK IT UP!

In 1973, the New York Dolls, a band made up of outer-borough immigrants and misfits, released a single called "Trash," a glorious, catchy swirl of a song. A live version opens with drummer Jerry Nolan's croaking scream of "One, two, three, four!" Half an instant later, singer David Johansen and guitarist Johnny Thunders explode in a chant of "Trash—go pick it up!" as the band bursts into three minutes of joyful noise. The lyrics flash images of romance, violence, and doubt. So many times while writing this book or reading documents and pre-code comic books, I heard "Trash" in my head. It is easy to imagine a parent in the early 1950s looking at piles of sexual, violent comics in their child's room and shrieking, "Trash!" just like the New York Dolls. It is equally easy to imagine that puzzled child looking up at her parent and asking, "So?"

Of course comic books are trash. They are art and popular culture and trash all at once. There is no shame in acknowledging them as such. Trash is wonderful; it is free from the expectations and restrictions weighing down "higher" culture. It is distinct from garbage culture. Both trash culture and garbage culture are designed to provide instantaneous, temporary satisfaction. But trash culture has value beyond money, and it survives; it floats to the top of our popular consciousness, while garbage culture simply sinks. One is sticky, the other slippery. There is something compelling about trash, something significant beyond the limits imagined by, or imposed on, its creators. Trash can surprise, terrify, and repel, and trash can enchant. Garbage culture is disposable, but trash culture is ephemeral. It can last a moment or imprint itself for years. More than a decade removed from his childhood, John Genzale, a kid from Queens, was inspired by a comic book character to change his name to Johnny Thunders. Perhaps it also pushed him to write an ode to trash and to scream along with David Johansen, "Trash—go pick it up!"

To millions of consumers around the world, comic books were and are wonderful trash—culture designed for a particular moment that survives many decades beyond. We read and reread comic books; we entomb them in plastic coffins; we remember them. This elusive power partially explains the American government's fascination with the medium. Had federal policy makers and propagandists probed a bit deeper, though, they might have learned that consumers do not necessarily extract intended meanings from comics. It is precisely this flexibility that elevates comic books to the level of trash rather than garbage culture; we find whatever we seek within comics: momentary distraction, comedy, terror, arousal, or something longer lasting and profound.

Describing the comic book as trash takes away none of its undeniable substance. And at the mid-twentieth century comics were very influential, uniquely American trash. Comics were an indispensable, state-sanctioned weapon against fascism and communism. They were simultaneously considered antisocial, quasi-fascist, and stupefying. Comics were so popular that people across Europe, Latin America, Asia, and the Middle East clamored for issues. And comics were also nearly invisible—their ubiquity functioned as camouflage, permitting for a time the distribution, in their pages, of grotesque, disturbing, and shocking images. Consumers demanded so many millions of comics that both readers and critics could find nearly anything they wanted in the resulting flood of culture. They were wonderful, terrible, ephemeral, important trash. Wertham and the anti–comic book crusaders on both sides of the Atlantic won only a temporary victory against the medium. What they managed to condemn as harmful garbage is now embraced as entertaining, compelling, and culturally significant.

Beyond the piles of documentary evidence, the nearly unavoidable presence of comic book characters in our culture, almost seventy years after a censorship code all but snuffed out the industry, is a testament to its strength. Comic book trash has spawned literal and metaphorical empires: initially as an instrument of American imperialism, and now as the creative engine behind the most globally visible and valuable form of American culture, the superhero blockbuster. The origin stories of Superman, Batman, Captain Amer-

FIGURE 1.4 Consumers referred to titles like this one, depicting an exaggerated female form, as "headlight comics." Some of the most memorable *Phantom Lady* covers—including this one from 1948—were drawn by Black artist Matt Baker and feature bondage imagery.

ica, and Iron Man are known to even the most casual consumers. My seven-year-old son has never seen a live-action superhero movie yet somehow knows the name of Thor's realm, the origin of Batman's sidekick, and the material used to make Captain America's shield. He might stumble over the names of characters from books we've read recently but remembers people and stories from comics read to him a year ago.

Comics are sticky; their impact lingers. It is why grown men and women collect, treasure, and even fetishize them. They hold meaning far beyond monetary value. Contrast this with the significance today of Wertham's research or postwar European fears that comic book violence would warp their youth. The concerns of an entire continent have disappeared from the story of the Cold War. Fairly or not, Wertham is remembered, where he is remembered at all, as a small-minded censor and villain. His complex life and unstinting support for progressive people and causes are largely forgotten. This is the power of trash.

Before the United States entered World War II, comics were enormously popular, but few thought they were important. They were everywhere, and yet they were nowhere; until the demands of wartime and imperialism made their contents into a political, global issue, comics went largely unnoticed by cultural critics, concerned parents, and religious groups at home and abroad. Their very status as disposable, juvenile culture freed them from the scrutiny paid to middlebrow publications. Comics were classless media: they appealed to people across the social striations of gender, race, class, and religion. This perception changed as the military, political, and cultural authority of the United States increased during the 1940s. Internationally, critics across the political spectrum cited the remarkable popularity of comic books as evidence of American cultural imperialism.

Despite the comic book's broad popularity and its use of adult themes and imagery, it was still widely considered a children's medium. Articles asked, "Are comics bad for children?"[7] Newspaper stories referred to "boys and girls" comic books, "the humble comic book for children," the "simplicity" of comic book artwork, and

children's comic book consumption habits.[8] In 1944, the Child
Study Association of America estimated that children consumed 70
percent of the twenty million comic books sold each month.[9] The
view of comics as strictly juvenile was rooted in their origins and
early successes, rather than its mass-produced and radically new
contents. In one early attack on the industry, a 1940 editorial titled
"A National Disgrace," critic Sterling North shamed parents for
permitting their vulnerable children to read comics. A 1941 *New York
Times Magazine* article noted that "the harmful influence of 'comic'
books" had already come under "vigorous" criticism from teachers
and parents.[10] These critiques, however, largely focused on the comic
book's shortcomings as a form, rather than on its contents. Even
North, who attacked comic narratives as "sadistic drivel," did not
single out a specific genre for criticism; he faulted the entire medium
as primitive and numbing: "Badly drawn, badly written and badly
printed—a strain on young eyes and young nervous systems. Their
crude blacks and reds spoil the child's natural sense of color."[11]

Josette Frank, of the Child Study Association of America,
dismissed criticism of the comic book as an overreaction: "There's
really nothing so new about the problem. Twenty years ago the
'funny sheets' in the Sunday papers were the target." Dr. S. Harcourt
Peppard, of the Department of Education, agreed, telling parents,
"Please let your children read the comics, and please—sometimes—
read them yourselves."[12]

Comic books were inseparable from the physical machinery of
World War II and the Cold War: they traveled abroad with soldiers,
with tourists, and through government agencies. They respected
neither borders nor local tastes and, to critics, proved quite capable
of infecting children and adults wherever American power left its
mark. To examine mid-twentieth-century history through comic
books is to see clear, undeniable connections between popular
culture and diplomacy, between race and propaganda, and between
an unfiltered, uncontrolled strain of American media and global
perceptions of American society. Through these people and their
agendas, we can come to see the American comic book in a new
way—it is not a juvenile medium, but one bound up with the hopes,

fears, and goals of its creators, American propagandists, and a global network of consumers. Together, these people, through comic books, shaped American diplomacy and policy making during the mid-twentieth century.

THE POWER OF POPULAR CULTURE

In 2006, I was studying nuclear weapons proliferation and interning at the Los Alamos National Laboratory. It was a heartbreaking path, and after years of nightmares and anxiety attacks stemming from my research, I sought advice from my father. He, too, suffered from nightmares of nuclear destruction. He told me of his memories of "duck and cover" drills during his childhood in Jersey City. Did he, I asked, ever believe that cowering under a desk would save him from the hydrogen bomb? Of course not. Even at age ten, he understood that what teachers told him about civil defense were well-intentioned fictions. He knew better, he said, because he read huge quantities of comic books full of violence and apocalyptic imagery. Such scenes appeared over and over, across a variety of genres and titles. Yet he felt that comic books were, above all, a lot of fun and that even gloomy narratives were entertaining. He didn't feel he had received specific messages from comics as much as a general feeling that some titles reflected the realities of his life.

The comic books that my father read were low-quality objects hastily printed on cheap, dull paper and sometimes difficult to read. Critics complained that the combination of poor printing and small type in commercial comic books caused eyestrain. The distribution and transmission of comic books were equally murky. Publishers created dozens of companies that existed in name only, often to skirt postal regulations and, eventually, to distance themselves from their products. The distribution system was arcane as well, difficult to understand even today. The biggest player in the field, the American News Company, distributed comic books to newsstands, drugstores, and small convenience or candy stores. Subsidiary branches outside of New York did business under a variety of names, such as the Great Western News Company and the International News Company, which handled the company's sizable overseas business in comic books and magazines. Abroad, propaganda comics traveled along similarly confusing distribution systems. In Latin America, the United States Information Agency (USIA) circulated anticommunist comics not at its displays or cultural exchanges but through discreet, "highly ingenious" methods. These included furnishing comic books at labor union meetings and stuffing comic books into customers' bags at food markets.[13]

Once purchased and consumed by its owner, a comic book took on a second, shadow life. It could be passed from child to child at school, dropped and retrieved on buses and trains, left for months in a dentist's waiting room, and read over and over until it fell apart. In this sense, comics were, literally, consumer culture: men and women read and transmitted them until they were consumed. The very design of commercial comic books suggested that the reader was expected to destroy them. They contained coupons to be cut out, full-page pinups to be ripped from the binding, and fold-in artwork on the inside back cover. By reading and engaging with a comic book, an individual or group of readers could tear it to bits. Parents who would have recoiled if a child shredded a book surely took no notice when their children tore up comic books. Comic books were the epitome of disposable culture, if they were considered culture at all. This apparent ability to hide in plain sight and travel from reader to reader across classrooms, bases, and bedrooms created a fear among critics that comic book narratives, traveling on dark pathways, might undermine the authority of teachers, parents, and policy makers.

As part of a two-pronged effort to quash the threat posed by dark commercial comic books abroad, federal agencies produced their own imperial, pro-American and anticommunist titles. The USIA, its predecessor agencies, and the State Department used comic books directly as cultural and strategic weapons in efforts as diverse as Operation Mongoose—a CIA-led program to overthrow Fidel Castro—and a long-term effort to promote cooperation between American diplomacy and private corporations, uniting commerce, policy making, and propaganda. What connected all the government's

FIGURE I.5 This image from a 1950 issue of *Spectacular Adventures*, with its depiction of a dark-skinned man selling a white woman, was the sort that posed problems for US policy makers and propagandists during the Cold War. The global distribution of comics like this one frustrated their efforts to present US-style democracy as a more sophisticated, inclusive alternative to Soviet-style communism.

efforts in this area was an unshakable belief in the fundamental comprehensibility of the comic book form and its unique appeal to less educated and non-White audiences. At the same time, the government sought to keep comics away from the White citizens of western and northern Europe, minimizing the embarrassment that might stem from its use of such a lowbrow medium. Comics lurked alongside pulps, pornography, and dime novels at the bottom of the cultural ladder. The racism, sexism, violence, and advertisements within their pages seemed actively opposed to the idea, promoted by the state, that the United States was modern and egalitarian. In response, federal agencies wasted little time appropriating elite forms of expression, including abstract expressionism and jazz music, to frame the United States as a more sophisticated alternative to the Soviet bloc and socialist realism.[14] The State Department enlisted musicians, modern dancers, and clothing designers, among others, in widely publicized global tours. It sought to associate the United States with modern sophistication, not *Modern Romance*.

During World War II and the early Cold War, commercial American comics were revolutionary: they entertained, thrilled, and outraged diverse audiences around the world, and they did so in defiance of the creative and distributive limits imposed on other forms of popular culture. In the hands of government propagandists, and in the wake of the comic book code, the medium became much more conservative—but no less significant. The first half of this book traces the creation of the comic book and its initial appropriation by wartime agencies and public intellectuals—that is, the formation and the beginning stages of the pulp empire. In that time, state intervention legitimized the comic book industry and created millions of new adult comic book consumers. The second half of the book focuses on the effects of this transformation, beginning with the postwar explosion in the popularity of violent, racist, and highly sexualized comic books and their global distribution through conventional commercial channels and America's far-flung Cold War network of military bases. This expansion of America's pulp empire triggered cultural, political, and diplomatic crises both at home and abroad. Nevertheless, federal agencies believed the comic book to be uniquely well suited to winning hearts and minds, particularly in the decolonizing world. As a result, they revolutionized and expanded the production of propaganda comic books, using them to battle communism and promote American-style consumerism.

At every point along this historical arc, the American comic book was bound up with matters of race and capitalism. Every decision made by federal agencies was, at its core, shaped by these two issues. And at every point political demands and policy priorities shaped the comic book industry and the medium's contents, both in commercial and propaganda titles. This intervention transformed the comic book into a political object and a weapon deployed around the world. The American comic book is inseparable from foreign policy, the great twentieth-century battles between capitalism and totalitarianism, and the political goals of the world's preeminent military and cultural power. The history of the American comic book is a story of visual culture, commerce, race, and policy. These four fields are analogous to the four colors used to print comic books: cyan, magenta, yellow, and black. They lie atop one another, smearing, blending, and bleeding to create a complete image. To separate them is to disassemble a coherent whole and to shatter a picture that in its entirety shows us how culture and diplomacy were entangled during the mid-twentieth century.

THE EARLY YEARS, 1935-1945

The period from 1935 to 1945 was defined by images of darkness and light. The comic industry itself—populated by otherwise unemployable immigrants, racial minorities, and political radicals—emerged from the shadows of the New York publishing world. In the mid-1930s, early comic books built on the sensibilities and style of newspaper comic strips like *Flash Gordon* and *Tarzan* and the crisp, fast-paced stories in mystery- and adventure-themed pulps like *Black Mask* and *Doc Savage*. These bold and incorruptible pulp heroes acted on behalf of the helpless and disenfranchised, meting out vengeance according to their own moral codes. Newspaper comic strips and pulps, though, were ephemeral; their stories and artwork appeared only once before landing in a trash can or a fishmonger's store. This changed in 1933, when the Eastern Color Printing Company produced *Funnies on Parade*, a collection of reprinted comic strips. Although intended as a promotional giveaway, *Funnies on Parade* hinted at a secondary market for newspaper comic strips, if suitably repackaged. Similar titles followed, and when publishers ran short of reprinted material, they bought new artwork and stories.

By 1938, both "the economics and the poetics" of the comic book form were set: the young and marginalized creators in New York City were organized into shops (what one early contributor termed the "artistic ghetto"), where their unfettered creativity was channeled through assembly-line techniques to produce sequential artwork, which was packaged and sold at ten cents for sixty-four pages of text and images.[15] From the outset, this combination of modern, industrial-scale production, uncensored talent, and low cost proved successful.[16] Typical early comic books sold between two hundred thousand and four hundred thousand copies per issue, while initial issues of *Action Comics*, starring Superman, reached sales of nearly one million copies each. Soon, dozens, then hundreds of new titles altered the geography of the newsstand, flooding it with bright, cheaply produced tales of superheroes, fantasy, and mystery. The comic book combined elements of existing mass culture—pulps, comic strips, and films—into something new: a medium with wide appeal and enormous popularity that became associated almost immediately with young consumers. The comic book was far more complex than simple juvenile ephemera or a straightforward physical expansion of the newspaper comic strip. It was an uncensored space where writers and artists could voice their own fantasies and fears and a way for consumers to access images of violence, sexuality, and fantasy unavailable in more traditional media.

Unusually for the time, people of all kinds, including Jews, Asian Americans, and African Americans, produced comics. Joe Kubert, a Jewish, Polish-born artist, recalled, "You could be a genius, you could be a nobody, a little kid from Brooklyn like me, or some kind of nut. The doors were open to any and all."[17] Artist Edd Ashe remembered working with Chinese and Japanese Americans who specialized in lettering dialogue in comic books.[18] Matt Baker, a Black artist from North Carolina, quickly established his expertise with "headlights"— comics focused on the female form. Artist and editor Al Feldstein, who worked next to Baker, recollected, "He could draw women— white women!—like nobody else."[19]

While the early comic book industry offered opportunities to writers and artists, it also extracted productivity from these men and women in ways that recalled the piecework laborers of New York City's garment district. In assembly-line studios, exploitative bosses paid by the page within a work-for-hire system in which artists and writers surrendered all rights to their creations and typically labored in anonymity. Nick Cardy, an artist in the Eisner-Iger shop, one of the earliest and most successful comic book content producers, said, "My mother used to work in a sweatshop making pants. Well, we made comics."[20] The early comic book industry, then, provided a means of employment to marginalized men and women but also exploited their creativity and vulnerability, while shop owners and publishers benefited from the medium's increasing popularity.

Not all early owners were capitalists. The "social idealist" and "bona fide communist" Lev Gleason, who left Eastern Color Printing in 1941, ran his company cooperatively with two editors, Charles Biro and Bob Wood.[21] Like other publishers, he hired Asian American artists, including Bob Fujitani and Fred Kida, and he also hired female writers like Virginia Hubbell.[22] Soon after founding his studio, Gleason encouraged his editors to create and produce a comic book that might attract the growing adult audience. They decided that a true crime–themed title would stand out among the dozens of superhero comics and named it *Crime Does Not Pay*. For Biro, truth and violence were inseparable; the reality of a criminal act was bound up in its brutality, which he insisted on depicting in lavish detail. Gleason and Biro's stories also portrayed the effects of unregulated capitalism, critiquing a society in which wealth, violence, and corruption inevitably lured Americans from a more responsible path. Within *Crime Does Not Pay*, the social systems of mid-twentieth-century America— families, schools, and communities—all failed to dampen the lure of profit. And while criminals inevitably faced a violent death or punishment in the title's final panels, the preceding pages suggested that dying young as a wealthy criminal might be preferable to living as a poor American.

But it was not only true crime comics that were full of the sort of violence, cynicism, and racism absent from newspaper comic strips. As early as 1938, in an adventure in *Amazing Mystery Funnies*, teenaged hero Dirk the Demon stabs an older villain to death with a knife, before seizing another criminal and announcing, "Now I'll just bang your head on the floor—pleasant dreams!"[23] In an issue of *Mystery Men Comics* from 1940, spies gun down FBI agents, and wild men choke women to death. Chinese villain Chen Chang "plots with fiendish wiles against the white race he hates" and tortures "worthless white man" Richard Kendall, his heroic opponent.[24] Even stories intended to combat racism, published by the progressive Gleason, included vicious images of non-White characters. In "The Lesson of Dr. Boggs," drawn by Dick Briefer—who also drew for the communist *Daily Worker*—the White Pirate Prince frees a group of enslaved Black people and attempts to sail them back to freedom in Africa. But the men and women speak in a singsong dialect and prove helpless without the aid of the prince. The prince and the liberated Africans are confounded by the evil Dr. Boggs, whose crew includes an Asian villain, replete with bright yellow skin, long mustache, and queue.[25]

Even the early adventures of Superman, who premiered in *Action Comics* in 1938, depicted the superhero as short-tempered and pessimistic. The character's young cocreators, writer Jerry Siegel and artist Joe Shuster, drew inspiration from science fiction and crime pulps, and in his initial appearances, Superman acts much like a superpowered Sam Spade, bound as much by street morality as the rule of law.[26] In his first adventure, Superman hurls an abusive husband through a wall, shouting, "You're not fighting a woman, now!" Then, while trying to save an innocent woman from the electric chair, Superman smashes his way into the governor's mansion, roughs up the governor's assistant, and when faced with a gun, screams, "Put away that toy. This is no time for horseplay!" Later, when investigating corruption in Congress, Superman drags a recalcitrant suspect by his foot, pulls him out a window, and threatens to electrocute him unless he talks. After a squad of crooks fruitlessly tries to machine-gun Superman, one thug exclaims, "He won't die!" Superman replies, "Glad I can't say the same about you," and then hurls the crooks out a window, their machine guns wrapped around their necks.[27]

Crime Does Not Pay and *Action Comics*, along with countless other titles, could include such graphic imagery and cynicism because, unlike movies and radio, they were unregulated and uncensored. But they were also disreputable, ranking, as Bradford Wright notes, just above pornography in the minds of much of society.[28] Not coincidentally, Harry Donenfeld, a founder of the company that became National Comics, was in the early 1930s the publisher of girlie pulps and "art nudies" like *Hot Stories* and *Gay Parisienne*. Victor Fox, publisher of titles including *Crimes by Women*, was a well-known hustler. He became notorious for ripping off Superman, for which Donenfeld successfully sued him, and for failing to pay the writers and artists who supplied him, by 1939, with four hundred pages of material every month. He was willing to spend money only on racy cover artwork, which he used to attract adolescent and adult consumers.[29] This was a world that rewarded production speed, lurid artwork, fantastic narratives, and new ideas, however exploitative.

THE WILD YEARS, 1945–1955

In August 1949, a new issue of *Crimes by Women* arrived at newsstands. It opened with "The Knife Woman," a western-themed story about Jean Terry, a young rancher who witnesses her father's murder by three thieving sheepherders. Renowned for her skills with a bowie knife, Jean sets out to avenge her father's death by killing the three men responsible. When she finds the first man, Jean wounds him with her gun, so that she may kill him with her bowie knife, a weapon "wonderful for carving up varmints like you." As the wounded man whimpers, Jean tells him, "Stop your blubbering. It's only a li'l nick on your gun hand! And nothing compared to the carving I'm gonna do." Jean kills the second sheepherder in a similar fashion, before hunting down the last of her father's murderers in a local town. She scoffs at his "blubbering," warning, "It won't help you," as she stabs him to death in full view of the local sheriff and townspeople. Now on the run, Jean chooses suicide over capture, stabbing herself in the chest as the sheriff and his deputies surround her.[30]

Within a nation that increasingly defined itself as advanced by the availability of jobs and power to women, comics like *Crimes by*

Women, crowded with brutal and cruel images, were an affront.[31] They depicted White American women as murderers, gangsters, and thieves and as both perpetrators and victims of violence. Comic book protagonists ran wild, killing innocents and criminals alike within a corrupt system that seemingly rewarded violence and revenge while mocking the concepts of family and friendship. Although the stories were billed as cautionary tales, criminals received justice only in the final panels of the narratives, often in a way that seemed insincere. The preceding pages made clear that crime could, in fact, pay; it was quite lucrative and thrilling for both women and men. Jean Terry not only murders the men that killed her father but also escapes justice by committing suicide. This was a profound shift from wartime superhero comics, in which the victims of violence were typically stereotyped Japanese characters or Nazis. In *Crimes by Women*, White women hurled acid at each other, fought with police officers, and forced men to dig their own graves. Like jazz or movies or Jackson Pollock's modernist art, American crime comics proved popular abroad, indicating a market for the least-constrained products of American popular culture. Which, though, would define the United States internationally?

THE COMIC BOOK CONTAINED, 1955–1965

In June 1952, Mohammad Ali, the Pakistani ambassador to the United States, brought his wife and sons to Los Angeles as guests of the Association of Motion Picture Producers. Before a luncheon in his honor, the ambassador and his family entertained a group of local reporters. One of the journalists noticed the ambassador's two sons, age eleven and thirteen, huddled in a corner with a stack of American comic books. Where, he wondered, had the boys acquired such sensational reading material? With a laugh, Ambassador Ali said, "They've been reading them at home, in Pakistan, since they have been able to read. Simply can't get enough of them. You could trail us by the comic books they leave behind in every hotel," Ali admitted. "Great stacks of them."[32]

The sheer complexity of the task facing American Cold War

propagandists, which, in the words of one despairing State Department official, required the creation of "material attractive equally to Saudi Arabians and existentialists," led back to the comic book's basic combination of words and images, which had proved popular, successful, and adaptable during World War II.[33] In the process, the comic book had become a symbol of America. As a result, elements of the American government at the local, state, and federal levels worked not only to censor but also to co-opt the medium. It could no longer go unregulated.

The domestic effort to pacify the comic book was largely successful, due to the sizable and politically inclusive anti–comic book crusade, spearheaded by Dr. Fredric Wertham, which cooperated closely with all levels of government. In late 1954, the American comic book industry accepted a supervisory agency, the Comics Code Authority. It implemented a code that was, as David Hajdu describes it, "an unprecedented monument of self-imposed repression and prudery." The code stripped the black humor, violence, and chaos from comic books. Among its requirements were bans on the words "horror" or "terror" in titles, any display of accurate details of a crime, and representations of horror, gore, and monsters. Also forbidden were drug use, nudity, any hint of corruption in law enforcement, and signs of disrespect to the clergy. The code additionally instructed that female characters were to be drawn without exaggeration of physical attributes and that romance should never be portrayed in a manner that stimulated "the lower and base emotions."[34] The code's general standards further warned that any display of bad taste or indecency—as defined by the code's regulators—regardless of whether it violated any specific requirement, was prohibited. After nearly twenty years of relative freedom, the comic book industry had been tamed.

In mid-1955, *Newsdealer*, an industry publication for periodical retailers, tallied ninety-eight distinct titles that disappeared in the wake of the code. The list includes virtually all the best-known and most popular crime and horror comics, like *Crime Does Not Pay* and *Tales from the Crypt*, along with many others.[35] In their place rose a new generation of superheroes, bearing more than a superficial resemblance to those popularized during World War II, emulating both their straightforward patriotism and, to a lesser but still significant extent, their racism. These new heroes, who began to debut in 1961, included Marvel's Iron Man, the Fantastic Four, and Thor, all of whom were creatures of the Cold War infused with characteristics honed during an earlier conflict. Like their patriotic predecessors, these new heroes embraced America's foreign policy priorities. Although created without any input from federal agencies, Marvel's new heroes straddled the line between purely commercial comic books and propaganda titles. These characters and narratives supported the Cold War consensus, a domestic coalition that crossed party lines and embraced the exertion of American power around the world and confrontations with communism wherever it surfaced.[36] By the early 1960s, comic book superheroes were waging war against the communists in Vietnam. Armed with the fruits of American technological prowess and wealth, Iron Man fought a one-man war against Soviet-style totalitarianism. Thor also went to Vietnam, where he used his godly powers to halt a North Vietnamese sneak attack.

Many of these new heroes gained their abilities through exposure to a strange, benevolent form of atomic energy, which supplanted comic book images of nuclear annihilation. In this post-1955 wave of comic books, radiation exposure granted new and remarkable powers to humans, rather than incinerating them. Within these pages, Americans once again became heroes, not targets; active cold warriors instead of cynical victims. These titles were hits with adult as well as juvenile audiences and laid the foundation for what is now the most recognizable and lucrative film franchise in history. The Cold War revitalized—saved, even—the newly hobbled American comic book industry, and the superhero genre in particular.

By the mid-1960s, with commercial comic books firmly backing the Cold War consensus, the use of propaganda comic books abroad had reached its peak—although there was no official end to the practice, and it continues to this day. With the end of major efforts to overthrow the Castro government in Cuba, the failure of President Kennedy's Alliance for Progress program in Latin America, and America's increasing commitment to the war in Vietnam, propaganda comics were less in demand. Moreover, with the United States deeply committed to the Vietnam War and rapidly advancing mass media technology bringing the results to audiences around the world, there was simply a limit to what comic book propaganda could now achieve.

Just as the nuclear balance constrained American military and diplomatic actions in Europe, the optics of America's war in Vietnam limited the effectiveness of the comic book as a means of promoting American values and policies. At the outset of the Cold War, the United States made a point of presenting itself as a nonimperial state and its embrace of capitalism as a model for the decolonizing world. America's intervention in Vietnam, revelations about the connections between Cold War culture and policy, and American complicity in the 1973 overthrow of the democratically elected Allende government of Chile, among other events, undermined those earlier efforts. As Ariel Dorfman and Armand Mattelart proclaimed on behalf of the entire decolonizing world in *How to Read Donald Duck*, "Donald, go home!"[37] For them, Donald Duck was synonymous with American power in all its forms: political, military, and cultural.

Yet today, Hollywood films based on comic books bolster American cultural influence around the world. Relative to World War II and Cold War–era comic books, they are scrubbed of most—but not all—overtly racist and jingoist imagery. Similarly, studios pack superhero films with violence but are relatively sparing with blood or gore. Sexuality, gender, and the issues they raise are on display, courtesy of the skintight costumes worn by most female heroes. But complex issues are typically glossed over in narratives that entertain and excite without offending or repelling. Happily, though, after nearly twenty years of overwhelmingly White, male superhero films and TV shows, studios are at last beginning to produce narratives featuring non-White heroes and women.

THE STRUCTURE OF PULP EMPIRE

This book is divided into seven chapters, arranged chronologically. Each chapter focuses on a particular aspect of the relationship between the comic book and the United States government during the mid-twentieth century. As a whole, they trace a history of local, state, and federal agencies nourishing, constraining, and appropriating the comic book in pursuit of victory over fascism and communism.

As in so many comics, major figures, beliefs, and organizations appear, vanish, and then reappear throughout this story. Also like a comic book, a few core ideas connect the chapters of this book as they wind through the decades. Above all, that at midcentury, comic books were powerful, political media. Comics were enormously popular at home and abroad, relatively uncensored, cheap to produce and buy, and closely associated with the United States. The US government alternately nurtured and choked the comic book industry as the two great twentieth-century battles against totalitarianism shifted and evolved. At any given time between World War II and 1965, government decision-making regarding comic books was driven by the matter of race and its role in US foreign policy. To tell the history, at the mid-twentieth century, of the comic book industry, foreign policy, and the American imperial project requires grappling with race.

The first chapter traces the earliest phase of the government's involvement with the comic book industry and its initial efforts at weaving covert and overt propaganda into comics. It explores how and why World War II–era federal agencies appropriated the comic book as a means of shaping popular perceptions of America's non-White citizens and its enemies and allies. Chapter 1 also lays out how federal intervention helped build the comic book industry into a colossus.

In late 1945, the federal government suddenly removed itself from the comic book industry. Chapter 2 analyzes the consequences of this decision, particularly the new waves of explicit crime, horror, and romance comic books that filled newsstands around the world after the end of World War II. Free from federal supervision or censorship and eager to cater to adult tastes coarsened by the war, writers and artists produced hundreds of millions of astonishingly violent,

sexual, and racist comics that spread around the world and proved a
national embarrassment in the new context of the Cold War. In contrast to World War II–era comic books supervised by the WWB, these
new comics depicted the United States as a dark place, populated
almost entirely by White men and women obsessed with money, sex,
exploitation, and brutality.

Chapter 3 shows how the sudden disappearance of governmental
supervision in 1945, along with a lack of censorship, also allowed
comic books to depict and debate atomic weapons in ways that more
traditional media could not. As with graphic crime, horror, and romance titles, the freedom enjoyed by comic makers enabled them to
create shockingly violent and pessimistic images of atomic war and
of an American society totally destroyed by global conflict. During
the brief period between the end of World War II and the beginning
of the all-out Cold War, these comic books boldly challenged the
utility and morality of the American nuclear deterrent and asked
whether world government might be preferable to an independent
United States under perpetual threat of nuclear attack. In an effort to
control the threat of these bleak, atomic-themed comic books, federal agencies reentered the comic book business, pushing publishers
to create positive, pro-atomic propaganda titles.

Chapter 4 records the forceful reentry of the American government into the comic book industry. It illustrates how local, state,
and federal authorities reacted to the postwar wave of violent comic
books by nourishing a vast, public anti–comic book campaign led
by the psychiatrist Dr. Fredric Wertham. This chapter then lays out
how comic book violence, sexuality, and racism created significant
problems for policy makers intent on building the United States into
a cultural, political, and military powerhouse capable of defeating
international communism. It concludes with a history of the 1954
comics censorship code, which shattered the industry and banned
the production of exactly the sorts of comics that sold hundreds of
millions of copies every year.

Chapter 5 focuses on the international anti–comic book campaign,
arguing that Dr. Wertham spearheaded it too. It traces the various
cultural and diplomatic crises triggered by the global distribution of

American commercial comics and the ways these crises complicated American Cold War policies. It shows how deeply the comic book was connected with mid-twentieth-century diplomacy and global perceptions of the United States as it embarked on a vast imperial project.

Chapter 6 illustrates the American government's return to and expansion of the World War II–era idea that comic books could be used to win hearts and minds in a battle against a totalitarian enemy. It is a history of the propaganda comic books produced by various federal agencies between the late 1940s and 1965. This chapter demonstrates the inseparability of race from the history of comic books, illuminating the process by which these federal agencies decided to use propaganda comic books among non-White peoples in the global south.

Chapter 7 explores the resurgence in the early 1960s of the American commercial comic book. It traces this revitalization through the wave of pro-American, anticommunist superhero titles created at Marvel Comics. It proposes that these comics alleviated much of the need for state-sanctioned propaganda titles. And at the same time that Marvel reenergized the superhero genre and the industry, policy makers acknowledged the reduced value of propaganda comics in the decolonizing world. The brutal realities of the war in Vietnam, the out-of-control nuclear arms race, and various American policies toward developing nations all overwhelmed the power of the medium to sway opinions.

FIT ONLY FOR BURNING

In the rich, eggplant-purple prose of the comic book, this book is a secret history.

The CIA has fought, with regrettable success, all my efforts through the Freedom of Information Act to drag their Cold War–era comic books out of the darkness. Even those propaganda comic books and documents not buried within the federal classification system are difficult to find. During World War II and the early Cold War, the State Department made frequent use of comic books as instruments of US diplomatic policy. But whatever evidence remains of this relationship lies scattered across boxes of documents stored

in vast archives around the country. And as I quickly learned, none
of these boxes are labeled "The Government and Comic Books, 1940–
1965." Rather, the secret history of the relationship between the
American government and the comic book is laced through the records of multiple government agencies, only some of which are open
to researchers. Compounding the challenge, policy makers were not
terribly proud of using comic books as instruments of foreign policy.
Many of the resulting propaganda comic books seemed often to have
been thrown out, rather than preserved. The story is much the same
for commercial comic books. As the nation's publishing storehouse,
the Library of Congress should have, at least in theory, received copies of every comic book published during the mid-twentieth century.
And the library does retain thousands of issues. Many more, perhaps
millions, however, were discarded. As one archivist patiently
explained to me, for many years the comic books were considered
trash; what serious scholar would ever want to read them? This book
is a political, cultural, and diplomatic history of an artifact whose
origins, sales numbers, and contents have been obscured through
shame, malice, and benign indifference.

Finding a box with information on comic books or, better yet, an
actual propaganda comic book was a cause for celebration. Because
so many people were or are comic book consumers, I happily shared
these triumphant moments with others. Once, in the Library of Congress, I cheered so loudly upon opening a box that a crowd gathered
around my table. An improbable group of researchers, tourists, and
unhoused men and women spent the rest of the afternoon huddled
over the box, trading their own experiences with comic books. Word
of the comic books spread so quickly that when I entered the library
the following morning, a security guard addressed me as "Captain
Marvel." During another trip, I opened a box from a congressional
investigation on juvenile delinquency to find a collection of mid-
twentieth-century pornography and, nestled beneath, what looked
like a small handgun. I closed the box, walked out of the room,
and returned with a few security guards and some very skeptical
archivists, unconvinced by my description of a box packed with smut
and a pistol. The guards quickly removed the box—I still don't know

if the gun was real or not—leaving me with a pile of government-curated pornography and the very palpable anger of my fellow researchers, whose work had been interrupted. Researching and writing this book has been an experience punctuated by these and so many other shocking and joyful moments.

When I was twelve or thirteen, I stopped reading and collecting comic books because of the common, unspoken understanding that they were strictly for children. This book is a rebuttal of that popular perception. It illuminates a very different time, when hundreds of millions of people from every region of the globe and from across the spectrums of politics, race, and ethnicity consumed enormous quantities of American comic books. It also reminds us of the value of the comic book and "lowbrow" culture in a period when American politicians feared, envied, and co-opted its power for the imperial project. Ultimately, this book offers a new interpretation of US foreign policy in the mid-twentieth century. Just as the American government shaped the form and content of the comic book, so, too, did the comic book shape US foreign policy. In this fluid relationship between policy and culture, between race and imperialism, lies a fresh understanding of the most significant and costly struggle of the twentieth century: the battle against totalitarianism.

CHAPTER ONE

THIS IS OUR ENEMY

GOOSE-STEPPING THROUGH HISTORY

In early 1945, the twenty-fourth issue of *All-Star Comics* went on sale at newsstands and drugstores and at US military bases throughout the world. A popular title, *All-Star Comics* traced the adventures of the Justice Society of America, a group of superheroes that included Wonder Woman, Green Lantern, and the Flash. On the cover of that issue, the Justice Society looks on in mute horror as the Four Horsemen of the Apocalypse, riding underneath a Nazi flag, lay waste to a city. A banner reminds American readers, "This Is Our Enemy." The issue included a nearly forty-page denunciation of Nazism and German people and culture, also titled "This Is Our Enemy." Although drawn in part by Joe Kubert, the Polish-born son of a kosher butcher, the issue was not simply the product of reflexive antifascism and patriotism.[1] It resulted instead from a long-term, cooperative effort between the publisher and the Writers' War Board (WWB), a quasi-governmental agency.[2] Throughout late 1944, members of the WWB crafted the plot and honed drafts submitted by writers and editors at National Comics, the publisher of *All-Star Comics*. The WWB even provided National with a list of potential titles, including "German

FIGURE 1.1   The cover of *All-Star Comics* 24 from 1945 depicts members of the super-hero team in a movie theater, horrified by the film of German atrocities unspooling in front of them. The related story, "This Is Our Enemy," created in cooperation with the Writers' War Board, presents all Germans—not just Nazis—as inherently violent and emphasizes that Americans are obligated to kill them.

Cult of Terror" and "Goosestepping through the Centuries."[3] The finished story condemns the German people as a thousand-year-old plague on decency, peace, and western civilization. National sold over half a million copies of the issue to civilians on the home front and servicemen stationed around the world.[4]

Ostensibly a private group staffed by volunteers, the WWB received funding and support from the federal government through the Office of War Information (OWI). Shielded by this veneer of independence, the WWB wove propaganda into popular culture to fuel a hatred of fascism, encourage racial tolerance in American society, and promote postwar international cooperation.[5] Beginning in April 1943, the WWB used comic books to shape popular perceptions of race and ethnicity as well as to build support for the American war effort.[6] WWB members saw that the core traits of the comic book form—its broad popularity, comprehensibility, emphasis on raw emotion, and distinct lack of subtlety—marked the medium as a potentially useful delivery system for propaganda and education. Additionally, because comics, unlike most other major media, were not subject to external censorship, writers and propagandists could freely use clear, unambiguous images and language; they did not need to obscure opinions beneath layers of allegory or abstraction. Soon, major comic book publishers were submitting story drafts to the WWB and even creating new characters and features at its behest.[7]

Through the WWB, comic books became political media.[8] Using racial stereotypes, WWB members and comic book producers promoted race-based hatred of America's enemies. Board-approved stories initially depicted Japanese and Germans as racially and culturally defective yet also eminently beatable opponents. But as the war dragged on, the WWB requested increasingly brutal depictions of Germans and Japanese as fundamentally, irredeemably evil and violent. Beginning in late 1944, this second wave of WWB-influenced comic books argued that unremitting violence was essential to creating a world in which democracy and tolerance could flourish. The board's embrace of comic book violence coincided with the actual escalation of the Allied war effort against Japanese and German civilians.

Paradoxically, the board also produced comic book narratives that promoted domestic racial harmony and international cooperation, in an effort to both bolster the war effort and portray the United States as an inclusive society, unlike its fascist opponents. WWB-approved comics presented racial tolerance—though not true equality—as essential to victory, highlighting the war effort contributions of Blacks and the nation's non-White allies. But these pro-tolerance narratives struggled to overcome the popular and long-lived stereotypes in American mass culture that denigrated Blacks, Chinese, and other Asian peoples, yielding complex and ultimately contradictory depictions of race and ethnicity.[9]

Admittedly, pro-tolerance comics were up against racism ingrained in American thought, culture, and even the military itself. The US armed forces were segregated, and this institutionalized bigotry was further complicated by the decision to send disproportionate numbers of recruits to the South for boot camp. And just two months after the attack on Pearl Harbor, the armed forces decided to separate Black blood serum from White serum; medics were not to provide those in need with blood from different races. This was a cruel and wholly political move unsupported by even a shred of scientific evidence, implemented to placate White southerners and their powerful federal representatives. The Jim Crow system was even extended to England, where Supreme Allied Commander Dwight Eisenhower instituted an "informal" system of segregation in an effort to avert conflict between White and non-White troops. Although far from free of entrenched racism, the British population paid little attention to these efforts, and Eisenhower marveled at what he saw as an obliviousness to the fundamental differences between White and Black Americans: "To most English people, including the village girls—even those of perfectly fine character— the negro soldier is just another man, rather fascinating because he is unique in their experience, a jolly good fellow, and with money to spend."[10]

Beginning in February 1942, Japanese Americans were interned in camps previously used to house animals. They were treated as presumptive spies and saboteurs, unlike German and Italian Americans, who were not assumed to be enemies of the United States. This was emblematic of the war in the Pacific—a conflict coded in racial terms, and one in which the potential extermination of the Japanese race was endorsed as sound policy. Such brutality was encouraged because Japan's early military successes challenged not only Allied hopes for victory but also the very foundations of White supremacy as a concept. As Undersecretary of State Sumner Welles tartly noted, "The thesis of white supremacy could only exist so long as the white race actually proved to be supreme."[11]

While the WWB worked to encode propaganda into commercial comic books for American audiences, another wartime agency brought propaganda titles to countries throughout Latin America. The Office for Inter-American Affairs (OIAA), headed by Nelson Rockefeller—a family name not traditionally linked with comics—spearheaded the use of propaganda titles outside the United States. While touring Latin America in 1939, Rockefeller noted a rise in fascist influence in the region. He conveyed his fears to President Franklin D. Roosevelt, who responded by creating the Office of the Coordinator of Inter-American Affairs, which soon became the OIAA.[12] Its employees worked to bolster economic, political, and cultural cooperation between the United States and the countries of Latin America. To this end, the agency laced propaganda into films, books, radio broadcasts, and comics. Domestically, the OIAA promoted Latin America as a culturally and strategically vital region. Throughout Latin America, the agency used propaganda to advance America's war aims and antifascism. The OIAA ultimately oversaw over one thousand domestic employees and three hundred others stationed throughout the Western Hemisphere.[13] In 1943, it, too, went into the comic book business.

PROPAGANDISTS DISCOVER COMICS

Comics appealed as propaganda tools most of all because they were popular, and the war made them even more so. In the wake of the Japanese attack on Pearl Harbor in 1941, federal policies further expanded the adult audience for comic books. Comic books were sold on military bases, while civilian buyers sent used copies to servicemen stationed wherever the war was waged.[14] Beginning in 1943, both the army and navy also worked directly with publishers on comic books designed to boost enlistment.[15] Ultimately, 44 percent of men in the army described themselves as comic book readers.[16] The army also circulated over one million copies per issue of an instructional comic book called *Army Motors*. Created by Will Eisner, artist, writer, and cofounder of the Eisner-Iger comic book studio, the comic traced the misadventures of the chronically incompetent Private Joe Dope. *Army Motors* taught the concept of preventive maintenance to the huge number of draftees tasked with caring for advanced vehicles and weapons. Soon after his own induction into the army, Eisner had encountered a group of illiterate soldiers and resolved to write *Army Motors* in simple, straightforward language. He replaced technical phrases like "Remove all foreign matter from the walls of the engine" with "Clean the crud out of the engine."[17] This simple text, when combined with clear, descriptive sequential artwork, made *Army Motors* a potent and popular educational tool.

Here and elsewhere, the Roosevelt administration downplayed overt propaganda in favor of a "strategy of truth." The Office of Facts and Figures, the initial agency overseeing much of the government's effort to build support for the war, aimed to inform Americans, rather than harangue them.[18] A focus on facts, not emotions, avoided unflattering comparisons with the state-controlled propaganda organs of Germany, Japan, and Italy. Building public support was essential to victory, however, and some policy makers sought to circumvent the "strategy of truth." Secretary of the Treasury Henry Morgenthau Jr., for example, wanted an agency that could insert propaganda into popular culture, promoting policies the government supported but did not want to overtly endorse. The WWB was the result in early 1942.[19] Frederica Barach, the board's executive secretary, confirmed Morgenthau's mandate, describing the WWB as devoted to the promotion of "government policy and popular support for the war effort while the government itself technically refrained from propaganda."[20] But the board did receive federal funding, with government agencies dictating much of its output. Even its own members tended to think of the WWB as a government agency.

The government did not pay board members, although by mid-1942, the Office of Facts and Figures (which soon became the OWI) was supplying an executive secretary, clerical assistance, and office space.[21] The board itself was staffed by volunteers from across the popular culture industry. Soon, the WWB exerted control over nearly five thousand professional writers and enjoyed access to thousands of newspapers and hundreds of radio stations.[22] The board additionally established a symbiotic relationship with many of the country's largest comic book publishers and influenced portrayals of some of the most popular comic book heroes of the day.

The WWB embraced comic books as a way to reach soldiers and civilians wary of more overt government-manufactured propaganda, noting that "many of its messages can be very effectively put over in the comics magazines, [including] combating race hatred, preaching the necessity for United Nations cooperation and unity here at home." Beginning in April 1943, it wrote various comic book publishers requesting cooperation from artists, writers, and administrators and convened a Comics Committee, headed by novelist Paul Gallico, to manage the relationships.[23] Publishers generally agreed. They had found that by promoting government policies, they could reach a larger adult audience, reap sizable profits, and earn a veneer of patriotic legitimacy. Over the next two years, committee members met with publishers, including National Comics, Fawcett Publications, Parents' Magazine, Popular Comics, Standard Magazine, and Street & Smith.[24] Cooperating publishers agreed to write stories based on ideas proposed by the WWB and to use the board's feedback and instructions in representing ethnicity, race, and other critical wartime topics in their publications.

The WWB saw comics as useful vehicles for propaganda for four reasons. First, comic books were already enormously popular. *Superman* alone sold roughly ten million copies in 1941.[25] Consumers bought over half a million copies per month of *Captain America*, which spawned a host of popular patriotic imitators. During the war, over one hundred titles battled for attention at American newsstands, and total annual comic book sales climbed into the hundreds of millions of copies. Indeed, comics proved so popular that when faced by wartime paper rationing, publishers declined to reduce the number of issues—instead they simply slashed the page count.[26]

Second, comic books enjoyed a large, diverse adult audience of civilians and members of the armed forces.[27] Beginning in 1943, the board discussed the usefulness of comic books for educating and entertaining servicemen. E. R. Ross, an editor at Famous Funnies, assured mystery writer Rex Stout, "The general trend in comic magazines [is] toward a more adult approach. Whereas the audience we reached was once primarily childish, our books now have their greatest percentage of sale in the Army and Navy bases, both in and out of the country."[28] Nearly half of all soldiers and sailors regularly consumed comic books, and the navy classified comics alongside water, food, and ammunition as "essential supplies" for the marines stationed on Midway Island.[29]

Both young and adult readers confirmed their devotion to comic books through letters sent to publishers. A letter from an army chaplain stationed overseas to publisher M. C. Gaines of National Comics noted, "We are at a hospital unit serving overseas, and before we left the states we took with us a small supply of your books titled *Picture Stories from the Bible*. These books have become so popular with our patients that we are now requesting that you ship us fifty more copies." Ever the hustler, Gaines forwarded the letter to the WWB along with a request for an exemption from paper rationing restrictions. A 1943 issue of *Wings Comics* contained a letter from a marine captain, who wrote with a compliment and a request: "While not on duty most of my time I spent reading your magazine. . . . I like every story in it. Jane Martin, G.G. and all the rest. I see nothing wrong in the clothes the girls in your stories wear and please leave the girls in your stories. Even though nothing like that ever happens (if it does, tell me where at) I would like to be stationed there."[30]

Third, WWB members appreciated the combination of simple text and images within comic books, which seemed to make the medium almost universally comprehensible. In 1944, the *Journal of Educational Sociology* devoted an entire issue to the idea that comic books possessed an overlooked means of educating Americans unwilling or unable to learn through more conventional methods. WWB members agreed that messages embedded within comics were more enjoyable and effective than overt, moralistic proselytizing.

Finally, because comic books, like the waves of dime novels and pulps before them, were categorized as lowbrow entertainment, they seemed an unlikely source of government propaganda. Recalling the virulent propaganda promoted during World War I by the Committee on Public Information and contemplating the dictatorial stranglehold over popular media in the Axis countries, many Americans associated explicit government propaganda with totalitarianism.[31] Comic books allayed this concern by cloaking patriotic exhortations beneath layers of bright colors, easily understood text, and imaginative characters. Appropriating the comic enabled the WWB to tackle controversial topics like race relations while tempering propaganda with humor, romance, and adventure. As a board member emphasized in 1943, "We believe that many subjects can be handled [by comics] without interfering with their entertainment value while making use of their power."[32]

Ironically, even the advertisements within comics—something that would never be found in explicit government propaganda—lent them a kind of "authenticity."[33] Wartime comic books included ads for a bewildering array of products, including creams to lose weight, pills to gain weight ("Skinny girls don't have oomph!"), toy guns, lingerie, male corsets, and, of course, war bonds. Other advertisements tempted adults with visions of products sure to be available after the war—tacitly promoting the government's advocacy of total victory through any available means.

The board decided, intriguingly, to use comic books to shape popular perceptions of race without putting the efficacy of cartoon propaganda to any kind of scientific test.[34] Rather, board members simply assumed that any medium as popular as the comic book doubtless exerted influence on its audience. Anecdotal evidence suggested their faith in the power of comics was misplaced. In 1944,

FIGURE 1.2   Comic book advertisements like this one for a weight loss gadget that doubled as a sex toy provided excellent cover for pro-American messages. Federal propagandists were sure that readers would not associate state-sanctioned narratives with a medium that also included such offerings.

Frederica Barach took home a copy of a "swell" board-sanctioned anti-racist comic book, only to find that her children interpreted it as a confirmation that racial intolerance was "inevitable and had always been part of history."[35]

DEFINING ENEMIES

Cooperation between the WWB and the comic book industry transformed cartoon images of race. When board members first grew interested in comic books, they asked publishers for stories about practical wartime issues, including labor relations and inflation.[36] But by late 1944, as US casualties mounted, the WWB focused on portrayals of Germans and Japanese. Fearing that comics treated America's enemies too lightly, the board encouraged very specific hatreds based on race and ethnicity. In cooperation with writers and artists, the board characterized Japanese and Germans by clearly defined racial stereotypes. Cooperating publishers—who may not have needed too much prodding down the path of cheap caricaturing—represented the fascists as racially defective, incurably violent, and responsible for their own destruction.

But this second wave of board-sanctioned racial representation worked on two distinct and potentially conflicting levels. On the surface, these images stripped America's opponents of their humanity, calling them deviant cultures and "plenty worthy of hate," however, the WWB hoped that stoking such hatred would result in a lasting peace.[37] By the end of 1944, WWB-backed comic books showed that the Japanese and German people were irredeemably aggressive, antidemocratic, innately bigoted, and cruel. By portraying all Germans as atrocity-committing Nazis and all Japanese as incurably evil, the board was encouraging American intolerance and hatred. Only by engaging in justifiable discrimination could the United States eliminate fascism and ensure a peaceful postwar world.

Prior to 1944, comic book artists and writers typically depicted Germans as either bloodthirsty criminals or buffoons. Often the distinction rested on whether a German character was a member of the Nazi Party or an average soldier. Either way, Allied heroes generally faced off against vicious Nazi officials, sneaky saboteurs, and oafish officers. These comic books implied that while specific Nazis were more evil than others, not all Germans were inherently aggressive or vicious. Allied heroes fought against evil individuals; the enemy was a person, rather than an ideology or a nation. Indeed, Germans sometimes even appeared as sympathetic, explicitly anti-Nazi characters.

"Hobo on a U-boat," from the comic book *War Heroes*, illustrates the different treatment initially accorded to individual Germans and Nazis. Merchant seaman Archie Gibbs survives a German torpedo attack on his ship and is pulled from the water by the crew of a U-boat. The sailors who save him wear civilian clothing, and even the ship's captain prefers a white sweater and shorts to a uniform. When Archie refuses to divulge his ship's cargo, however, he is brought before a menacing gestapo officer in full Nazi regalia. Archie senses tension between the U-boat crew and the brutal gestapo officer. Confident that the German seamen will protect him, Archie mocks his interrogator. Enraged, the officer tortures Archie and leaves him to die. Behind the officer's back, the German sailors tend to Archie's injuries, give him food and medicine, and make up a bed for him. One of the crewmen even mocks Hitler, thumbing his nose while mimicking the Nazi salute. When the submarine founders under an Allied depth charge attack, the Germans give Archie a life jacket and urge him to leap overboard. Thanks to the warmth and bravery of the non-Nazi crew, Archie survives his encounter with an individual villain.[38]

When not depicted as merciless thugs, comic book Nazis appeared as easily defeated fools. In *Young Allies*, oafish Nazis—including Adolf Hitler himself—prove incapable of defeating a group of American and British children. The Young Allies are a collection of five kids with a shared hatred of fascism, all but one of whom boasts specific skills. The nominal leader is Captain America's sidekick, the bright and brave Bucky Barnes. Aiding Bucky is Toro, young partner to the Human Torch, who can ignite his body, fly, and hurl balls of flame at his opponents. The Young Allies also include the intellectual Jefferson Worthing Sandervilt and Percival Aloysius O'Toole, better known as Knuckles, a Brooklyn-born punk without fear or peer as a fighter. Only Whitewash Jones, the lone Black member of the team, lacks intelligence or raw courage, although the other members acknowledge his fluency in "the crass ways of the world," praising his skill with a harmonica.[39] On their first mission, the Young Allies encounter and defeat several Nazi villains, including a strutting, bloodthirsty Nazi officer with the gloriously absurd name of Fritz Flootzendootzen. When the young heroes reach Berlin, they trick the Nazi supervillain Red Skull and a group of Nazi guards into pummeling a notably chunky Adolf Hitler. Fuming helplessly after his beating, Hitler cries, "Zuch a fool they make of me yet!"[40] Despite his demand for vengeance, the Young Allies escape.

This approach changed in late 1944, when the WWB provided publishers a clear template for German characters. Above all, the board urged writers to conflate Germans with Nazis. Americans needed to believe that Germans, along with Japanese, were incurably hostile; they could be reeducated only after a necessarily brutal conflict and total Allied victory. The board encouraged writers to de-emphasize individual villains in favor of fascism and "German-ness." The German nation—and all of its inhabitants—was the enemy of democracy, freedom, and equality. There was thus no need to create unique and buffoonish Nazi comic book villains. The very real atrocities committed by average German soldiers offered plenty of raw materials for comic book condemnations of fascism.

To disseminate its new perspective on Germany, the WWB commissioned an anti-German narrative from National Comics. Board members drew up the plot and refined the text, inserting changes to emphasize that "the German people have willingly cooperated with their leaders, rather than being unwilling dupes." National had provided an early draft that placed responsibility for Nazism on Germany's leaders instead of average Germans, but WWB executive secretary Barach rejected it, insisting on "radical" changes. She reminded editor Sheldon Mayer, "The emphasis on leaders who tricked their people into war strikes entirely the wrong note from the board's point of view. Emphasis should be rather that the people were willing dupes, and easily sold on a program of aggression."[41] Mayer

FIGURE 1.3 For every pro-tolerance comic book narrative crafted by the propagandists at the Writers' War Board, many more racist representations of Black characters appeared in wartime comic books. This one depicts Whitewash Jones in the first issue of *Young Allies*, published in 1941.

complied, and the story, which appeared in the spring 1945 issue of *All-Star Comics*, presented Hitler as simply "a mouthpiece" for the malignant beliefs and policies embraced by the German people.[42]

According to the final, board-approved version of "This Is Our Enemy," World War II occurred because Germans—all Germans—

were inherently violent. In one of several scenes emphasizing this point, an old Teutonic knight gazes across a battlefield and reminds his young comrade, "There is nothing like battle. It is like wine to a man, filling him with excitement and eagerness." The younger knight agrees, confirming "that is what we Germans have always been taught." "This Is Our Enemy" also demolished any distinction between Germans and Nazis. It condemned all Germans as members of "a degenerate nation whose people throughout the centuries have always been willing to follow their military leaders into endless, bloody but futile warfare."[43]

Through this portrayal of the German people, the narrative endorsed hatred and violence as the only solutions to German militarism.[44] Justice Society member Johnny Thunder proclaims, "Until their mad ideal of world conquest is broken forever, Germany will always be an aggressor nation. Well, if they want total war, we'll give it to them!"[45] "This Is Our Enemy" also included a board-sanctioned vision for the postwar world. Since Germany's inherent aggression posed a permanent threat to Europe and the United States, durable peace required three steps. First, the Allies had to shatter the nation, society, and culture responsible for plunging the world "into a maelstrom of blood."[46] Second, the United States had to reeducate and deprogram the German people. Finally, peace required a world organization devoted to nonviolent conflict resolution. Should these steps fail to eliminate violence in the postwar world, the United States also needed a standing peacetime army and universal conscription. This issue of *All-Star Comics* sold a satisfactory six hundred thousand copies, reaching an estimated several million adults and children. The board viewed its cooperative effort with National Comics as a resounding success and as a template for further collaboration between its members with the comic book industry.[47]

The WWB ultimately encouraged similarly paradoxical sentiments—hatred and brutality as the solutions to fascist aggression and bigotry—in comic books aimed at America's enemy in the Pacific. But while the board feared that Americans did not sufficiently loathe Germans, it had little doubt that Americans held a deep hatred for Japanese. This was due to both the humiliating and devastating attack on Pearl Harbor and the long-standing derogatory representations of Japanese and other Asian peoples in American mass culture, not least comic books. Beginning before Pearl Harbor and continuing after the US entry into the war, Japanese characters inhabited a curious dual role in American comics. Japanese were viewed simultaneously as subhuman—defined, in John Dower's words, "in terms of primitivism, childishness, and collective mental and emotional deficiency"—but also as members of a powerful, pan-Asian threat to American society, the "Yellow Peril."[48] In wartime comic books, there was no Japanese analogue to the "Good German."[49] These widespread cultural assumptions significantly defined the Japanese during the war.[50] Beginning in mid-1943, the WWB shaped and directed these stereotypes in support of specific policies and perspectives.

Perhaps the quintessential example of a menacing Asian villain first appeared in the December 1939 issue of *Silver Streak Comics*, starring Daredevil, "the World's Most Daring Man of Action." Daredevil's nemesis was the Claw, a mysterious "God of Hate," the unchallenged ruler of a nation of "strange religions and mysterious customs." The Claw embodied and amplified the pervasive prewar conception of the Yellow Peril.[51] He was enormous, dwarfing New York City skyscrapers, and had dripping fangs instead of teeth. Tufts of yellow hair hung over his sharply slanted eyes and his oversized, pointed ears. He lived in a subterranean pit of fire, emerging to issue instructions to his enslaved army. Bent on destroying America, "the most unfortified country in the world," the Claw ordered wave upon wave of his enslaved forces to invade the United States. The strong among his army were worked to death, and the weak crushed beneath his enormous yellow feet.[52] He was a superhuman monster, obsessed with America's complete destruction. Average American civilians or soldiers were no match for him. Only Daredevil, a super-hero, could defeat him.[53]

In other comic books where Japanese people were not depicted as superhuman, they often appeared as incompetent and subhuman. In these titles, they were likened to monkeys or rats that could be easily exterminated by larger, stronger Americans—in some cases, even by

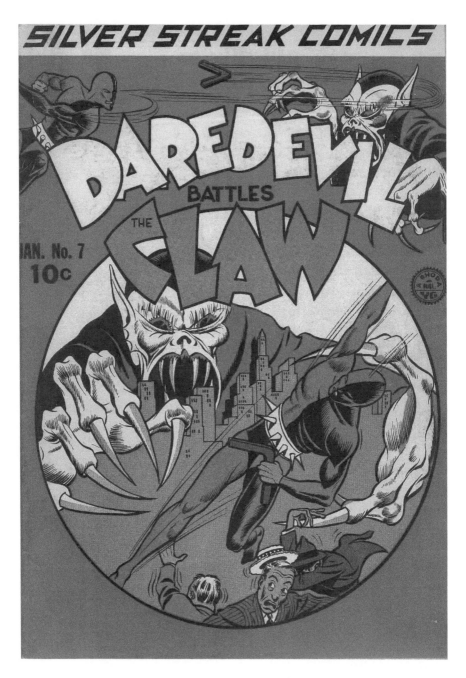

FIGURE 1.4 The character known as the Claw combined multiple elements of the anti-Asian sentiments prevalent for decades in American popular culture. This cover from January 1941 predates the Japanese attack on Pearl Harbor by nearly a year.

American children or the elderly. In an *Our Gang Comics* story from 1944, several children are shipwrecked on a desolate island in the Pacific. Aided by a short-tempered, old sailor named Cap'n Dan, they explore the island and begin building a raft. A White child named Froggie and Buckwheat, again the lone Black character, are sent to find fresh water in the jungle. The two boys stumble upon a secret Japanese radio station hidden in the island's interior and attack the befuddled, incompetent Japanese soldiers manning it. The battle rages across two pages and includes several panels in which Buckwheat appears alongside equally crude representations of Japanese soldiers. One of the hapless Japanese soldiers receives a brutal kick from Froggie, while Buckwheat looks on and exclaims, "Once again ah is thankful ah is no Japoon." Meanwhile, Cap'n Dan stakes out a spot near the Japanese hideout and tells the gang, "They're in a spot the minute they start goin' down that Jacob's Ladder!" When a child asks why the Japanese will be in trouble, Cap'n Dan retorts, "A Jap pilot machine-gunned my own lad when he was parachuting down over the Coral Sea—and ol' Cap'n Dan isn't one to let an opportunity pass!" After killing two Japanese soldiers in front of a member of the gang, Cap'n Dan laments, "I'm sorry you had to see that, lad. It's never a pretty thing to kill even a rat." The frighteningly desensitized child replies, "That's okay—an' that was some shot!"[54]

These conflicting images of the Japanese soon attracted the attention of the WWB. Neither Asian enemies like the Claw nor patronizing representations of easily defeated Japanese soldiers met the board's criteria for effective propaganda. One board member cautioned, "The comics are drumming up a lot of hate for the enemy, but usually for the wrong reasons—frequently fantastic ones (mad Jap scientists, etc.). Why not use the real reasons—they're plenty worthy of hate!" Perhaps, fretted board member Milton Kramer, comic books had done too good a job of mocking and stereotyping the Japanese, lulling American readers into expecting an easy victory in the Pacific.[55] Compounding this problem, as an OWI survey of comic books lamented, comic book creators "do not understand that this is a global war. Americans win alone. The enemy is a pushover. The allies are non-existent or subordinate." Such simplistic, condescending representations of Japanese implied that the United States had no need for allies. This "Americocentric" image of the war worked against government assertions that the four Allied powers—the United States, Britain, the Soviet Union, and China—all contributed to the fight against fascism.[56]

When the board issued its guidelines for representations of Japanese characters, they coincided with a general increase in the ferocity of the Pacific conflict, and some comic book publishers toughened their stance without any input from the board. Increasingly vicious images of Japanese appeared in parallel with the increasing US commitment to total war against Japan, typified by the strategic bombing campaign against the Japanese home islands. Before Pearl Harbor, the US government had condemned the strategy of aerial bombardment. In 1938, for instance, a Senate resolution had named Japan as the chief perpetrator of terror bombing, branding it a "crime against humanity" and "reminiscent of the cruelties perpetrated by primitive and barbarous nations upon inoffensive people."[57] During World War II, however, the United States launched its own massive strategic bombing campaign against Japan and Germany. The army air force concluded that "the entire population of Japan is a proper military target," and American bombers assaulted virtually every major Japanese city with explosives, phosphorus, and jellied gasoline.[58]

The comic book series *United States Marines*, published with the cooperation of the Marine Corps, typified comic book representations of Japanese during the last years of the war.[59] A 1944 issue included a story entitled "The Smell of the Monkeymen." Told from the perspective of Eric, an American guard dog stationed with marines on a Pacific island, the story depicts Japanese soldiers as simian brutes whose sickening body odor betrays their concealed locations. In the course of a Japanese attack on a marine emplacement, Eric joyfully mangles one of the onrushing soldiers: "The smell of the 'monkeyman' was so strong that it choked him. The dog's teeth sank into a corded throat, a snarl ripped up into his mouth and into the soft flesh that choked his jaws." Drenched in blood, Eric returns to his master, who praises him for "killing that monkey." The next issue

No. 3

THE UNITED STATES

MARINES

10¢

15¢
IN CANADA

A LEATHERNECK FLAME THROWER

★ AUTHENTIC U.S. MARINE CORPS PICTURE STORIES ★

FIGURE 1.5 This image from 1944 is typical of the effort, supported by the Writers' War Board, to represent Japanese characters as deserving of extermination by the Allies. Board-sanctioned stories assured readers that such violence was not only acceptable but also essential to preserving peace in the postwar world.

of *United States Marines* boasted "Nippon's Sun Starts Down," a vivid retelling of a US attack on a Japanese base in the Pacific. The story contains detailed images of Japanese soldiers burned alive by American flamethrowers manned by laughing marines. Another story in the same issue, "Jap Souvenirs from the Solomons," describes the pleasure of picking over Japanese corpses in search of mementos. Alongside drawings and photographs of mangled Japanese bodies, the text informs readers, "Next to killing Japs, American servicemen in the South Pacific like best to collect Jap souvenirs."[60]

Ironically, as the comic book campaign against Japan grew increasingly brutal, participants raised concerns about the usefulness of fanning racial hatred. In late 1944, publisher M .C. Gaines notified the WWB that he was ready to begin work on a story about Japan as a complement to the anti-German story in *All-Star Comics*. But Gaines and his editor Sheldon Mayer worried that a virulently anti-Japanese story would encourage "an increase of race feeling" on the home front.[61] As an alternative, Mayer suggested a more evenhanded story about a fictional, antifascist underground movement in Japan. Clifton Fadiman flatly rejected National's proposal. The story, he complained, depicted an attractive Japanese "wench," encouraged "a soft peace with Japan," and suggested that the Japanese people disliked fascism. He appealed to Mayer to abandon the idea, reminding him, "Our attitude towards the Japanese must, if anything, be more stringent than our attitude towards the Germans."[62]

DEFINING ALLIES

Just as board-sanctioned images of Japanese drew on racial caricatures, so, too, did comic book representations of America's Chinese allies. Depictions of Chinese characters as heathens or primitive "coolies" were commonplace by the early twentieth century, particularly in political and editorial cartoons.[63] These representations both fed and were fueled by federal legislation, beginning with the 1882 Chinese Exclusion Act.[64] By the time the United States entered World War II, negative perceptions of Chinese were an established part of mass culture as well as the nation's legal fabric. Not until

December 1943 did Congress modify the Chinese exclusion laws. Even then, Congress was driven not by altruism but by concerns that discriminatory legislation provided the Japanese with powerful anti-American propaganda material that might drive China from the Allied alliance.[65]

Any effort to use comic books to present a more positive image of America's Chinese allies therefore had to overcome the pervasive, cumulative effects of stereotyping and discrimination. The WWB, however, did not provide publishers with a racial template for non-White allies like China, the Philippines, and India. In the absence of direction from the board, comic book publishers generated very few complimentary depictions of non-White heroes. A 1943 WWB review of comic books lamented, "Hate for the enemy is practically the only good propaganda put across," and it noted the absence of positive, non-American characters.[66] That same year, Street & Smith Publications notified the WWB of an upcoming series in *Air Ace* called "The Four Musketeers." With members from the United States, Britain, China, and the Soviet Union, the group promoted the cooperative fight against fascism. Although the WWB's Barach railed against the images of Chinese characters as "awful," she provided neither instructions for how to improve the feature nor any support for the idea of non-White heroes.[67]

Board members reacted similarly to a 1944 narrative in Fawcett's *Captain Marvel Jr.* The story included images of Soviet and Chinese characters, with the Chinese defined as drug addicts and smugglers. In it, a Soviet diplomat warns that unless the Chinese stop smuggling opium across the border, the Soviet Union will invade China. Concerned that the Soviet ultimatum showed an American ally in an unfavorable light, the board requested that Fawcett take greater care with future depictions of Soviet characters and with the implication that China weakened the Allied war effort through drug use and smuggling.[68] As with "The Four Musketeers," the WWB did not clarify how the publisher might change the story to encourage positive perceptions of an Asian ally.

Still, the board did approve of an independent effort to promote the contributions made by America's non-White allies. *Comic*

FIGURE 1.6 The plaintive title of this 1944 story, created in cooperation with the Writers' War Board, testifies to the anti-Asian feelings prevalent in American society in the mid-twentieth century. Images of Filipinos in the story are virtually impossible to distinguish from the vicious caricatures of Japanese characters with whom they share pages.

Cavalcade, a National publication, included an ongoing series of stories produced in cooperation with the East and West Association, a private agency headed by WWB member Pearl S. Buck and committed to improving American perceptions of Allied Asian nations. Issue nine boasted a story with the depressingly unambitious title, "Filipinos Are People."[69] Despite the low bar this set, Fadiman praised the story as "a fine job" and assured the publisher, "the Board applauds the folks who are responsible for it."[70] Yet within its pages, Japanese and Filipino characters are visually indistinguishable. Both groups have grotesque buckteeth, tattered clothing, and bright yellow skin. American soldiers ultimately identify a Filipino only after he speaks in a singsong sort of American slang. And "Filipinos Are People" made no mention of the larger Filipino population, only the contributions of a single Filipino character. Thus, Filipinos may have been people, but like other comic book minorities, they were still different—human yet not quite White.

These halting efforts were buried beneath the sheer quantity of negative comic book depictions of America's non-White allies. Perhaps the best-known Chinese comic book character at this time was Chop-Chop, a member of the Blackhawk Squadron who appeared in *Blackhawk Comics*, *Modern Comics*, and *Military Comics*. Blackhawk, a Polish pilot, first appeared in the August 1941 premiere issue of *Military Comics*. Despite bravely battling the German Luftwaffe, Blackhawk lost all his squadron mates and family to a sadistic Nazi pilot, von Tepp. Intent on continuing the fight, Blackhawk assembled a new squadron that included refugees from the western European lands occupied by Germany. The squadron also acquired a mascot, a diminutive Chinese man nicknamed Chop-Chop. Unlike the rest of the Blackhawk Squadron, Chop-Chop did not fly a plane. Rather, his buffoonery often inadvertently aided Blackhawk through pratfalls and accidents. Colored in the same yellow hue as his Japanese opponents, Chop-Chop dressed in garish, old-fashioned clothing, wore his hair in a queue, and had enormous buckteeth that nearly reached his chin. Like the characters in "Filipinos Are People," Chop-Chop spoke in a singsong dialect, threatening to "smack Japs until they

FIGURE 1.7 This drawing of Chop-Chop, a Chinese member of the crack team of Allied pilots, the Blackhawks, typifies the offensive representations of America's Asian allies in wartime comics not created in cooperation with the Writers' War Board. The board sought to counteract images like this one with stories highlighting the contributions of Allied nations.

yell 'Remember Kobe Harbor!'"[71] He personified the stereotype of the "coolie."[72]

Confounding WWB efforts, characters like Chop-Chop appeared at a time when the board tried to represent the United States as an inclusive society. In 1943, the same year that the Chinese exclusion legislation was modified, board members acknowledged that comic books provided a particularly useful means of "combating race hatred, [and] preaching the necessity for United Nations cooperation and unity here at home."[73] In spite of this faith in the power of the medium, the WWB did not assign the same priority to pro-Chinese and pro-Allied comic books that it bestowed on narratives designed to foster hatred of Germans and Japanese.

DEFINING RACE

At the same time that the WWB nurtured increasingly vicious representations of America's opponents, it also commissioned comic book narratives designed to encourage racial tolerance both on the home front and overseas. Believing that victory overseas demanded domestic cooperation, the board worked with publishers on stories depicting the United States as racially and ethnically tolerant.[74] These tales promoted unity among Americans within a very specific context and for a single purpose: victory over fascism. This was a call for public rather than private tolerance; a demand for unity in service of war production and military service, not civil rights.[75] Comic book makers complied.

As with the board's endorsement of anti-Japanese and anti-German sentiment as a war-winning measure, its embrace of racial tolerance on the home front emerged from concern that Americans were unprepared to work together in a long-term battle against fascism. In mid-1944, the Comics Committee initiated a joint project with the WWB's Race Hatred Committee. Members appealed to four comic book publishers for stories promoting the contributions of non-Whites to American culture. The board stressed that the need for such stories stemmed from practical concerns and potential dangers to civil society. Board members warned publishers, "Some good judges actually fear that a civil war may come about in this country unless all men of good will put their shoulders to the wheel" to fight intolerance. A racial war at home threatened not only liberal democracy but also the country's ability to wage and win a global war. The board argued the need for comic book makers' help because "we have got to begin from the ground up with the run-of-the-mill, average American citizen who reads the pulps and the comics and who is decisively influenced by them."[76]

The board's race-based outreach made sense because Americans of all races consumed comic books. In particular, both Black civilians and soldiers read comic books and were therefore likely to encounter and, hopefully, appreciate the messages of tolerance in board-sanctioned stories. In 1944, Enoch Waters, Pacific correspondent for the *Chicago Defender*, a historic Black newspaper, reported on the morale of troops stationed on the island New Guinea. Noting how hard it was for Black soldiers to entertain themselves on the isolated island, Waters stressed the significance of comic books. As a means of distracting soldiers from the horrors around them, "comic books rate high," he wrote. Indeed, they were so significant that comic books with a cover price of ten cents traded hands for $3.25 among Black soldiers on New Guinea.[77] It was important, then, that race-based WWB propaganda reach Black as well as White consumers, both in and out of uniform.

As the Comics Committee geared up to produce pro-tolerance narratives in support of the war effort, Fawcett Publications boasted the best-selling comic book in the United States: *Captain Marvel Adventures*, which featured Captain Marvel, "the World's Mightiest Mortal" and alter ego of young orphan Billy Batson. Billy transforms into Captain Marvel whenever he utters the magic word "Shazam." *Captain Marvel Adventures* sold approximately one million copies every month. In 1944, Captain Marvel's fan club included half a million members.[78] The captain's popularity spawned several companion comic books, including *Captain Marvel Jr.*, starring disabled newsboy Freddy Freeman as the alter ego of Captain Marvel Jr., a teenaged variation on the original.[79]

The August 1944 issue of *Captain Marvel Jr.* included an anti-lynching narrative called "The Necktie Party" that emerged from Fawcett's enthusiastic cooperation with the WWB.[80] Fawcett submitted story drafts to the board for comment and even created a new character, Radar the International Policeman, as part of the board-mandated effort to promote internationalism. WWB members enthused over the message of tolerance and justice embedded in "The Necktie Party," which criticized the attempted lynching of an innocent, impoverished White man. The WWB, wrote Fadiman, had "nothing but the warmest kind of praise" for the story.[81] "The Necktie

Party" exemplified the WWB's cautious, practical approach to promoting tolerance at home: it condemned extralegal punishment and attacks on the poor but did not describe lynching as a crime overwhelmingly inflicted on Blacks by Whites. Indeed, the story included no Black characters at all.

At the same time, racist images of Black characters appeared in other Fawcett titles like *Captain Marvel Adventures*, typified by Steamboat, the captain's valet. Steamboat embodies the worst excesses of minstrelsy; he has thick lips and kinky hair, speaks in dialect ("Cap'n Marvel, thank heab'n yous heah!"), and bumbles into danger, confounding Captain Marvel and letting criminals escape. Although the WWB criticized racial discrimination as detrimental to the war effort and convened the Race Hatred Committee, it did not request that Fawcett remove Steamboat from *Captain Marvel Adventures*.[82] Eliminating Steamboat required the determined efforts of a Black youth group from Junior High School 120 in New York City who met with Fawcett editor Will Lieberson in mid-1945 and demanded Steamboat's removal. Initially, Lieberson refused, arguing that *Captain Marvel Adventures* included many kinds of caricatures "for the sake of humor." The students responded by showing Lieberson a picture of Steamboat, telling him, "This is not the Negro race, but your one-and-a-half million readers will think it so."[83] Ultimately, Lieberson relented, and Steamboat quietly disappeared from the pages of Fawcett comic books. He was not, however, replaced by any more positive depictions of Blacks.

In June 1944, Fadiman sent a letter to M. C. Gaines of National, requesting a comic narrative "with a negro hero." Fadiman suggested a tale built around the exploits of the Black 99th Army Air Corps Pursuit Squadron and offered to send the necessary background materials to National.[84] Gaines's staff duly crafted a story including the 99th Pursuit Squadron, nicknamed the Red Tails and better known as the Tuskegee Airmen. The story, "The 99th Squadron," appeared in the winter 1945 issue of *Comic Cavalcade*, a series with a circulation of four hundred thousand copies per issue.[85] In spite of the issue's title, the protagonist is not a Black flyer but a White pilot named Hop Harrigan. Aided by Sergeant Tank Tinker, his sidekick and mechanic,

Hop fights fascism all over the world. "The 99th Squadron" finds him stationed in the European theater alongside the Tuskegee Airmen.

Hop and his fellow squadron mates must fly Luftwaffe general Fritz Schlange, a Nazi Party member, to a prisoner of war camp. After boarding the transport plane with Schlange, Hop delights in informing the Nazi that their pilot is named Izzy Epstein. Hop then sets up a movie projector and screen and offers Schlange the opportunity to watch some in-flight movies while the plane wings toward the prison camp. Schlange accepts, and Hop rolls a film depicting the 99th Pursuit Squadron's P-40 fighter planes shooting down German aircraft from Schlange's own squadron. Deeply impressed by the bravery and skill of the American pilots, Schlange exclaims, "Those pilots of the 99th must be your best veterans. No doubt men of the superior races." Hop smiles as the Nazi watches the planes of the 99th Squadron land. Schlange is horrified as the film shows the victorious Black pilots of the 99th descending from the planes. Shaken, he exclaims, "Donnervetter! Those—*those* are the pilots who shot down my men?" Hop responds angrily, "So much for your 'superior race' nonsense."

Stunned, Schlange submits to one last film recounting his defeat in aerial combat and subsequent capture by the Allies. He gloats as the film silently unspools, showing the Nazi pilot's plane as he strafes a Red Cross convoy. Then a member of the 99th Squadron shoots down Schlange's plane, wounding the general and forcing him to crash-land near the wreckage of the Red Cross convoy. Deflated, Schlange stares at his own wounded, unconscious body on the screen as first a Jewish soldier and then a Black man volunteer for blood transfusions so that the Nazi might live. Schlange murmurs that he is no longer a true Aryan, to which Hop retorts, "You should feel better for it." Chastened, the Nazi asks to apologize to Epstein, the Jewish pilot at the controls of the transport plane. Epstein refuses to speak with Schlange or accept his apology, telling Hop, "The herrenvolk learn too little and too late. The blood of the millions of innocent minorities that have suffered and died under Nazi brutality may not be erased by a word."[86]

The WWB applauded the finished story, which appeared in not only *Comic Cavalcade* but also the *CIO News*, a publication of the

FIGURE 1.8 The Writers' War Board worked with National Comics on this positive, pro-tolerance narrative from 1944 about the Black 99th Pursuit Squadron. Within the story, though, White characters share virtually no physical space with Black characters.

Congress of Industrial Organizations (CIO) with a circulation of half a million copies per issue.[87] Still, in spite of its anti-Nazi language, the narrative contains few specific references to the Tuskegee Airmen, and images of Black aviators appear in just three of the fifty-three panels in the eight-page story. The pilots of the 99th Squadron have no dialogue and do not interact with Hop Harrigan or his Nazi captive. Black and White pilots do not share a single panel. The pilots of the 99th Squadron are virtually invisible. Epstein, the Jewish pilot, remains hidden as well. Readers "hear" his disembodied voice from behind the closed cockpit door but never see his face. Neither policy makers nor propagandists sought to weaken "the power of whiteness."[88] Wartime culture could not be allowed to interfere with the essential reasons why many White Americans agreed to fight.[89]

In mid-1945, at the request of the board, National began work on a story about the formerly enslaved abolitionist Sojourner Truth. The WWB provided Gaines with a biography of Truth and also solicited help from Walter White, head of the National Association for the Advancement of Colored People (NAACP).[90] National submitted a draft to the WWB, which the board passed on to the Bureau for Intercultural Education.[91] Shocked by the narrative, the bureau warned, "The author unconsciously deepens the image of the 'Negro type' and so defeats the purpose of the story. It inspires repugnance." Far from praising the contributions of Truth, the story perpetuated stereotypes "associated in the minds of many whites with illiteracy and ridicule." Specifically, the bureau insisted that National not depict Truth when she was enslaved because this implied the superiority of Whites, and it requested the deletion of the word "nigger" and the phrase "faithful slave." It also questioned why the WWB and National Comics had assigned a White artist to the story.[92] In reality a Black artist, Alfonso Greene, *did* draw the story and even signed the first panel. Apparently, neither the members of the Bureau for Intercultural Education nor those of the WWB knew that Greene was Black.[93]

The finished story presented Truth as brave but also dependent on the courage, knowledge, and open-mindedness of White Americans. It appeared in the summer 1945 issue of *Wonder Woman* as part of an ongoing series of historically themed tales called "Wonder Women of History." As with the earlier story on the 99th Pursuit Squadron, the biography of Truth did not expressly mention civil rights or contemporary racial injustices. It simply focused on the bravery of an individual Black woman while simultaneously suggesting that White Americans facilitated this bravery.[94] One of the White enslavers, "a good-natured man named Martin Scriver," sells her to another man for $350, a price based upon her amusing "independent airs." After freeing herself from her new enslaver, she turns to the legal system in an effort to reclaim her infant son, whom she was forced to

FIGURE 1.9 This story about abolitionist and suffragist Sojourner Truth appeared in a 1945 issue of *Wonder Woman*. Illustrated by Black artist Alfonso Greene, it was part of the paradoxical, state-sanctioned effort to use comic books to generate race hatred abroad and racial tolerance at home.

leave behind. When a White judge mocks her appeal, a White lawyer intercedes and retrieves her child. Significantly, Truth appears more as an advocate for women's rights than as a crusader for civil rights. And in a reversal of the sort of segregation imposed on characters in the Hop Harrigan story, Truth appears overwhelmingly with White people; she shares panel space with other Black people only while she is enslaved. In accordance with the board's limited endorsement of racial equality, the biography of Truth represented her as an individual who, with the help of sympathetic Whites, solved personal rather than larger social problems.

These timid efforts at teaching tolerance competed with vast numbers of stories containing racist images of Black characters. In addition to offensive Black characters like Steamboat, comic books offered similarly repellent depictions of Black men and women around the world. In issue after issue of *Wings Comics*—a popular title aimed at older readers—pilots and adventurers like Jane Martin, Suicide Smith, and Captain Wings battled Black characters in Africa and on Pacific islands. In one such story from 1943, the women of a USO troupe called the XYZ Trio are marooned along with Captain Wings on a Pacific island. After a few panels in which the women repeatedly change their clothes in front of Captain Wings, a Black native approaches the group. One of the trio uses a ventriloquist's dummy of Uncle Sam to terrify him. When another native gawks at her dummy, she quips, "Oboy! What a publicity still, if we only had a camera!" The rest of the story offers a baffling and grotesque flurry of anti-Asian and anti-Black stereotypes. Initially, the islanders are sympathetic to the Japanese soldiers stationed there, but the ventriloquist convinces them to back the Americans when her dummy exclaims, "Yellow men are weaklings! Liars! Unworthy of your trust! They dare not fight in equal combat!" Speaking mangled, nearly incomprehensible English, the islanders then rise up against the Japanese soldiers, as one shouts, "White man's juju talkum true! Take yellow bang-bang!"[95] What meaning might a consumer extract from such viciously racist imagery? And would it be tempered by the sort of vague, pro-tolerance narratives in select, WWB-affiliated titles? The board did not attempt to answer these questions.

PALADINES DE LA LIBERTAD

As the WWB worked behind the scenes to shape popular perceptions of race among English-speaking consumers, the OIAA labored to convince Latin American audiences of the need to fight totalitarianism. The agency, however, took a rather different approach to the "comic book technique" than the board. OIAA offices throughout Latin America utilized noncommercial propaganda comic books, instead of existing superhero titles. Creating these propaganda comics posed both an opportunity and a challenge. As the agency supervised the contents of its own comic books, it was able to tailor the contents to the country in which it was distributed.[96] The OIAA also streamlined the cost of propaganda by farming out comic book production to local businesses. But because its propaganda comics remained the product of a government agency, OIAA publications— like those of the WWB—could not address certain key issues, for fear that American elected officials would object. OIAA comic books therefore avoided any mention of racial tensions at home or between the United States and its continental neighbors. OIAA operatives worried that an official pronouncement on race not only could anger citizens of Latin American nations but also might "light a domestic political bonfire" in the United States.[97] As a result, the agency's comic books focused on less controversial themes: the shared dangers from fascism, the need for cooperative hemispheric security, and the role of the United States in defeating Germany and Japan.

While the WWB established a symbiotic relationship with commercial comic book publishers and camouflaged its propaganda within popular titles, the OIAA made no effort to hide its propaganda. Again, the reasoning behind these decisions was due, in large part, to the racial composition of the intended audience. The WWB strove to differentiate itself from the more obvious, state-sponsored propaganda produced by America's fascist opponents. Its members feared that American consumers would be repelled by overt state intervention in the culture industry or transparent manipulation of culture for the sake of patriotism. WWB propaganda sought to change minds while also entertaining them and to win hearts by demonstrating, without embellishment or interference, the true evils of totalitarianism. The OIAA, however, presumed its non-White audiences were less educated and less discriminating than those in the United States. There was no need, then, to embed comic book propaganda within commercial titles or to emphasize subtlety rather than a more heavy-handed approach. The most effective propaganda, OIAA operatives concluded, employed clear messages and acknowledged its origins.

OIAA comic books built support for the nation's foreign policies by narrating the lives of prominent Americans, outlining American sacrifices made in the name of hemispheric security, and representing Germany as a mortal threat. In 1943, the OIAA Coordinating Committee in Uruguay printed and distributed *Paladines de la libertad* (Freedom fighters), a comic book biography of American statesmen and soldiers, including Franklin D. Roosevelt, George Marshall, Henry Wallace, and Cordell Hull. OIAA members reported "numerous favorable responses" to the comic book, which attempted to humanize America's political and military leadership.[98] It includes glimpses of "a typical day in the life of President Franklin D. Roosevelt" and a reminder that Vice President Henry Wallace woke up early every day to play tennis before work.[99] Absent, however, were any non-White or female American heroes, though later OIAA titles did note the wartime contributions made by these groups, both in the United States and Latin America.

In 1944, several OIAA offices produced two hundred thousand copies of another pro-American propaganda comic, *Estados Unidos en la guerra* (The United States in the war). The title was printed in Ecuador and distributed there as well as in Uruguay, Paraguay, Bolivia, Peru, and Chile. Its outward appearance mimics that of a contemporary American commercial comic book, boasting a glossy, action-filled cover. But on the inside panel, which precedes pages of basic black-and-white artwork printed on cheaper paper, the consumer finds the attribution, "Published by the Coordinator of Inter-American Affairs, Washington, D.C."

The comic extols the material and military contributions made by the United States on behalf of all free nations in the fight against fas-

FIGURE 1.10 Issued in 1944 for distribution in Latin America, this title became a model for many of the federal propaganda comic books sent by the millions to the decolonizing world during the Cold War.

cism. In promoting "the sacred contribution of free men toward the final victory of the United Nations," *Estados Unidos en la guerra* also emphasizes that in the United States, this effort included both White and non-White Americans. "If the Axis develops a new weapon," it notes, "someone, maybe a soldier on the front or a dark worker, suggests a way of fighting it."[100] It emphasizes the sacrifices made by all Americans on behalf of the war effort, including "housewives of the United States" who "give their valuable cooperation towards a just distribution of all scarce food." The comic also reminds readers that American wartime innovations would eventually yield higher standards of living for all humanity. It makes a very practical appeal for support, echoing domestic advertising and propaganda that encouraged Americans to fight on behalf of a peaceful and prosperous future. At its core, *Estados Unidos en la guerra* presents the United States as both a reliable, selfless ally and a potential source of labor-saving technologies and products.

The following year, OIAA Coordinating Committees in Cuba, Ecuador, and the Dominican Republic printed at least twenty-five thousand copies of another comic-type pamphlet, *La sórdida amenaza* (The sordid threat), for use in Latin America and the Caribbean.[101] The title is physically plainer than *Estados Unidos en la guerra*, lacking a glossy cover and containing artwork of varying quality. It differs in content as well, offering an attack against Germany and fascism, rather than support for America's wartime sacrifices and contributions. In a style reminiscent of domestically distributed comic book propaganda like "This Is Our Enemy," it describes Germany as a nation with a single historical goal: "To dominate the world through force of arms." *La sórdida amenaza* includes images of German brutality, including a scene titled "Peace, Nazi-style." It depicts a German soldier reading a collection of Goethe's work amid the ruins of the Czech town of Lidice, which was virtually erased from the earth and whose population was slaughtered.[102] In contrast to the upbeat *Estados Unidos en la guerra*, its tone is cautionary. It warns that any collaboration with fascists will lead to similar destruction in Latin America and an inevitable Third World War.

CAMOUFLAGED PROPAGANDA

The WWB and OIAA made the bold decision to use comic books because their members believed the medium possessed several unique traits. (Imagine if decades later the federal government successfully snuck pro–Vietnam War sentiment into rock music.) Comic books were cheap, popular, portable, and comprehensible. Unlike film or radio, comic books were not subject to any sort of external censorship. They seemed capable of communicating with a remarkably diverse audience deemed out of reach of more conventional propaganda through the sort of language and violent imagery considered unacceptable in more middlebrow media. Children and adults, civilians and servicemen, the semiliterate and the well-heeled—all enjoyed and understood the combination of action, words, and images woven throughout comic book narratives. Most crucially, books did not *seem* like propaganda.

From the outset, the relationship among the comic book industry, the WWB, and the OIAA was inseparable from the issue of race. By 1943, the agencies had identified comic books as a particularly useful means of shaping popular perceptions of America's enemies as not only different but also deserving of destruction. The agencies were aided in this effort by the nature of the comic book medium and industry. Free from the censorship and constraints imposed on more established mass culture like Hollywood films, comic book creators and propagandists could utilize remarkably high levels of violence and racism in the service of US policy.

In some cases, derogatory racial tropes and conventions appeared on the same pages as patriotic, inclusive imagery. A single, frantic full-page image from a 1943 issue of *Young Allies* exemplifies this contradiction. In it, the Young Allies are engaged in a vicious fight with several Japanese soldiers. One of the squad's White members, Knuckles, is busy pummeling an adult Japanese soldier. Nearby, Bucky Barnes struggles to restrain a Japanese officer intent on stabbing Whitewash Jones, the squad's Black member. The faces of the Japanese officer and Whitewash are nearly touching, and both are rendered in the crude, racist visual language of the time. Whitewash has thick purple lips and wears a bright green checked suit with a garish tie. Above Whitewash, the straining Japanese officer peers through round spectacles perched on a piglike nose and grits a set of enormous buckteeth.[103] What messages were alert readers to extract from this and similar stories? Surely they noted the conflicting appeals for tolerance and cooperation juxtaposed with demands for the utter destruction of non-White, non-American nations.

This juxtaposition highlights the major challenges created by the comic book. While board members helped shape stories like "This Is Our Enemy," it competed on the newsstand with roughly one hundred other titles, the majority of which were assembled without input from the WWB. For every image of domestic harmony or German treachery carefully crafted by the board, there were thousands, even millions, of potentially conflicting comic book narratives full of fantastic Japanese supervillains, buffoonish Nazi officers, and viciously stereotyped Black characters. And although some contemporary scholars endorsed the comic book as a powerful propaganda weapon, the WWB had no real evidence that audiences absorbed the "correct" messages.

The use of comic books by the WWB and OIAA ended with the Japanese surrender in 1945. The OIAA and the OWI were first shrunk and then absorbed into the State Department's Cultural Division, which in 1946 was renamed the Office of International Information and Cultural Affairs.[104] For a time, cultural warfare seemed vastly less important than nuclear warfare.

CHAPTER TWO: THE WILD SPREE OF THE LAUGHING SADIST

THE CONFERENCE ROOM TECHNIQUE

In 1950, Guatemala elected progressive former army officer Jacobo Árbenz to the presidency. The election was a significant test of civic participation in a country emerging from decades of dictatorship and domination by the American United Fruit Company, the nation's largest landowner and employer.

While not a declared communist, Árbenz promised social and economic reforms aimed at modernizing Guatemala, moderating United Fruit, and ending the nation's economic dependence on the United States. Interpreting these plans as communist-inspired mischief, the CIA branded them "an intensely nationalistic program of progress colored by the touchy, anti-foreign inferiority complex of the 'Banana Republic.'"[1] By the time Árbenz took office in March 1951, the CIA and State Department were already planning his overthrow. This effort gained momentum with the 1952 election of President Eisenhower, who installed Allen Dulles as head of the CIA and his brother John Foster Dulles as head of the State Department. The Dulles brothers had close ties to United Fruit and enthusiastically endorsed the plan, optimistically code-named Operation Success, to

75

overthrow Árbenz and replace him with a leader who would priori-
tize anticommunism, stability, and United Fruit.

In December 1953, Allen Dulles approved Operation Success,
which included a list of fifty-eight Guatemalans targeted for
assassination.[2] A CIA officer summarized the operation as "a terror
campaign to terrify Árbenz particularly, to terrify his troops," and to
provide an opening for American-backed rebels to take over.[3] Within
months, news of the looming Operation Success reached Árbenz in
Guatemala, and his government set about trying to defend itself. But
the United States had already stopped selling military equipment to
Guatemala and now moved to block purchases from other countries.
Trapped, Guatemala sought arms from communist Czechoslovakia, a
decision that confirmed the American leadership's worst suspicions
of Árbenz. Within the closed loop of Cold War thinking, Árbenz's
desperate bid for Soviet bloc weapons—an act the United States practically engendered—only confirmed the need for Operation Success.

High-ranking members of the Guatemalan army cooperated with
the CIA, and Árbenz realized he no longer controlled his country's
armed forces. Hoping to preserve some semblance of his reforms,
along with Guatemalan independence from the United States, he ab-
dicated the presidency in late June 1954. Árbenz and his family were
driven into exile, and after being refused citizenship in Switzerland
and France, they sought refuge behind the Iron Curtain. His daugh-
ter committed suicide in 1965, and Árbenz died under confusing
circumstances six years later, having never returned to Guatemala.

True to its code name, Operation Success brought Guatemala
a stable, anticommunist government sympathetic to American
political, military, and economic goals. But this victory and the
agency's recent success in overthrowing Iran's elected government
established dangerous precedents. They normalized political assassinations, the subversion of governments that posed little or no danger
to the security of the United States, and the idea that deviation from
American-style capitalism justified illegal and even violent regime
change. In their wake, one CIA officer recalled, "Many of us . . . did
not feel bound in the actions we took as staff members to observe all
the ethical rules."[4]

Among the materials prepared by the CIA for Operation Success is an astonishing nineteen-page document. It is essentially a step-by-step guide for assassinations, complete with cartoon images of how to conduct a political killing. The document begins by laying out the history of political assassination and various justifications for its use. After noting that murder is illegal, the anonymous author adds, "Killing a political leader whose burgeoning career is a clear and present danger to the cause of freedom may be held necessary. But assassination can seldom be employed with a clear conscience. Persons who are morally squeamish should not attempt it." The text then instructs CIA agents how to select appropriate assassins and manipulate them into committing political murder.

The last page of the guide, blandly titled "Conference Room Technique," is broken into six panels, much like a page in a comic book. Beneath each scribbled panel is a bit of text; the words and images walk two assassins through the killing of ten people seated around a conference table. Each step is laid out in detail: the first gunner enters the room, then "opens fire on first subject to react. Swings across group toward center of mass. Times burst to empty magazine at end of swing," as the second gunman "covers group to prevent individual dangerous reactions, if necessary, fires individual bursts of 3 rounds." Finally, after everyone around the table is dead, the second assassin "leaves propaganda" in the room, and the pair escape with guns loaded.[5] The CIA diagram is, in essence, a crime comic book.

The battle for Guatemala played out in commercial comic books as well. But despite a relative lack of censorship, none of the comic book images of Guatemala were as violent as those found in the CIA's "Study of Assassination." In a 1952 issue of Racket Squad in Action, a group of criminals take advantage of the chaos in the country to sell shares in the "Guatemala Sweepstakes," a lottery scam run by "some guys who are down there dodging extradition!" The story implies that the Guatemalan government is crooked and complicit in—or at least tolerant of—schemes hatched by American criminals hiding in the country. By depicting Guatemala as a lawless haven for gangsters at a time when communism was synonymous with illegal and unethical behavior, the story implicitly supports the state-sanctioned

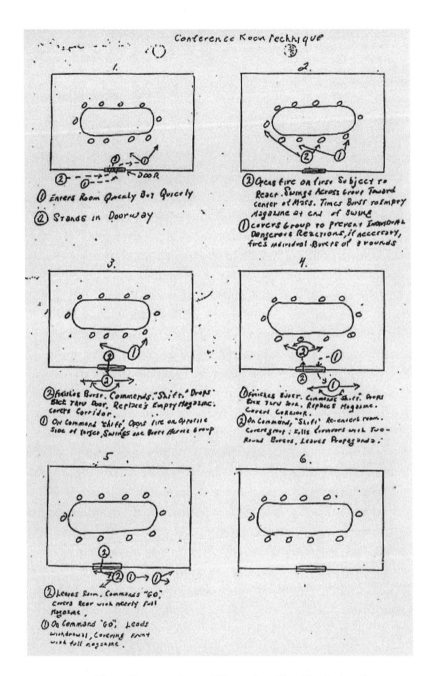

FIGURE 2.1 These diagrams, from a CIA-produced booklet designed to teach Guatemalan insurgents how to murder communists, echo images from commercial comic books criticized by activists like Dr. Fredric Wertham for their depictions of various crimes.

view of Guatemala as a threat to American security. When contrasted with the images in the "Study of Assassination," however, the illegal schemes, fistfights, and gunplay in "Guatemala Sweepstakes" seem amateurish. The savagery in the commercial comic book unfolds on a small, personal scale, as petty criminals punch and shoot each other without harming anyone else around them. The violence is economical, rather than political, in both substance and style.[6]

Even after the CIA-led coup that overthrew Árbenz, another story entitled "The Commie Fire Bomb Plot" depicts Guatemala as a country riddled with unrepentant communists out to destroy the reputation of the United States in Latin America. This appears in an issue of *T-Man*, a Cold War–themed comic that catalogs the globe-trotting exploits of Treasury agent Pete Trask. At the outset of the story, Guatemalan-American relations are strained by a series of explosions aboard American ships sailing off Central America. Trask is sent to investigate and quickly realizes the saboteurs are using a communist jai alai player to run an extremely convoluted scheme. Stationed on a beach, the player uses his jai alai basket to lob incendiary bombs down the smokestacks of passing American ships. When the ships accelerate to full speed, the bombs explode. The resulting loss of property angers the United States and makes a mockery of the pro-American government in Guatemala.

The story undoubtedly reinforced contemporary concerns about communists infiltrating Latin America and the need to meet this challenge with alacrity. Although Trask solves the crisis largely through a sort of smiling brutality, the story involves no killing. Ultimately, Trask defeats the communists simply by shooting one of their incendiary bombs out of the sky. "The Commie Fire Bomb Plot" is packed with racism, political intolerance, and physical violence, but it still remains less chilling than the step-by-step guide to murder in the CIA's crime comic book.[7]

Comics like *T-Man* and the "Conference Room Technique" resulted from a postwar shift in the relationship between the federal government and the comic book industry. During World War II, the government nourished the comic book industry and helped create millions of adult comic book consumers. Following the Allied victory, federal agencies quickly relinquished control over the raw materials and content of commercial comic books while still appropriating the comic book form in support of foreign policy goals. The WWB was dissolved, but comics were still incorporated into government programs both overt and covert, like the Marshall Plan and Operation Success, and distributed to American service members waging the Cold War in many parts of the world. It was as though policy makers imagined that the comic book industry had frozen in time during World War II, perpetually churning out stories full of patriotic superheroes, pro-tolerance narratives, and state-mandated characters of color. This was not so.

The federal government's speedy exit from the commercial side of the industry had significant effects on the content of postwar comic books. Publishers could cater to the rougher, more graphic tastes of their adult readers in the United States and around the world. New genres focused on crime, horror, and romance soon outsold and overshadowed the superhero titles so popular during World War II. Free from federal supervision, substantial characters of color rarely appeared in these new varieties of comics. They depicted the United States as a society in which prejudice referred to class, religion, or gender, rather than race. At the same time, absent any guidance from agencies like the WWB, comic book creators directed violence at new targets. Crime and horror titles, in particular, turned their extreme brutalities inward on to new sorts of villains, who greatly differed from the external, racialized villains popularized during the war. American men and women—overwhelmingly White—were now the victims of increasingly graphic violence. Similar scenes, though less overtly violent, also appeared in romance titles.

This inversion took place not only because it *could* but also because comic book consumers demanded it and comic book makers were willing and able to produce new and challenging narratives. The crime, horror, and romance genres, so novel and confrontational, emerged as the country established a global military and cultural presence as part of the Cold War. These comic books reached wide international audiences as American publishers sold their products, both in English and in translation, in dozens of countries.

At the same time, federal agencies incorporated these new and unfettered comic books into the Marshall Plan, a massive effort to rehabilitate the economies of Western Europe. The postwar comic book, cut loose from the federal supervision imposed during World War II, was now a popular worldwide phenomenon. Wherever the United States sent tourists, soldiers, and diplomats, these problematic comic books went too.

By the early 1950s, approximately four hundred comic book titles spanning dozens of genres jostled for attention on newsstands in the United States and abroad.[8] A popular crime comic book could sell half a million copies per issue (*Crime Does Not Pay* self-reported sales of over a million) at a time when the best-selling children's books sold one-tenth as many copies in an entire year.[9] On a per-issue basis, newsdealers sold more copies of *Roy Rogers Comics* than *Good Housekeeping* magazine and larger numbers of *Looney Tunes Comics* than *Look* or *Better Homes and Gardens* magazines.[10] One study from 1949 showed nearly 90 percent of children aged thirteen or younger read comic books every week. Another contemporary study indicated that more than 80 percent of teens and 90 percent of children consumed comics.[11] Comic books were, as Carol Tilley suggests, "the most dominant cultural force in children's lives in the 1940s and 1950s."[12] Children bought, consumed, and traded comics, and they could be found in locations as varied as the dentist's waiting room, local stores, or classrooms, where teachers used them to educate students about topics ranging from atomic energy to mental health.

Children were not the only audience for American commercial comic books. The government's support for the industry during the war ensured that millions of adults consumed comic books too. A 1947 study conducted on behalf of Fawcett Publications interviewed two thousand city dwellers and concluded that 55 percent of urban families read comic books, with the largest number attributed to families with older children. Nearly half of adults aged eighteen to twenty-five identified as frequent or occasional readers, as did 35 percent of adults between twenty-six and thirty-five. Although the number of self-identified urban readers decreased with age, 27 percent of adults aged thirty-six to forty-five read comics, along with

13 percent of adults over the age of forty-six. Among these adult age groups, the number of comic book consumers was nearly evenly split between men and women. Intriguingly, the study also noted that because adults outnumbered children in urban areas, the actual number of mature readers was larger than the number of younger ones. Both men and women over the age of eighteen admitted to reading at least six comics in the month preceding the survey, with the most going to middle-income families. In total, these urban adults bought more than three million comic books during the month of the survey.[13]

Another market research study conducted in 1949 indicated that over 30 percent of adults identified as regular comic book readers, including members of the armed forces based around the world. One veteran, upon returning to an unfamiliar United States, despairingly told the *Washington Post*, "The only thing I have in common with my son is the comics."[14] An early postwar issue of *Boy Comics*, from Lev Gleason Publications, contained letters from an army soldier noting, "In *Boy Comics* we really escape from the rigors of Army life. *Boy Comics* are passed bunk to bunk, and believe me, there's a long waiting list."[15] Some titles boasted of their military readership, perhaps to use it as a legitimizing, patriotic veneer and to emphasize the titles' adult contents. One such comic book was *Wings Comics*, a popular anthology title that was distributed internationally in both English and Spanish.[16] Many issues included a page dedicated to letters from readers, often including members of the American armed forces and men and women in Britain, Burma, Canada, the Philippines, and South Africa.[17] The covers of *Wings Comics* frequently boasted images of women in bondage, while the stories within depicted women as both the victims and perpetrators of sexualized violence. French characters were inevitably female and voluptuous and a source of excitement to male Americans who alternately beat and rescued them. Black characters, when they appeared at all, hewed to vicious stereotypes. Chinese men were communist troublemakers, while the women appeared in turn as alluring red sirens and helpless pro-American dolls.[18] These images found ready audiences among service members and civilians during the postwar decade and also

FIGURE 2.2 Sold around the world in English and Spanish, this bondage- and violence-filled 1947 issue of *Wings Comics*, and millions more like it, caused many problems for US policy makers. Uncensored commercial comics were distributed abroad by formal and informal Cold War networks of publishers, service members, diplomats, and tourists.

argued against the state-sanctioned image of America as a culturally advanced and politically inclusive society. The wartime support for and subsequent abandonment of the comic book industry by the federal government made it all possible.

MAPS FOR CRIME

In 1954—the same year the CIA unleashed Operation Success—the most visible American critic of comic books, Dr. Fredric Wertham, published *Seduction of the Innocent*. It was a blistering, four-hundred-page assault on the very form and content of the medium as a significant contributor to juvenile delinquency. Comic books, Wertham argued, provided a "map for crime"—they were instruction manuals for acts of violence. In the middle of *Seduction of the Innocent* are sixteen pages of images, reproduced without context, from various crime and horror comic books. Intended as a visual warning to parents, the gallery showcases what Wertham believed were the very worst images and ideas available in crime and horror comic books. Beneath each picture, Wertham includes a tart comment; under a drawing of a gangster screaming, "I don't need nobody! I'd shiv my best friend's back if it would get me an easy buck! Friendship is for suckers!" he writes, "Comic-book philosophy." And following a full-page diagram of the human body, labeled to indicate physically sensitive areas, he simply writes, "How to hurt people."[19]

The diagram is crude with simpleminded suggestions for inflicting pain like "Shins: kick" and "Pit of stomach: fist blow or kick."[20] It is a rough guide for schoolyard bullies that shares essential similarities with the sequential artwork in the CIA's guide for assassinations. Both are divided into panels and use a powerful combination of simple images and text to explain how readers might inflict violence on others. And both presume that this blend of words and pictures was comprehensible to virtually anyone, from schoolchildren to assassins abroad, along with non-English-speaking CIA operatives. The CIA and Wertham both saw the comic book form as an instruction manual for crime—a means of conveying violent directions to those who were not "morally squeamish," whether through youth or training. The CIA's assassination diagram was the culmination of the crime comic and the manifestation of Wertham's worst fears about the medium.

Within the frightening new context of the Cold War, American activists, parents, and law enforcement officials feared that susceptible children would use comic book crimes as templates for illegal behavior. In August 1947, at its annual national convention, the Fraternal Order of Police condemned crime comic books as guides to "unrestrained, bold, vicious, salacious, and immoral" conduct.[21] The following year, police in Oklahoma blamed crime comic books for teaching two young boys how to steal and then fly a plane over one hundred miles from their home. A few months later in Indiana, authorities warned that such comic books taught young children how to torture each other. That summer, three boys between the ages of six and eight told police they were reenacting a comic book story when they abducted, stripped, bound, and burned a seven-year-old boy from their neighborhood. Acknowledging the apparent power of the comic book form, local officials affirmed that the three delinquents came from "good families," suggesting that the positive influences of parents and siblings were no match for the allure of comics.[22]

Postwar American crime, horror, and romance comic books grew popular within a very specific political and cultural context. The immediate postwar period witnessed labor strife, atomic tests, the Soviet Union's transition from ally to enemy, and a civil rights movement energized by its wartime achievements. It was within this singular swirl of dread, optimism, and newfound American power that violent and sexual comics captivated millions of readers. By their very nature, these comic books posed a challenge to the growing domestic consensus that the survival of American-style democracy required a long-term confrontation with international communism. In a society that imagined itself as a more inclusive alternative to Soviet-style dictatorships, these comic books raised uncomfortable questions about the true state of race relations, gender roles, and economic inequality.

Equally significant were the changes wrought by the war on the medium and its audience. Malcolm Kildale, a comic book writer, artist, and editor who had worked for more than ten publishers since the very dawn of the industry, tried to explain these profound shifts to Wertham in a long and impassioned letter. They were, he lamented, simple matters of money and pride: he had never met anyone who wanted long-term employment in comics; everyone dreamed of working in more reputable fields and saw comic books as nothing more than a means of staying alive, clothed, and fed. Because writers and artists did not care about the quality of their work, they took the path of least creative resistance: rather than inventing new stories or characters, they simply bought comics from a particular publisher, read them, and then banged out copycat narratives and images, with only a few changes. If the publisher had already printed a nearly identical story, odds were good they would do so again. Its competitors likely sought proven formulas too, not innovation.

The core problem, Kildale explained, was that the comic book originated as entertainment for children but had, during World War II, become wildly popular with adults. Left unmentioned was the role of the federal government in promoting and shaping the wartime comic book industry and the ways in which this intervention encouraged adults to consume comic books. The growing popularity of comic books among adults, Kildale continued, forced the production of content aimed at servicemen, many of whom were deeply affected by their wartime experiences. "I was in the Navy," he wrote, "and watched comic books sink lower and lower in editorial taste. The books were slanted at men in the armed forces. Think of that—comic books aimed at men, using a format established primarily for children. What is to be done?" Once publishers realized the size and scope of their newfound audience, there was no going back "because the publishers are catering to adults with low mentality, and not children." Kildale despaired because outside of censorship—an unacceptable step—he could think of no other way to curb the excesses of comic book creators. Violent and antisocial comics, he warned Wertham, were not going anywhere.[23]

As the Cold War took shape, the family became an essential element in the battle between democracy and communism. A "domestic ideology" emerged as Americans sought relief from postwar fears in their homes and private lives. Men and women committed themselves deeply to the family both as a defense against the stresses of postwar life and as a means of nurturing the nation's children, a vulnerable—and valuable—resource in a long-term ideological battle.[24] Mirroring the nation's quest for security in a complex and fluid international system, families sought safety through a policy of containment that would keep dangerous cultural and political forces at bay.[25] For these millions of Americans, comic books came to present a clear challenge to the concept of a safe home.[26] Within these titles, there were few caring mothers or strong male authority figures, and children were often transformed into criminals, rather than responsible citizens.

It was not simply the images and narratives within postwar comic books that posed a threat. The processes by which Americans purchased and consumed comic books additionally suggested a loss of control over segments of the population—children, young adults, the uneducated, and the impoverished—deemed either vulnerable or dangerous within the context of the Cold War. Crime comics dealt in the themes of lust and fright. They became private objects of desire among people who, by the standards of the time, were thought not to possess such capacities.[27] Compounding these challenges, comic books also circulated away from the eyes of authority. They could be smuggled into homes, churches, and classrooms, even tucked between the pages of textbooks. It was this combination of invisibility, ubiquity, and availability that made comic books so powerful. Anyone, of any age, could buy a comic. The comic then lived its second, shadow life in the hands of multiple consumers who read the issue, passed it along, and brought it into new spaces previously presumed safe.

In a society increasingly concerned with the menace of decay from within, comic books represented a contagion. They were transmitted to and among consumers without regard for traditional dividing lines like age, race, and geography. In 1947, a coroner's jury in Pittsburgh cited crime comic books as a contributing factor in the suicide of a twelve-year-old boy. The jury concluded that he had

learned how to hang himself from diagrams and images in a crime
title. "I burned every one," his mother assured the jury, "but Billy
always found ways of hiding them."[28] As long as publishers churned
out millions of violent and sexual comic books each month, and
stores continued selling them to consumers of any age, there could
be no effective vaccine. Readers, it seemed, would always find ways
of hiding them.

The new wave of crime and romance comic books was a global
phenomenon. Beginning in 1947 and accelerating through the early
1950s, America's international military commitments expanded
at the same time that the comic book industry became a major
economic and cultural force. The strategy of containment, coupled
with federal support for American companies involved in global
trade and a growing emphasis on international tourism, ensured the
steady circulation of uncensored comic books around the world.[29] In
addition, a variety of unsanctioned channels spread American comics internationally. Friends and relatives shipped copies to soldiers
serving overseas, where they fell into the hands of local readers,
while American tourists scattered comic books on their travels.
Comic books traveled along these unofficial Cold War networks, connecting an unregulated form of American mass culture with local
consumers, who read them, then traded or sold them to others.

Comic books also traveled through official, state-sanctioned channels. Working independently and under the auspices of the Marshall
Plan, private American companies shipped comics and artwork to
resellers in Europe, Asia, the Middle East, and Latin America. Curtis
Publishing received a contract from the Economic Cooperation Administration (ECA) worth forty-one thousand dollars for comics sent
to Germany.[30] This order, from a single comic publisher in a single
year, was larger—in some cases more than five times larger—than
the ECA orders with *Reader's Digest*, *Time*, Bantam Books, and Pocket
Books during the same time period. To Germany and other countries
that participated in the Marshall Plan came a steady stream of comic
book violence, paid for and distributed by the government of the
United States. Even as the federal government relinquished control
over the medium, its agencies continued to use the comic book as a

weapon against totalitarianism both overtly, through the distribution of commercial titles, and covertly, through documents like "Conference Room Technique."

CRIME PAYS

The crime comic books loathed by Wertham and appropriated by the CIA first emerged in the months before the United States entered World War II. In July 1941, comic book publisher Leverett "Lev" Gleason launched his own war against Nazi Germany with the first issue of *Daredevil Battles Hitler*. On the cover, clad in a costume of red and blue, Daredevil launches a boomerang at an enormous image of the Nazi leader's face. Another of Gleason's superheroes, Silver Streak, lands a devastating punch on Hitler's jaw. Below, the text promises the heroes will "deal the ace of death to the mad merchant of hate!" Gleason was a veteran of World War I and, despite his advanced age, would reenlist in the army after the Japanese attack on Pearl Harbor.[31] As discussed in chapter 4, he was also an avowed leftist and likely a member of the Communist Party USA. Similar to many other publishers, he produced several patriotic superhero titles during World War II, including *Silver Streak Comics*, *Boy Comics*, and *Daredevil Comics*. They sold well enough but did not stand out among the dozens of patriotic superhero titles that flooded newsstands during the war.

Then in 1942, Gleason, along with coeditors and artists Charles Biro and Bob Wood, produced the first issue of *Crime Does Not Pay*—the first of many millions of crime comic books to follow. It was notably different from other comic books available at the time, and newsstand employees were not quite sure how to display it.[32] Gleason, at least, seemed to think it would appeal to adults. He ran advertisements in his other comic books screaming, "Get *Crime Does Not Pay*! Show it to Dad, he'll love it!"[33] But it was sold alongside the superhero and funny animal comics available at the time. On the cover of the first issue, there is no brightly clothed hero or patriotic imagery. Instead, gunmen shoot at each other from across a saloon. A dead body plummets toward the ground, as a wounded man slumps onto the bar. Another shooter chokes a curvaceous woman while leveling a tommy gun at his opponent. The interior contents are equally violent. An early story opens with a full-page picture of a man laughing as he smothers his mother with a pillow and lights her body on fire.[34] Rather than tracing the adventures of a costumed, patriotic crusader, *Crime Does Not Pay* boasted stories about real criminals, both contemporary and historical. Ostensibly full of cautionary tales, its narratives actually suggested that an abbreviated life of crime might be preferable to a longer but more constrained existence.

Above all, *Crime Does Not Pay* was shocking. An early cover illustration depicts a typical domestic scene with a young, well-dressed man and women in a tidy modern kitchen. The floor is covered in a cheery linoleum checkerboard of green and black, and in the background a row of spice bottles perch on the countertop. In the foreground, the man laughs as he forces the woman's head down against a lit burner on the spotless white stove, setting her face and hair aflame. Her bright red dress clings to her body and rides up her thighs as she struggles. Through a window, a police officer surveys the scene, his gun at the ready.[35] Although he may shoot the man, it will be too late for the woman. The cover presents the literal, gleefully transgressive immolation of the feminine ideal. The kitchen, a traditionally feminine and familial space, is transformed into a crime scene. Nonconsensual sex and violence intersect as the woman is bent over her own stove and set on fire. Americans who generally viewed comic books as juvenile entertainment—whether parents, educators, or politically conservative organizations—were unprepared for the onslaught of images of bondage, sexual assault, and crimes committed by and against White Americans, including women and children.

Crime Does Not Pay did not sell particularly well during World War II. But as Americans emerged from the war, the title found a new and growing audience. Its combination of more realistic settings and extreme violence not only propelled sales of *Crime Does Not Pay* toward a million copies per month but also spawned many similar titles from competing publishers, including *Crime Must Pay the*

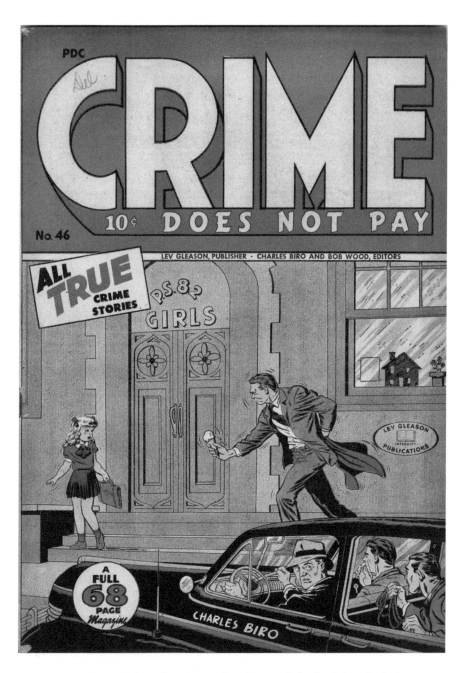

FIGURE 2.3 Some of the ugliest images in crime comic books did not include any explicit violence or bloodshed. In this particularly chilling image from a 1946 issue of *Crime Does Not Pay*, armed thugs wait in a car as one of their gang kidnaps a young girl from outside her school.

Penalty, Justice Traps the Guilty, and *Crime SuspenStories.*[36] Gleason, along with his editor and artists, had launched a new and popular genre: the crime-themed comic book. Soon, violent titles took over the newsstand. Eager to keep ahead of competitors, Biro instructed illustrator Bob Fujitani to "forget about art. Go in for the detail, the nuances: bullets going through the head, brains blowing out the back. . . . That's the thing that sells."[37] Fujitani took Biro's advice to heart, as did artists at other competing studios. The result was a torrent of vicious imagery available to anyone with a dime, just as Malcolm Kildale described to Fredric Wertham.

Copycat titles typically lacked the social commentary laced throughout the original. When *Crime Does Not Pay* told the life story of a criminal, the tale often began with a few panels highlighting his difficult childhood or other factors that led him to commit crimes. Perhaps he was a poor, unintelligent, or mistreated child whose frustrations pushed him to become a petty thief or the pawn of an established gangster. From there, he learned that violence generated attention, money, and respect. Only then, after exposure to other criminals and a variety of abuses, was he transformed into a savage, irredeemable killer. Finally, in the last few panels, he was himself killed or jailed. Imitators generally dispensed with the sort of background details included in *Crime Does Not Pay,* and there was little attempt to explain why someone might become a crook. The violence, rather than the reasons behind it, was the point.

An early issue of *Crime Does Not Pay* tells the story of mobster Lucky Luciano. Although it depicts Luciano as a greedy, murderous thug, it also suggests that his brutality stems, at least in part, from his harsh upbringing in a crime-ridden city and a country that cared little for the millions of European immigrants landing on its shores. The story opens with the Luciano family emigrating to the United States from Italy early in the twentieth century. Luciano's father hopes his son will grow up to be a lawyer or a doctor, and an elementary school teacher assures him, "In our American schools, a boy can study anything he wants to." Luciano's mother marvels, "Theysa letta my bambino go to school-a, free!" But Luciano finds school too challenging and degrading. He receives little help from teachers, and his classmates mock his learning difficulties. Soon, Luciano quits school and becomes a low-level thug in his crime-filled neighborhood. After being caught and jailed, his fellow inmates teach Luciano how best to hurt, kill, and commit more profitable crimes. Upon his release, equipped with this alternative education, Luciano returns to his old neighborhood. A mob boss, Joe Masseria, soon promises Luciano "good-a pay and tough-a work!" Armed with a pistol and brass knuckles, Luciano quickly earns a reputation as a brutally effective thug and killer.

It is not until the advent of Prohibition, though, that Luciano transforms himself into a sophisticated boss of other killers and criminals. Suddenly wealthy, he is able to hire skilled lawyers to keep himself out of jail and in charge of lucrative bootlegging and extortion rackets. But even these resources cannot keep Luciano safe from other mobsters. He is kidnapped by a pair of thugs that first tie up Luciano before torturing him with stilettos. One chuckles that it is no different than stabbing a pig, and the other cracks, "Pigs smell better." Left for dead, Luciano bribes a doctor to heal his stab wounds, then kills his kidnappers. Protected by both his money, which allows him to bribe police officers and judges, and his terrifying reputation, Luciano again thrives. Only when he confronts a district attorney unwilling to accept a bribe does Luciano go to jail. After thirteen pages of cruelty, murder, extortion, and torture, Luciano's fate is dispensed with in four panels.[38]

The contents of *Crime Does Not Pay* and its imitators defied the state-sanctioned image of America as a sophisticated, egalitarian democracy. These comic books included implicit critiques of American society, the relationship between poverty and violence, and the treatment of women. An early postwar issue of *Crime Does Not Pay* simultaneously depicts American women as victims and criminals and American men as bullies and rich cowards. On its cover, two wealthy, overweight men are tied up alongside a blonde woman in a backless dress and glasses, also bound to her chair. A table in front of them displays an open straight razor, a dagger, a length of rope, a handgun, and an ominous bottle. A slim, young man looms over the trio, leering at the helpless woman. Gesturing at her, he says, "OK

I'll start with **you**, Four Eyes—I'm gonna let ya choose your **own** way out! **Take your pick!**" His partner, a bored-looking platinum blonde woman in a low-cut dress, pearls, and fur, says, "He's crazy, I tell you—He means it!"[39]

Within crime comic books, America was a primitive society driven by the basest and most aggressive of emotions. It was a country in which young White men faced poverty, physical abuse, and an ineffectual educational system. They grew up in mob-run city neighborhoods or quiet rural homes with parents who either ignored or beat them. Shaped by these brutal circumstances, they responded with indiscriminate greed and violence directed at anyone—man, woman, parent, or police officer—unlucky enough to stumble across their path. Innocence, kindness, or weakness meant nothing to the criminals in crime comic books; the vulnerable and sympathetic died alongside everyone else. On the first page of a 1947 issue of *Crime Does Not Pay*, mobster Louis "Lepke" Buchalter mows down a police officer, who topples onto a towering pile of average-looking dead men and women killed for no reason at all.[40] In a particularly nightmarish narrative from the same year, "The Wild Spree of the Laughing Sadist—Herman Duker," the teenaged protagonist burns a cat alive, beats his father, and murders a store owner and a milkman.[41]

In contrast to Lucky Luciano and many other crooks depicted in *Crime Does Not Pay*, Herman Duker receives no introduction explaining his descent into crime. Instead, in the first image of the story, Duker titters into the ear of a woman with a black eye and bleeding mouth. With one hand he pulls at her hair, and with the other he presses a gun to her throat, while inches away, a corpse bleeds out through a bullet hole in the middle of his forehead and a long slash down his cheek. Alongside, a text box warns, "Some fools commit crimes for money—some because of jealousy or a sudden rage. But Herman Duker was one of those queers who robbed and killed out of sheer pleasure—experiencing delight in others' terror and agony, he laughed his way through crime, until fate refused to crack a smile."

Across the next two panels, young Herman is discovered killing his family's pet goldfish and cat. While his father spanks him, Herman vows, "I won't change! I won't! You'll see! I'll be worse!" After a friend tries to stop him from drowning a dog, Herman beats him to the ground, produces a knife, and threatens to carve his initials in the boy's face. When a neighborhood pal sees Herman holding a cat, he asks, "Ain't ya gonna drown him like always?" This time, though, Herman dunks the cat in kerosene before setting it on fire, as his friend looks on in horror. Told of the killing, Herman's father tries to beat him with a leather belt, but Herman breaks free and pummels his father until the older man orders his son out of the house. Herman leaves, but not before stealing the family's meager savings. It is, he gloats, "enough to buy duds and a gun! I'm set!"

Armed with a revolver, the teenaged Herman transitions from killing animals to murdering people. A witness to his murder of a shopkeeper tells the police that she cannot identify the murderer but will never forget how he laughed while shooting the defenseless man. A second shopkeeper swears his cash register is empty, but Herman shoots him anyway, standing over the empty register and giggling, "See what ya get for bein' so honest?" When a police officer discovers Duker looming above his second victim, the killer is sent not to jail but to a reformatory. Where *Crime Does Not Pay* depicted Lucky Luciano as further warped by his time in lockup, Herman Duker is so twisted that he terrifies his fellow prisoners and even the guards. When the warden of the reformatory tries to explain to Duker that good behavior is the fastest route to freedom, Duker retaliates: "Shove it. There's a quicker way than that!" He becomes even more savage, assuming that the authorities will soon tire of dealing with him.

Once free, Duker looks up Dale, an old friend and partner who has since gone straight. Dale protests that he no longer wants to be a criminal, and Duker asks, "You want me to skin you alive, like I skinned them alley cats? Remember, Dale?" Terrified, Dale agrees to help Duker steal from a milkman. Instead of simply robbing him, though, Duker shoots the milkman dead, laughing as blood drenches his victim's white uniform. Summoned by a witness, the police soon surround Dale and Duker. In the final panel, Duker is killed in the electric chair. But the preceding six pages are crammed with new

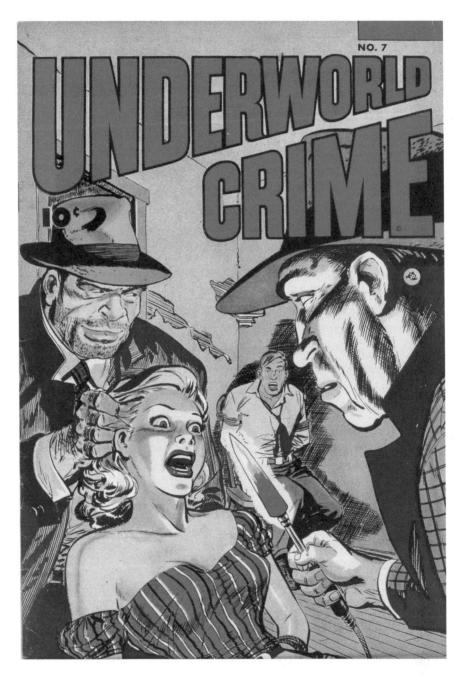

FIGURE 2.4 *Underworld Crime* was published by Fawcett, a company better known for good-natured superheroes like Captain Marvel. The implied sexual violence on the cover of this 1953 issue, depicting the moment before a thug assaults a woman with a red-hot tool, is much darker.

and unsettling images. Readers were accustomed to adult superheroes beating up male, often non-White foreigners, but here was the graphic murder of authority figures and average-looking men and women by a savage, freckle-faced American teenager.

The most chilling of all crime stories, however, involved Bob Wood, one of the editors of *Crime Does Not Pay*. In the wake of the 1954 comics code, Wood struggled to find work. An alcoholic, he sank deeper into the darkness of his addiction. In 1958, a blood-soaked Wood hailed a taxi in Manhattan. Once inside, he confessed to the driver that he had just killed a woman in a hotel room. The cabbie alerted the police, who went to the room and found a scene right out of *Crime Does Not Pay*. A woman in a negligee lay dead, her head smashed in by an electric iron. Wood did not deny killing the woman and was sent to Attica prison. After just a few years, he was released. What exactly happened next is unclear, but Wood was soon dead. Some in the comic book industry thought he had committed suicide, but writer and artist Joe Simon believed Wood was murdered by men he had met in prison. Just like the abused women in so many crime and horror comics, justice—or revenge—came too late for Wood's victim.[42]

CRIMES BY WOMEN

When comic books published during World War II gazed inward at American society, they emphasized the attributes of White culture and the racial and gender status quo.[43] The imagined American home front was overwhelmingly male, with women typically restricted to roles as secondary characters in need of rescue or sexually suggestive victims in bondage.[44] Through issue after issue of *Superman* and *Action Comics*, Superman raced to the rescue of reporter Lois Lane. In the world of Captain Marvel, women were virtually absent except as incidental characters. Other popular war-time characters, including Captain America and Batman, focused on relationships between male superheroes and villains. In comics that did feature secondary female characters, they were mostly spared beatings, immolation, or stabbing.

The young and comparatively open comic book industry did offer writers and artists the freedom to create some strong female heroes as well. Wartime issues of *Wings Comics* often included one or two stories starring women as Allied fighters waging war far from home. One was Jane Martin, at various times a nurse, pilot, and secret agent. In all these incarnations, she supported and ministered to American fighting men stationed around the world. As Jane tells a rescued flyer, "My job is to heal, not to destroy." When pressed, though, she was capable of battling Axis agents and soldiers. In one issue, she is stationed in Crimea, serving as a Red Cross nurse alongside a group of British soldiers sent to aid the Soviet Union. When the soldiers find themselves under attack by German dive-bombers, Jane leaps into the cockpit of a nearby plane, directing a male soldier to sit behind her and man a machine gun. Thanks to Jane's aggressive piloting, her back seat gunner downs one of the German planes. Later that same day, while walking the streets of a Crimean city, Jane spies a German soldier abusing some Ukrainian peasants. Without hesitation, she leaps at the German and grabs his rifle, shouting, "Dog! You'll pay heavily for this, and soon!"[45]

But Jane's hand-to-hand battles with Axis soldiers devolved into full-panel displays of dress-bursting bondage as often as they depicted her outmaneuvering German dive-bombers. While Jane fights the Germans in Crimea, one attacks her from behind, bursting her undershirt and bending her down. When she leaps for his rifle, her skirt rides up, showing her legs and a pair of high-heeled shoes. Images of Jane as she fights a group of German soldiers are shown from above, with the reader looking down the front of her uniform, even as she lashes out at a mob of enemy troops. Senorita Rio, another female hero featured in the popular anthology title *Fight Comics*, similarly combined aggression with submission and violence with sexuality in expeditions far from the American home front. In a South American adventure from 1942, Senorita Rio angrily bashes an Axis agent over the head with a rock, chuckling, "Can this be what they mean by the womanly touch?" The man tumbles to the ground, either seriously wounded or dead. The same story, however, includes multiple panels of Senorita Rio in her underwear, close-ups of her stockinged legs, and an image of men grabbing her from behind, forcing her breasts out toward the reader. The issue also boasts a two-page spread of war-themed pinups, including one woman reclining in negligee, telling her friend, "The air raid warden thinks I deserve special attention. He says I'm a military objective."[46]

By the late 1940s, comic book violence toward women became much more personal and intimate—and this brutality took place in the United States, rather than abroad. American women were strangled, burned, beaten, and sexually assaulted. Scenes of women being assaulted or killed became staples of crime and horror comic book covers. A cover from *Fight against Crime* features a man stuffing a woman's body, clothed in a very tight red dress, down a manhole. He keeps one hand free, the better to hold the woman's severed head.[47] A *Crime SuspenStories* cover shows, in extreme close-up, a woman's face and neck submerged in water, while a disembodied pair of muscular, hairy arms chokes her to death. The perspective of the image places the viewer underwater, suffering along with the woman.[48] Another from *Underworld Crime* depicts a simian goon pulling a woman's hair, as another thug menaces her face with a red-hot—and undeniably phallic—soldering iron.[49] On a cover from *Uncanny Tales*, bright yellow text screams out, "I live with corpses!" as a headless, decaying male body carries the dead body of a woman wearing a skimpy dress.[50] These images of American women, and thousands like them, were transmitted around the world through a combination of official and unofficial channels, including publishers, soldiers, tourists, and diplomats.

Perhaps the most brutal assaults on postwar conventions of the American family and femininity appeared in the pages of *Crimes by Women*. Published by Victor Fox, the contents lived up to the title. Within a nation that defined itself as modern and egalitarian based on the roles available to women in society, comics like *Crimes by Women* were an affront.[51] Stories offered scene after scene of White American women as liars, cheats, bullies, and murderers. Images of extreme violence crowded the covers, as women hurled acid at each other, fought with police officers, and forced men to dig their own graves. In a typical story, Ruth Carter ("The Terror from Tacoma") murders her boyfriend after he proves to be a coward. She then embarks on a brutal crime spree, becoming a gangster's hired gun and earning a second nickname, "the Sentinel of Death."[52]

In another story, entitled "Madame Murderer," young Lila Horne becomes a killer for hire. Her mother, who teaches Lila to do whatever is necessary to survive, sets Lila on her dark path. When Lila objects to her brother's theft of a box of candy, her mother slaps her across the face and screams, "Don't be such a little dope! Our kind takes anything, regardless of where it comes from. You go to bed, Snow White, no sharing in the loot for you!" Lila absorbs this cruel lesson, becoming first a swindler and then a hired killer for the local mob. After committing her first murder, she gleefully robs the corpse, to the shock of the men in the gang. Lila then methodically murders the mob's leadership, taking control of its rackets. As her wealth, power, and reputation grow, so does her fear of betrayal. Afraid that her underlings will kill her, she recruits her brother Ben into the gang. Ignoring their mother's childhood admonition that even family cannot be trusted, he agrees to protect Lila. After joining the gang, he helps Lila kill the male members plotting to take her place only to become another victim of her greed. Pleading for his life, Ben asks, "You wouldn't kill your own brother, would you! Put the gun away, sis!" Before killing her brother, Lila replies, "I'll put the bullets away, Ben, right in your worthless hide!" She then tries to kill a police officer, who barely manages to shoot her first, ending the career of the "money mad killer who was called Madame Murder."[53]

Such violence and contempt for law enforcement, which would have been unthinkable in Hollywood films or children's books, appeared over and over in postwar crime comics. Insulting depictions of police officers were a staple of crime titles, as typified by the cover of a 1951 issue of *Fight against Crime*. There, in a scene at a cement factory, a pair of crooks—a man and a woman—gloat over two police officers handcuffed in a storage vat. One officer is already dead, and the other, horrified, struggles against his restraints. The woman points a gun at the officer and pleads with her partner to "let me plug him!" Her male partner refuses, gloating instead as he turns on a flow of cement into the vat.[54] Other equally transgressive stories

FIGURE 2.5 Comic books like this 1949 issue of *Crimes by Women* presented an image of postwar American womanhood at odds with those promoted by federal policy makers and propagandists.

showed modern American women let down or betrayed by law enforcement and pushed to make their own justice outside the law. Although these stories were billed as cautionary tales, punishment—when it happened at all—occurred only after many pages of greed and mayhem. The preceding pages made clear that crime could, in fact, be quite lucrative and thrilling for women as well as for men.

The highest-ranking law enforcement agent in the nation—a man widely considered the paragon of patriotism—criticized the endings of stories in crime comic books. In a 1947 article on juvenile delinquency, J. Edgar Hoover singled out the comic book industry as uniquely dangerous. Publishers, he claimed, "are as responsible as the sex fiends they incite by their wares." Crime comics were particularly problematic because of their twist endings. Hoover recalled a conversation between a police officer and a fifteen-year-old gang leader: the officer asked the gang leader whether crime comic books did indeed end with scenes stressing the futility of crime. "Sure," replied the teenager, "but we never read the end."[55]

THE STRANGE CASE OF HENPECKED HARRY

As crime comics displaced superhero titles, horror-themed comics became popular as well. The postwar wave of horror comics began in 1947 with the first issue of *Eerie*. It established the formula for the genre with the story "The Strange Case of Henpecked Harry," which featured excessive violence, an abusive female character, and a twist ending. "The Strange Case of Henpecked Harry" tells the story of an unhappily married man, Harry, who is physically abused by Helen, his domineering wife. One night when he arrives home late, Helen smashes Harry over the head with a frying pan. She then beats Harry so thoroughly that some rough neighbors overhear and joke, "They're better'n ever tonight!" Lying stunned on the floor of their apartment, Harry decides that the only solution is to murder his wife, making her death appear as an accident.

The next day, he follows a woman wearing his wife's distinctive green coat into the subway and pushes her into the path of a train. The train runs over and kills the woman, who turns out to be Margie, a friend of Helen's who has borrowed her coat. Later that night, Margie's corpse, still wearing Helen's coat, turns up at the couple's apartment. Mangled and soaked in blood, Margie chases Harry onto the roof of the apartment building, where a spectral subway train bears down on him. Desperate to escape, Harry slips and falls off the roof, hitting the ground with a sickening crunch. When Helen arrives home, she takes the news of Harry's death with a chuckle, exclaiming, "No kidding! Isn't that funny? Then Margie died the same day as my Harry, and my coat was on her back!"[56]

Soon, across the pages of thousands of similar comic books, women were beaten, drained of blood, vivisected, and drugged. Men were blinded, stabbed, drowned, and murdered. Children killed adults and escaped punishment. Victims had to fend for themselves, often by resorting to torture or murder. As in many crime comics, police officers, when they appeared at all, were frequently incompetent. Driven by greed or abuse, average-looking American husbands and wives tore each other apart. A company called EC—detailed in chapter 4—specialized in such dark images of the postwar American family. A cover from the EC title *Crime SuspenStories* features, in close-up, the torso of a paunchy man, clad in a dress shirt and belted slacks, holding a bloody axe in one hand and the head of a blonde woman in the other.[57] The woman's eyes tilt upward, as though staring at the unseen face of her killer, and her mouth gapes, dripping blood and saliva. Behind the man, her body lies on a clean, tiled bathroom floor, revealingly clothed in a short skirt and high heels. Despite the obvious violence and gore, it is the everyday banality woven through the image that makes it so unsettling. The killer is no costumed villain or gangster. He is White, of unflattering build, dressed in respectable clothes, and standing in a spotless bathroom. His victim is an attractive blonde woman whose location on a bathroom floor implies that her body is about to be chopped up in the bathtub. Their clothes suggest that the act was unplanned, as though a typical American man simply put down his pipe, rose out of his chair, and hacked off his wife's head. This cover summarizes, in just one image, EC's chilling credo: "Virtue doesn't always have to triumph."[58]

Similarly unsettling imagery appears in "The Orphan," from EC's

Shock SuspenStories. The story opens with a little girl, Lucy Johnson, describing the abuse she suffers at the hands of her alcoholic father, Sam. Lucy's mother, Mildred, although not a drinker, is similarly cruel. Mildred makes clear that Lucy is not wanted and that the child is the result of Mildred's rape by Sam. Mildred then proceeds to demand a divorce, so that she can be free of both Sam and Lucy. In an aside to the reader, Lucy screams, "I hated them! I hated them both! I don't know who I hated more, Daddy, because he beat me and yelled at me and came home drunk all the time, or Mom, because she never wanted me and never showed me any love and was willing to give me up just like that!" When Lucy asks her kind Aunt Kate to adopt her, Sam lashes out, swearing, "No dried-up old maid's gonna bring up my kid!" Although horrified, Aunt Kate does not alert the police or local child protective authorities. She simply leaves.

Soon, Lucy discovers that her mother is having an affair with a man named Steve. Initially, Lucy likes Steve, and she promises to keep her mother's secret. Lucy daydreams of a life with Mildred and Steve, far away from her abusive father. Then one night Lucy discovers Mildred and Steve frantically packing a suitcase. She realizes that they plan to leave Lucy behind with her father. When Mildred expresses regret about abandoning Lucy, Steve screams, "It was your idea to play up to her! You know how I hate kids! Let her old man have her!" Mildred quietly agrees, admitting that she has never loved Lucy. As Lucy sobs in silence, Mildred and Steve sneak out the front door. They stumble upon Sam, Lucy's father, in a drunken stupor. Suddenly, Sam is shot in the head. Aghast, Steve flees, leaving Mildred to deal with the police, who only now appear in the story after hearing the gunshot.

The tale then becomes even darker, as Lucy testifies in court that she saw her mother and Steve kill her father. Over two images of electrocution, she tells the reader, "In our state, murderers die in the electric chair. Mommy went first. Then Steve." The story ends with an image of Lucy winking at the reader, sitting happily near her Aunt Kate. Smiling, Lucy admits that it is she who killed her father, and she who framed her mother and Steve for the crime. To her, "Everything worked out swell."[59] The story is shocking not only for its cruelty but also because it treats a manipulative, murdering child as a hero. It depicts the United States as a country where women and children are verbally and physically abused without any interference from the police. It presents an American woman as a victim of spousal rape and as incapable of loving or even protecting her own child. The only worthy adult in the story—Aunt Kate—is derided as a "dried-up old maid" who knowingly abandons Lucy to mental and physical abuse. Indeed, Lucy has to trick her aunt into caring for her, a task she accomplishes by first killing her own father and then framing her mother for murder.

WHITEWASHING ROMANCE

Romance comics grew popular alongside postwar crime and horror titles and emerged from the same creative team, Joe Simon and Jack Kirby, that created Captain America. In the wake of the war, Simon noted the large numbers of adults reading comic books and wondered why so few titles were aimed at women. From this realization sprung the concept of the romance comic book. Their first title was *Young Romance*, which appeared on newsstands in 1947 with the warning, "Designed for the More Adult Readers of Comics," emblazoned on the cover. Simon's son Jon was born the same year, and while on the way to visit him at the hospital, Simon and Kirby stopped at a local candy store for some small gifts. Once inside, they found a swarm of teenaged girls huddled around the comic book racks, reading the first issue of *Young Romance*. Buoyed by this chance encounter, Simon and Kirby soon received even better news: *Young Romance* had sold out completely. The creative duo immediately began work on subsequent issues. Simon and Kirby did make one change to *Young Romance* at the behest of Martin Goodman, publisher of the Timely Comics line. The phrase, "Designed for the More Adult Readers of Comics," was removed. Although not the publisher of *Young Romance*, Goodman was concerned that the disclaimer "bordered on pornography" and would harm the entire comic book industry. The distributor of *Young Romance* instructed Simon and Kirby to comply with Goodman's warning.[60]

Romance comic books were wildly popular, and not just with teen-aged girls. Hank Williams, the country music king, wrote haunting, romantic lyrics that earned him millions of fans in the late 1940s and early 1950s. His songs offered a harrowing image of postwar America, populated by jobless men and women just "one step or careless deed" from misery.[61] An alcoholic, Williams battled his disease at sanitariums, where friends and family brought him horror and romance comics. His second wife, Billie Jean, recalled, "I brought him every weird, crazy funny book on the stands. Hundreds of them. He called them 'goof books' and he never read anything else, not even a newspaper."[62] Williams built songs from the narratives and language used in these uncensored comic books. Fellow songwriter Merle Kilgore remembers, "He would read *True Romance* comic books. My sister had *True Romance* comic books, and I'd say, 'What do you read those sissy comic books for, Hank?' And he said, 'Sissy, hell! Where do you think I get my ideas from?'"[63] Williams divined the sadness, brutality, and dark humor that made these comic books so popular, particularly at a time when many American adults prioritized family, consumption, and patriotism. Through the darkness of their lyrics, Williams's songs offered a means of resistance to those unconvinced by the promise of the atomic age.[64]

Elvis Presley was also an avid comic book fan, and his favorite character, Captain Marvel Jr., even inspired his personal style and clothing.[65] Like Williams, Presley offered his listeners a means of rejecting more conventional styles of expression. Unlike Williams, whose challenge mostly came through his lyrics, Presley's resistance was complete: aural, visual, and physical. In the heat of a late July evening in 1954—the year that *Seduction of the Innocent* became a phenomenon—a very young Presley walked onstage at the Overton Park Shell in Memphis, Tennessee. He and his band played just a handful of songs. Nervous, Elvis began to dance, grinding his hips as he stood on the balls of his feet. Soon, the sounds of shrieks and screams washed over the stage. Within the pulp empire, Presley's performance, and the reaction he received from young women, posed a problem. This was a new kind of sexuality made public, as Presley and his largely young, female audience danced, shouted, and swayed in unison. Presley's performance provided a space for women to express and embrace their sexuality. Written and illustrated primarily by men, romance comic books offered a similar, although more private, space for American consumers to confront their status as sexual members of postwar society. The meaning and significance of the images and narratives were a matter of perspective: in American society during the late 1940s, romance comic books presented exciting images of White, female sexuality to audiences eager for realistic entertainment. During a time in which film and television were severely restricted in their representations of sex, romance comic books offered excitement.

Although the cartoon narratives and text stories in each issue of *Young Romance* were presented as the true confessions of young women, they were written and drawn by men. Men even wrote the monthly advice column, credited to "Nancy Hale." To their surprise, Simon and Kirby received thousands of letters documenting women's fears and hopes along with intimate details of their love lives. In return, recalls Simon, "Thousands of girls were eased into puberty by a couple of comic book artists who were too cheap to hire a competent female counselor. . . . We took turns being Nancy Hale, answering letters to the column, giving comfort and advice. Advice was easy to dispense, and surprisingly, we got away with it."[66] Although Simon intended *Young Romance* as a title for heterosexual women in their teens and twenties, its contents had much to offer people across the spectrums of age and sexuality. Readers of any orientation could find sexually exciting content in romance comic books. The titles offered a more private space to engage with titillating imagery, graphic advertisements for sex toys, bras, corsets, and vibrators, and letters to the editor ostensibly written by their peers.

In one issue of *Young Romance*, Nancy Hale responds to a reader stuck in an abusive relationship. The reader writes, "I have been going with a fellow I like very much. In fact, we plan to be married next year. But whenever he gets angry with me, he slaps me. My friends all say that if he slaps me now, it is a sign that he will beat up on me after we're married. What do you think?" The male writer (or writers) behind Nancy Hale provided some sensible advice: "Any

man who slaps a woman is no gentleman. . . . Lay down the law
to him, Wanda. . . . If this doesn't break him of the habit, we think
you should find yourself a more considerate boyfriend—one who
has more respect for you."[67] Unpacking this interaction, though,
raises multiple questions. Is the letter writer really a heterosexual
woman? It seems equally possible that a gay woman or a man unable
to solicit advice from more conventional sources wrote the letter
and fabricated a planned heterosexual marriage. Regardless of the
reader's identity, this interaction makes clear that men and women
engaged in a sort of theater when writing to the editors of romance
comic books. None of the actors necessarily represented themselves
truthfully. Yet the experiences and advice they offered may well
have provided comfort to men and women trapped in difficult
situations and lacking access to support or advice within their own
social circles. Either way, they demonstrate how comics provided a
safe space and typify the unique, intimate sort of correspondence
possible between comic book producers and consumers in the 1940s
and 1950s.

Even romance comic books were filled with crime plots. In
mid-1951, the newest issue of a romance comic called *My Secret Life*
arrived at newsstands across the United States, Western Europe, and
Latin America.[68] In the lead story, "Glamour Turned My Head," Jari, a
lonesome and overweight young woman, moves from the small town
of Centerville to New York City. She attends a finishing school, loses
weight, and returns, triumphant, to Centerville. At first, Jari revels in
the attention paid to her by men who once mocked her for being shy
and overweight. Soon, she falls for Kirk, a glamorous out-of-towner
who works as a fundraiser for the Red Cross. "Completely under his
spell," Jari agrees to marry Kirk and help him with his charity work.
But before the wedding, she learns that Kirk is actually a con man
using her to steal ten thousand dollars intended for the Red Cross.
When Jari protests, Kirk points a .45 at her chest and snarls, "You're
up to your neck in this, too!" Smirking, Kirk tells her that ripping off
the Red Cross makes for an easy life. Torn, Jari ultimately decides to
abandon Kirk and cheers when Steve, her only childhood friend, ma-
terializes along with the local police force. Jari, chastened, realizes

it is Steve she has loved all along and falls into his arms, grateful for her escape from "dangerous romance."[69]

Although its protagonist eventually chooses a conventional man and marriage over a more thrilling and dishonest "easy life" with Kirk, "Glamour Turned My Head" remains a rather bleak representation of life in early Cold War America. It is a landscape studded with swindlers, shallow city dwellers, and suffocating small towns. Honesty is framed as the dowdy, responsible alternative to a life of crime. Similar images and characters appeared in the tens of millions of romance comic books sold during the first postwar decade.

Romance comics were also able to take on other once-taboo subjects. The February 1951 issue of *Young Romance* contains a story entitled "Different." It tackles the issue of anti-Semitism through the experiences of the Williams family, who have just moved from the city to a small town called Jayville. The eldest Williams child, Irma, soon attracts a circle of friends and falls in love with a young man named Gil Soon, but word circulates that the Williams family was once the Wilheim family: German Jews that immigrated to the United States. Irma finds herself snubbed by her former friends, and her father's furniture business falters, as the townspeople refuse to do business with him.

The story confronts discrimination through coded language. Neither the word "Jewish" nor any racial slurs actually appear in the story, and we hear the townspeople refer to the Williams family only as "foreigners." Desperate, Mr. Williams decides to move his family back to the city, away from the bigotry lurking in small-town America. The wealthiest man in Jayville, Jeremiah Standish, happily visits the Williams home and boasts of his open-mindedness. His absence of prejudice and willingness to do business with anyone, claims Standish, are why he is so much wealthier than anyone else in town. He laughingly refers to his own ancestors as "scoundrels" and offers to help the Williams family settle down in Jayville. Gil then reassures the family that "Old Jerry sets the pace in this town. Once the others find out where he stands, they'll change their tune, pronto!"[70]

"Different" illustrates how romance comics operated on multiple simultaneous planes, offering readers transgressive or conservative interpretations. The narrative decries discrimination but also suggests that prejudice is overcome only by following the example set by wealthy Americans. By reducing anti-Semitism to an issue of class, "Different" neatly sidesteps the idea that middle- or upper-class Americans might be prejudiced. Discrimination is treated as an anomaly—a quirk of those with comparatively less education and money. Similarly, "Glamour Turned My Head" offers multiple experiences. At the outset, Jari is sad, shy, and overweight. It is clear that in this condition, she is unappealing to both men and women. Only when Jari loses weight and learns to dress in a more feminine style do men take an interest in her. Still, she initially spurns the "good" men in town to date a glamorous outsider. The town itself is simultaneously safe and suffocating: although it provides Jari with a husband, its population is dull and small-minded. By settling down with Steve, Jari resigns herself to life in a small town, away from all the opportunities and people she so enjoyed in New York City.

Despite the relative freedom accorded comic book creators, one topic remained taboo in romance stories: interracial relationships. As with crime and horror comic books, the world within romance titles was virtually all White. In this sense, postwar comic books were little different from their wartime predecessors, which typically relegated non-White characters to roles as villains, servants, primitives, or buffoons. Wartime comics presented the outside world—that is, anywhere but the United States—as full of dangerous non-Whites. When in 1944 the WWB asked publishers for comic book narratives advocating racial tolerance, its members made clear that any non-White characters could appear only in secondary roles. In a remarkable display of tone deafness, the board reassured comic book publishers (many of whom were themselves Jewish, and some of whom employed African Americans or Asian Americans), "While your readers cannot be expected to accept heroes or heroines belonging to minority groups, it is possible to give subsidiary characters Jewish names or depict them as Negroes, etc."[71] Comic book makers complied, typically limiting non-White characters to supporting roles or segregating them from White heroes.

This wartime whitewashing was a calculated attempt to keep the

FIGURE 2.6 Like crime, horror, and jungle-themed comic books, romance titles included images and narratives depicting postwar America as a violent, sexualized society. This issue of *Romantic Love* dates from 1952.

home front calm without upsetting racists in the federal government. The near-total absence of non-White characters in postwar crime and horror comics is equally troubling. A fairly diverse community of men and women wrote and illustrated crime and romance comic books, so why were their contents so White? Asian Americans,

African Americans, even Western and Eastern Europeans virtually disappeared from the pages of crime, romance, and horror titles.[72] They even became difficult to find in their traditional roles as villains. Overwhelmingly, crime and romance comics created for their readers an environment free of accents, ethnicity, or color. Even in a story from *Love Confessions* called "Love Conquers Bigotry," it is faith in a "different church," rather than race, that causes friction between lovers.[73] The result of this tempering is an eerie, homogenous world where criminals, heroes, bystanders, and children are all White. It is a gritty, highly detailed landscape, populated by engaging characters, yet quite unreal. Hateful wartime figures like Steamboat and Whitewash Jones are gone, but so are the token Black heroes commissioned by the WWB. Above all, it is a construct within which being American is synonymous with being White.

The phenomenon is much the same in horror comic books. Finding scenes of dismemberment, torture, sexual assault, and child abuse is as straightforward as thumbing through a pile of issues. Non-White characters are much tougher to find. Those that do appear are more likely in the form of zombies or "witch doctors" than anything recognizable in postwar American society.[74] This was due to not only a combination of ingrained prejudices and commercial fears but also the removal of government influence from the comic book industry. Without an agency like the WWB compelling publishers to include racially varied characters, there was little motivation to risk sales over a moral and ethical matter like diversity. No matter how many different sorts of people worked on comic books, these men and women had virtually no economic or political clout. They were not unionized, they were easily replaced, and some had few employment options outside the comic book industry.

UNTIL THE END OF THE WORLD

No single factor explains the rise of crime, horror, and romance comic books in the late 1940s. But significant causes include the rapid split between federal agencies and the comic book industry, the brutalizing effects of World War II, and the advent of atomic weapons. Millions of young and adult comic book readers were traumatized by the war. Perhaps thousands more were employed by the comic book industry. During the war, fantastic superheroes in colorful costumes dispensed punishment to buffoonish German characters, crudely rendered Japanese soldiers, and fanciful super-villains. But in a world of atomic weapons, death camps, and spies, superheroes seemed a holdover of a time past. Publishers struggled to maintain sales numbers no longer buoyed by wartime patriotism and government intervention. How could they sell millions of comic books to adults conditioned by military service, the loss of loved ones, and the revelations of atrocities committed by both fascist and democratic nations?[75]

The Cold War was fundamentally different from World War II. Although crime, horror, and romance comic books remained overwhelmingly White during the early Cold War, the world in which they were consumed turned their treatment of race into a liability. World War II was a total war, a conflict based on racial and ethnic hatred in which extermination was essential to victory and the subsequent peace. It was also an atomic war in which the United States twice used these weapons against non-White targets. The organizing principle of the Cold War, in contrast, was indiscriminate, automated terror—human savagery kept in check by the threat of a total, final conflict. It was a time when policy makers all over the world embraced peace through terror and purpose through perpetual conflict. Thus constrained, the Cold War overwhelmingly was waged across the global south, where the superpowers labored to sway hearts and minds without inadvertently triggering an international holocaust. Because the federal government removed itself from the comic book industry immediately after Japan's surrender, agencies like the WWB and OIAA no longer directed or tempered the appearances of major non-White characters.

It is tempting to view the sudden popularity of crime, horror, and romance comic books as an inevitable reaction to the atrocities committed by and on people during World War II. And this perspective can be supported with similar examples in other media, including film noir and the novels of Mickey Spillane. But it gives scant credit to the role played by governmental policies, wartime agencies, and the unique freedom accorded the comic book relative to other forms of popular culture. In time, comic book narratives would return to the patriotic violence and racial tropes popularized during World War II. For a brief period during the late 1940s and early 1950s, however, publishers focused their rage inward, toward American men, women, and even children. Consumer demand drove this inversion, and the newly freed comic book industry found itself able to provide the sorts of adult-themed narratives that took the place of wartime superhero stories.

The first postwar generation of crime comic books was not simply different from what had come before; it was objectively more confrontational and less patriotic than its superhero predecessors. The new breed of comic books also created very specific and potentially troublesome issues for American diplomacy within the emerging system of American empire. Crime and romance comic books equated violence with realism and provoked shock and outrage—along with record sales numbers—exactly because they bore little in common with earlier titles.[76]

In a time of great political, social, and strategic shifts, when the United States was simultaneously the most powerful nation on earth and vulnerable to subversion and atomic attack, the comic book form offered a unique outlet for contemporary fears and passions. In such a time, the relative freedom of the comic book industry yielded narratives full of cynicism, sexuality, violence, and doubt. What made these new comics so unique was their distortion of violence—their reversal of traditional victims and perpetrators of crimes. They presented a very dark view of American society when the United States was, for the first time, the dominant global power. Rather than celebrating the sacrifices that made this possible, new comics emphasized the shortcomings of democratic capitalism—flaws like economic inequality, crime, and institutionalized racism.

Looming over all these changes, above the first postwar wave of comic books, above CIA murder manuals, above life itself, was the atomic bomb. First the United States and then the Soviet Union suddenly based their security on weapons of extermination and the threat of indiscriminate death on a global scale. Atomic bombs were instruments of terror, designed to kill so many people that politicians would never dare to use them. In such a world, the brutality in crime and horror titles seems almost prescient. Perhaps the images of the United States in postwar comic books were more realistic than many Americans were comfortable admitting. That these same Americans were scandalized by titles like *Crime Does Not Pay* and *Crimes by Women* but found ways to live, love, and work at the edge of the end of the world is remarkable. And comic books had a role to play in this new atomic world. Unfettered by censorship, they provided a unique space for debate over atomic weapons.

CHAPTER THREE

DONALD DUCK'S ATOM BOMB

TRUE MONSTERS

By early 1945, many thousands of men and women labored in the American atomic archipelago, a network of secret installations tasked with building a new weapon of unprecedented power. In March of that year, about five micrograms of plutonium, the toxic metal at the core of an atomic bomb, were sent to Dr. Hymer Friedell of Oak Ridge, Tennessee. The plutonium was then injected into a "colored male," Private Ebb Cade, who had been hospitalized with a broken bone in the Oak Ridge Army Hospital. The Oak Ridge doctors sought to learn how the recently discovered metal, suddenly so critical to national security, would affect Cade's body. Code-named HP-12 (for "human product"), Cade neither asked for nor consented to the injection of plutonium. Two months later, with the radioactive metal settled in his bones and liver, a fellow soldier observed Cade suffering and thought, "He seemed in terrible shape. He looked to me like he was not going to make it." Then, Cade simply disappeared. One source claims he dressed himself and walked out of the hospital; another suggests he went blind and died in 1953. Cade never learned that his own government had poisoned him.[1]

116

The practice of covertly injecting unwitting human subjects
with radioactive toxins continued after the end of the war. In April
1946, four-year-old Simeon Shaw was admitted to the University of
California Hospital in San Francisco with a rare bone cancer. His
condition quickly worsened, and ten days after entering the hospital
his fever spiked to 104 degrees. That same day, doctors injected him
with a radioactive brew of plutonium, yttrium, and cerium. There
is no evidence that his parents were informed. After a month or so
of observation, Simeon was released, and his doctors never saw him
again. But a couple of years later, a hospital administrator reached
out to Simeon's mother, eager to know how her son was feeling. Mrs.
Shaw did not reply; Simeon had died in January 1947, just months
after leaving the hospital.

Six years later the Atomic Energy Commission (AEC) launched
Project Sunshine—an effort that would not have seemed out of place
in the pages of a horror comic book—seeking a better understanding
of the effects of radioactive fallout from atmospheric nuclear tests.
AEC Commissioner Willard Libby argued Project Sunshine was
essential to national security because if public fears about fallout
could not be soothed, "weapons testing may be forced to stop—a
circumstance which could well be disastrous to the free world." So in
an effort to safeguard atmospheric nuclear weapons tests, scientists
collected six hundred fetuses, thousands of bone samples, and
body parts from more than fifteen thousand human beings. Project
Sunshine was secret, and its scientists often appropriated body parts
or even entire corpses without asking permission or contacting
the next of kin. At one point, eager to acquire more corpses for the
study, Libby told his fellow scientists, "If anybody knows how to do a
good job of body snatching, they will really be serving their country."
Decades later, the federal government would reveal that Project
Sunshine was only one of fifty-nine "tissue analysis studies" directed
by American atomic scientists during the Cold War.[2]

So many of today's most beloved comic book and film
characters—the Hulk, the Fantastic Four, Daredevil, Doctor Manhattan, and, most famously, Spider-Man, gained their superpowers from
exposure to radiation. The reality of radiation exposure was quite

different, leading to intense suffering, organ failure, and death. Its uninformed subjects, in contrast to radiation-fueled superheroes, were often ill, impoverished, and ignorant of the experiments inflicted on their bodies. They were oblivious conscripts in the Cold War.

Remarkably, comic book images of nuclear weapons predate by five years the first test of an atomic bomb. In the winter of 1940, *Target Comics* 11 landed at newsstands throughout the Western Hemisphere.[3] It features a striking, all-black cover with three brightly colored heroes—the Target and the Targeteers—sprinting toward the reader. Inside, Lucky Byrd, an Army Air Corps pilot and spy, stars in a narrative entitled "The Atomic Bomb." It is an eerily accurate fictional description of things to come. Five years before the first detonation of an actual atomic bomb at Alamogordo, New Mexico, the story describes a nuclear weapons test in the New Mexico desert. It is likely the first depiction of atomic weapons in a comic book. Many hundred more would follow during the second half of the decade.

The comic book was, in many respects, the ideal medium for depicting and debating atomic power. The relative lack of censorship imposed on comics allowed artists to show the more gruesome aspects of an atomic explosion. Comic book artists, having spent years crafting superhero narratives, were also used to illustrating fantastic and nearly incomprehensible abilities. It was as if the world had caught up to their fevered imaginations. As the WWB learned during World War II, comic books were additionally able to break down complicated subjects into a comprehensible combination of simple text and pictures featuring familiar characters. Even the complexities of basic physics and US foreign policy were less daunting when unpacked through sequential images. Because many titles included a page full of letters from readers, the medium also allowed consumers to discuss the depictions of atomic energy. By late 1945, the commercial comic book offered a unique site for debates over the atomic bomb and the foreign policies surrounding its use.

Initially, these atom-themed stories carried on in the tradition of WWB-sanctioned narratives from World War II. In the wake of the war, American society was divided over the potential risks and benefits of nuclear power. An initial wave of euphoria soon gave way to a creeping dread—a fear that the United States could soon fall victim to the same weapon it had unleashed at Hiroshima and Nagasaki. Comic books replicated this societal division, providing a unique space for dissent and negotiation within mass culture. Early comic book reactions to the atomic bomb ranged from cheery predictions of radioactive supermen and world government to grim visions of an America ravaged by nuclear war. A victim of the crumbling relationship between the United States and the Soviet Union, the window for debate over the global arms race closed by 1950. In the wake of Cold War crises and the first Soviet atomic test in August 1949, America committed itself to a security strategy based on ever-more powerful nuclear weapons. As the Korean War erupted in 1950 and domestic anticommunism devolved into a Red Scare, the internationalist approach to nuclear armament virtually disappeared from the pages of commercial comic books. In its place came bleak depictions of all-out nuclear conflict in titles like *Atomic War* and *World War III*. These were unpopular with readers, who no doubt turned to comic books for a thrill or scare, rather than a reminder that they might die in an atomic war.

In the charged atmosphere of the early Cold War, the essential characteristics of the commercial comic book—affordability, portability, and comprehensibility—also marked it as out of control.[4] In an effort to combat the graphic and often disturbing images of atomic power in comics, government agencies appropriated the medium for their own purposes. During the late 1940s and early 1950s, the Federal Civil Defense Administration (FCDA) attempted through comic books to soothe Americans' fear of atomic war. It participated in the distribution throughout public schools of propaganda titles like *Bert the Turtle Says "Duck and Cover"* and *The H-Bomb and You*. But despite distribution numbers in the millions, these propaganda comics were swamped by the hundreds of atomic-themed images and stories in commercial comic books. Propaganda titles also suffered for their simplistic artwork, stiff, educational text, and lack of colorful advertisements.

THE H-BOMB AND YOU

As the Cold War took shape in the late 1940s, a corporate infrastructure emerged to meet the growing demand for targeted propaganda comic books. At the same time, propagandists reached out to established American corporations for funding and branding opportunities. Cold War propaganda comics would be made by a new breed of publisher and distributed with corporate cooperation. One of the largest and most prolific companies to specialize in propaganda and corporate comic books, Commercial Comics, was founded in 1946 by Malcolm Ater. After serving in the navy during World War II, Ater briefly worked in the New York City comic book industry. During this time, he noted a small subset of the industry that produced customized titles for educational and advertising purposes. Sensing a potentially lucrative niche driven by the rising popularity of comic books and their ability to reach a wide range of readers, Ater founded his own company.[5]

During the buildup to the 1948 presidential election, Ater offered his services to the Republican Party. Although a Democrat, the business-minded Ater believed, "If anybody needed comic books—and could afford them—it was the Republicans."[6] When the Republicans proved uninterested, Ater presented his idea to the Democratic National Committee. Its members were sufficiently impressed and ordered three million copies of Ater's proposed comic book biography of President Harry S. Truman. In telling "the thrilling story of our thirty-third President," the comic stressed that Truman "made the awesome decision to use the atomic bomb, and thus saved thousands of American lives." It also blamed a group of cigar-smoking Republicans and "big business" for the postwar recession and depicted a grateful European thanking Truman for "helping us without trying to run our governments."[7] Ater's biography was the first comic book used as part of a federal election campaign, and it led to additional contracts with politicians from both major parties, both houses of Congress, and several governors. Perhaps as a result of his growing work on behalf of federal agencies, Ater moved his company in 1950 from New York City to Washington, DC.[8]

FIGURE 3.1 Cheap to produce, easy to distribute and share, and simple to understand, political comic books seemed an excellent way to reach voters. Commercial Comics published this issue for the Truman campaign in the lead-up to the 1948 presidential election.

One of Ater's next projects was a series of pro-segregationist, anti–civil rights comic books for southern governors. Sized to fit inside a standard mailing envelope, they could be sent to constituents and consumed in private. Some of the titles attacked civil rights leaders as communist dupes and troublemakers. Others presented segregationists as defenders of the South's institution. In a comic book for Louisiana gubernatorial candidate Chep Morrison, two men chat about politics as they walk down a peaceful, leafy street. One asks the other if Morrison is in favor of segregation. The other man answers, "Of course, son. Why, he's been sued so many times by the NAACP that he's lost count." In the next panel, Morrison himself appears, promising the reader, "I will use all the powers of the governor's office to maintain segregation in Louisiana." In other comic books for segregationist candidates like John Patterson and George Wallace, characters use more coded language, speaking of "states' rights" and "race agitators," rather than segregation and specific civil rights leaders.[9]

All these titles, however, promoted a policy—racial segregation—that caused substantial difficulties for American diplomats and propagandists during the Cold War. Segregation not only made a mockery of American pronouncements about fairness and equality but also provided a rich and endless source of material for communist propagandists. The embarrassments associated with segregation were not abstract: the nation's racism complicated efforts to win allies in the decolonizing world. And at home, because Washington, DC, was in the American South, non-White dignitaries and diplomats visiting the capital were subjected to the same humiliations as Black Americans. Ater's willingness to work for segregationist politicians made him part of a confusing cycle: even as federal agencies hired Ater and Commercial Comics to create pro-American titles designed to win hearts and minds abroad, domestically, the company promoted the same racist policies that created so many international problems in the first place.

Commercial Comics played a significant role in America's postwar propaganda efforts, creating comic books on behalf of federal agen-

FIGURE 3.2 Sized to fit in an envelope that could be discreetly mailed to potential voters, this comic book touts an Alabama gubernatorial candidate as an enemy of civil rights and attacks the NAACP as a "gang of agitators." It was produced by Commercial Comics.

cies for use in a variety of regions.[10] Ater's comics typically featured realistic characters tailored to each assignment. One early product for the State Department entitled *The Free World Speaks* critiqued international communism. It depicts events like the Soviet occupation of Eastern Europe and includes negative portrayals of figures like Joseph Stalin and Andrey Gromyko, the Soviet representative to the United Nations. By omitting references to popular characters and superheroes, propaganda comics maintained the more serious tone sought by policy makers. Yet they retained the inherent benefits of the comic book form: comprehensibility, broad popularity, and affordability.

In 1949, Ater and his staff began work on a short, eight-page civil defense comic book script entitled *If an A-Bomb Falls*. Although intended for publication as a comic, it eventually appeared as a full-color strip on the first page of the *Washington Post* in July 1951. The text emphasized that it complied "in every respect with instructions issued by both the district Civil Defense authorities and the Federal Civil Defense Administration."[11] The FCDA grew out of an earlier government organization, the National Securities Resources Board (NSRB). The board was a product of the 1947 National Security Act, which created the NSRB as a means of assisting President Truman with national mobilization in the case of war.[12] In addition to dealing with strategic and economic mobilization, the board also handled matters of domestic civil defense through the Office of Civil Defense Planning (OCDP). The Civil Defense Act of 1950 reclassified the OCDP as a separate organization and renamed it the Federal Civil Defense Administration (FCDA).[13]

In April 1953, Ater met with representatives of the FCDA who requested a script for a thirty-two-page comic book explaining how to survive a nuclear attack.[14] By this time, *If an A-Bomb Falls* was out of date. Fission-type atomic bombs had been dwarfed by the detonation, in November 1952, of a new fusion weapon known as the hydrogen bomb. The first hydrogen device, code-named Ivy Mike, produced an explosion equivalent to approximately ten million tons of conventional explosives—many hundreds of times more powerful than the atomic bombs that destroyed Hiroshima and Nagasaki. Ater

FIGURE 3.3 This terrifying cover, depicting a bloodred hydrogen bomb blast looming over the title text, undercuts the message within, which encourages readers to believe that Americans will invent a defense against such weapons. Commercial Comics produced it for distribution by civil defense agencies.

titled the new comic book *The H-Bomb and You*. Commercial Comics prepared to produce an initial run of two hundred thousand copies, and local and state civil defense agencies in California, Illinois, Louisiana, Ohio, and Michigan placed additional orders for the comic book throughout 1954 and 1955.[15]

The H-Bomb and You follows a group of elementary school students learning about civil defense from a variety of adults. Initially, the students watch a classroom film on the hydrogen bomb, which leads young Johnny to comment, "It was a swell film, all right, but seeing that H-bomb tear apart a make-believe city seemed awfully real." In case of an attack on a real city, he asks, wouldn't all its inhabitants be killed? His teacher dismisses Johnny's concerns as rumors and "the kind of talk an enemy would have you believe." *The H-Bomb and You* emphasizes that taking reasonable precautions will blunt the effects of a nuclear attack. "No matter what the weapon is," stresses the teacher, "there is a defense against it. The best defense against the H-bomb is a well-trained, alert Civil Defense to back up our military forces." American children must not only acclimate to life under the constant threat of nuclear war but also become a component of America's national defense. As combatants in the Cold War, the comic book argues, they could ensure their nation's survival by volunteering two to four hours per week with Operation Skywatch, a program designed to scan the nation's skies for incoming Soviet bombers. But a visiting official from a local civil defense office admits, "We must accept the facts: even though our Air Force is on the alert 24 hours a day, many enemy planes may break through our defenses."[16]

By the late 1940s, key American policy makers believed the nation was in the midst of a long-term, zero-sum battle against communism. Victory in this era of permanent conflict required not only massive government investment but also the commitment of millions of average American citizens.[17] Indeed, the unstated goal of the FCDA under President Truman was to ensure that Americans were willing to endure any price—even nuclear war—to defend their nation, society, and way of life.[18] This was a massive task, requiring the FCDA to change popular perceptions of atomic weapons and warfare.

The FCDA used the comic book medium to domesticate the horrors of nuclear attack. Beginning in 1951, the agency provided American schools with millions of copies of *Bert the Turtle Says "Duck and Cover,"* a decidedly upbeat comic book full of instructions on civil defense.[19] Because the FCDA was a "supervisory and inspirational agency," it busied itself with creating pro–civil defense propaganda materials and campaigns, rather than with matters of funding and implementation. The job of the agency was to motivate other civil defense agencies at the local and state levels to pay for and deploy FCDA-approved materials. Most FCDA products found their way to citizens through public schools, an effective distribution channel for large quantities of printed matter.[20] *Bert the Turtle Says "Duck and Cover"* offered young readers a straightforward and soothing message: the world was full of commonplace dangers like crossing the street, and an atomic attack was little different. The FCDA comic book presented the atomic bomb as "a new danger," but one that could be neutralized through education and preparation. As a turtle, Bert carried his own protection on his back. Because kids had no protective shell of their own, they had to learn the signs of an atomic attack and react accordingly. After seeing the flash of an atomic explosion, kids would survive by ducking "behind walls and trees, even in a hollow in the ground. In a bus or auto, duck down behind or under the seats. . . . Do it instantly, don't stand and look, duck and cover!"[21]

THE ATOMIC MAN

Despite the federal government's early and enthusiastic embrace of the comic book as a means of waging the Cold War, there existed no professional consensus on the utility of comics as educational tools. There were, however, a number of advocates for comic books. These men and women—many of them academics—not only saw commercial titles as generally benign but also argued that comic books created expressly for educational purposes had a place in postwar classrooms. The medium's comprehensibility, along with its popularity, offered educators a chance to teach complex scientific subjects to students that struggled with conventional science textbooks and lectures.

In December 1944, and again in December 1949, the *Journal of Educational Sociology* devoted an entire issue to potential educational applications of comic books. In addition, the January 1949 issue included multiple articles on the use of comic books as a means of teaching Americans about atomic power.[22] Within these three issues, a diverse group of men and women from the academy, the military, and the arts argued that comics were an undervalued means of educating people who struggled to learn from traditional classroom materials. Sociologist Harvey Zorbaugh of New York University noted that in 2,500 classrooms, students learned reading skills from *Superman* workbooks, while other comics taught subjects as diverse as foreign languages, classic literature, and science.[23] Even Sunday schools used comic books to teach students about religious history, tolerance, and the dangers of communism.[24] Comics, argued W. W. D. Sones of the University of Pittsburgh, used a language nearly "universally understood" by both young and adult readers.[25] This comprehensibility marked the comic book as a medium uniquely suited to distill the complexities of life in the atomic age into language understandable to the widest possible audience.

In the December 1949 issue of the *Journal of Educational Sociology*, Katharine Hutchinson laid out the academic defense of comic books. She reviewed the results of a joint experiment conducted by New York University and the University of Pittsburgh on the suitability of comics as educational tools. Over two thousand teachers in twenty-seven states agreed to participate in the experiment by using a weekly collection of comic artwork in the classroom.[26] The results suggested that students in elementary school and junior high were particularly receptive to comics in the classroom. Science teachers noted that even the "pseudo-science" in *Flash Gordon* proved beneficial as a gateway to discussion of proven scientific concepts.[27] Other educators commented that comics proved "particularly useful" as a means of reaching underperforming students. The combination in comics of basic language and more complex, adult situations encouraged these students to practice their reading and comprehension skills.[28] Based on this study, Hutchinson concluded that comic books were useful classroom tools and excelled at simplifying technical subjects.[29] When invited to respond to the articles in this issue of the *Journal of Educational Sociology*, Dr. Fredric Wertham wrote, "I am afraid I have neither the time nor the inclination to dignify their phony comics issue with a reply."[30]

Also in 1949, Volta Torrey, managing editor of *Popular Science Monthly*, warned that public ignorance of atomic power posed a threat to national security. Torrey argued that only when average Americans comprehended the benefits and risks of nuclear energy could they make informed decisions regarding the newfound atomic bomb. Because so few newspaper journalists understood the science behind nuclear weapons, and because journalists faced daily deadlines, Torrey suggested that monthly magazines, and even comic books, offered more useful forums.[31] In this way, writers and artists could take the time to educate themselves about nuclear power before attempting to relay this knowledge to their readers. American citizens were being asked to accept the atomic bomb as their nation's primary means of defense in a very new and uncertain sort of war. Before accepting the long-term challenge of competition against communism, Americans deserved to understand the capability, promise, and dangers posed by atomic energy. Comic books seemed a plausible means of providing the necessary information.[32]

Accordingly, in 1949, Blondie and Dagwood (stars of the *Blondie* comic strip and comic book series) entered the atomic age to teach Americans the fundamentals of physics and the basic science behind nuclear reactors and weapons.[33] The impetus behind Blondie and Dagwood's recruitment was Lieutenant General Leslie Groves, the head of the Manhattan Project that produced the first atomic bomb. Groves himself, who was particularly fond of *Blondie*, proposed that the characters be incorporated into an educational comic book on nuclear energy for distribution at a traveling exhibit entitled *Man and the Atom*.[34] Working with a physicist, artist Joe Musial drafted a comic starring the Bumstead family—Dagwood, Blondie, and their children—and other popular King Features characters like Mandrake the Magician, Popeye, and J. Wellington Wimpy.

The issue opens with a photo of General Groves and Joe Musial above a signed introduction attributed to the general. Groves hopes that the comic book "will bring a clearer understanding of atomic energy. Many will understand what has formerly confused them. Mere words need not frighten them in the future—words such as fission, isotope, proton, chain reaction, and atom bomb. This book will reassure the fearful that the future can be made bright." The narrative within continues in this upbeat tone, with Mandrake the Magician shrinking Dagwood down to the size of an atom so he can better understand basic nuclear physics. The issue ends with Blondie, charmed by her trip through an atom, exclaiming that physics is simpler to understand than her husband.[35] *Dagwood Splits the Atom*'s chipper attitude toward atomic energy was shared by a

number of commercial comic book characters created during the last
half of the decade.

These new heroes—modernized, nuclear-fueled versions of
earlier superheroes—suggested that atomic power was a manageable force, one that held enormous promise for Americans. First
appearing in *Headline Comics* in November 1945, the Atomic Man
was originally a World War II veteran named Adam Mann. While
in combat overseas, Mann sustained serious wounds and a case of
malaria. He returns home, where a doctor tells Mann that he also
has leukemia. With a dark chuckle, Mann replies, "What a laugh! I
survive six months of malaria and live through another six months
of operations while the medics dig the shrapnel out of me—I survive
all of *that* for *this*." Depressed, Mann decides to spend his last
months alive working on a "heavy water experiment" at his atomic
laboratory. Dizzy from his injuries, Mann inadvertently drinks a glass
of water full of powdered uranium-235. His leukemia disappears,
and he becomes indestructible. Mann soon learns that he is also able
to explode any object simply by touching it with his right hand, an
ability he controls by donning a leather glove. So equipped, Mann
reflects, "I've been transformed! I'm no longer a man! I'm a human
atomic bomb!"[36] For all his enthusiasm, the Atomic Man did not find
a significant audience and appeared in just six issues of *Headline
Comics*.

In February 1946, two new atomic-powered costumed heroes
appeared on newsstands. The first was the Atomic Thunderbolt.
Before his transformation, William Burns was a "wharf rat"—a
veteran of the merchant marine whose mind faltered after surviving
a Nazi torpedo attack. Like many actual combat veterans, Burns has
trouble reacclimating to American society after the war. Unhoused
and alone on the docks, he sits on a shipping crate full of plutonium.
When the crate's recipient, Professor Rhonne, warns Burns to move
or risk death, Burns tells the scientist that he's ready to die because
he's "no good for anything anymore." The professor realizes that
Burns is the perfect test subject for a dangerous atomic experiment.
He hopes to change the very structure of human tissue, so that all
mankind will be able to survive a nuclear attack. By making all hu-

FIGURE 3.4 The Atomic Man was an early atom-powered superhero, depicted here in 1945 as the nearly divine result of a fortuitous radioactive accident. Appearing soon after the atomic bombings of Hiroshima and Nagasaki, the Atomic Man lasted for just a few issues before disappearing.

mans indestructible, Rhonne believes he will put an end to warfare. The experiment goes wrong, destroying the laboratory and killing Professor Rhonne, but leaves William Burns transformed into the indestructible Atomic Thunderbolt.[37] Despite his newfound power, the Atomic Thunderbolt disappeared after a single issue.

Atoman told the origin of another atomic superman. Atoman was the alter ego of nuclear scientist Barry Dale, who realizes that he has, like the Atomic Man, became immensely strong and resistant to injury. Initially baffled, Dale concludes that atomic energy was responsible for his transformation. Triumphant, he exclaims, "An atomic explosion occurred—inside of me! Madame Curie, who discovered radium later found that her body had become radioactive. I've handled radium for years . . . radium and uranium . . . can I be radioactive?" Dale is, indeed, radioactive; his body "so geared as a result of working with radium and uranium that it can explode atoms, and give me atomic strength." He decides to use his new abilities to defeat a gang of foreign agents intent on using the American government's "atomic formula" to build their own nuclear plants. Atomic power, Atoman declares, "cannot belong to one man, or group of men, or even one nation! It belongs to the whole world. My own power must be used to help all people, regardless of race, creed, or nationality. I am strong—therefore it is my duty to help the weak."[38] Atoman's appeal for global unity and fairness is virtually identical to the slogans approved for use in wartime comics by the WWB. These sentiments, though, were fast falling out of favor as the confrontation between East and West hardened. Global events ensured that he, like the Atomic Thunderbolt, vanished after just two appearances.

SUPERBOMBS BEAT SUPERMEN

From the mid-1930s through the mid-1940s, superhero comic books dominated the industry. Titles boasting popular characters like Captain Marvel, Superman, and the Human Torch sold hundreds of thousands or even millions of copies per issue. To generate such impressive sales numbers, publishers forged an unwritten compact with their readers: writers and artists created an entertaining, formulaic world for their superheroes, and in exchange, readers accepted the premise of altruistic, superpowered characters fighting for universally positive institutions. Superhero comic books subsequently followed a fairly standard formula: good trumped evil, male heroes rescued women, and non-White characters functioned as villains or comic relief. This formula required comic book artists and writers to craft worlds in which the ultimate authority resided with superpowered, pro-American heroes. The atomic bombings of Hiroshima and Nagasaki, however, fractured this formula and, with it, the compact between comic book creators and consumers.

The atomic bomb loomed over American public thought during the late 1940s. It dwarfed everything and everyone and challenged the very idea of human survival. The bomb proved even more dangerous to comic book superhumans. Maintaining the comic book formula required overwhelmingly strong—in many cases, invulnerable—heroes. During the war, this proved a tidy formula, as lone superheroes battled hundreds of soldiers. But in the atomic age, this premise was painfully, intolerably unrealistic. Even at a time when comic books enjoyed relative freedom from censorship, writers and artists struggled to combine superheroes and atomic weapons. The horrors suffered by the citizens of Hiroshima and Nagasaki were public knowledge, as was the sheer, terrifying power of the atomic bomb. How were superheroes to compete with a weapon able to level entire cities and menace the very idea of human life?

Wartime superhero comic books encouraged readers to side with their heroic protagonists. These characters existed in a world of patriotic American men and women and skilled, sympathetic authority figures. But after Hiroshima and Nagasaki, it was no longer so simple to pull readers into a system populated by kind heroes, accommodating police officers, and right-thinking governments. The bomb brought a new and brutal darkness into the world of the superhero. And atom-powered vigilantes did not resonate with postwar consumers. Despite the lure of atomic-powered factories and homes and infinite supplies of energy, there was an element of fear to the first wave of atomic superheroes. No matter how altruistic they might be, their very existence was a danger to Americans. A radioactive superhero was doubtless a menace to criminals, but he was equally dangerous to law-abiding citizens.

Why were atomic superheroes such commercial failures, while violent and sexual comic books grew extremely popular? The postwar wave of crime, horror, and romance comics were gritty and "real" in the sense that they depicted American men and women without any superpowers engaging in acts of violence and sexuality. But this was violence on a human, intimate scale: men and women shot, stabbed, and tortured each other. Despite their shared brutality, these images remained quite different from the implied immolation of hundreds of millions of people. Atomic war was a distinct degree of atrocity. Ultimately, consumers did not accept the concept of altruistic, atom-powered heroes. Recent history made clear that exposure to radiation produced not superpowers but suffering and horror. Comic book readers needed more time to accept life under the atomic cloud before embracing nuclear-powered superheroes.

Heroes like Mary Marvel and Batman relied on more conventional, bloodless imagery than their new competitors. They solved crimes with their fists, rather than with knives, guns, or implements of torture. Atomic power, though, was on a wholly different and more terrifying scale of violence. Some exceptionally strong heroes like Captain Marvel and Superman could, and did, survive atomic explosions, but many others were simply humans in costumes, as vulnerable to blast, heat, and radiation as any inhabitant of Hiroshima. But unlike the citizens of Hiroshima, these superheroes were White and American. Depicting Japanese soldiers incinerated by napalm during World War II was one thing. Portraying the immolation of superheroes by communist-built atomic weapons was quite another.

During the weeks and months following the atomic bombings of Hiroshima and Nagasaki, a torrent of atomic-themed stories and commentaries appeared in America. Paul Boyer notes that this period resembled nothing so much as a "national town meeting on the atomic bomb and its meaning."[39] Cultural reactions fell into one of two broad categories: cautious optimism regarding the transformative capacity of atomic energy and a gnawing fear that humanity, at least in its contemporary stage of political, cultural, and intellectual development, was not equipped to deal with the dangers posed by atomic explosives. Nuclear power seemed to offer a path to national security and a revolution in fields as varied as engineering, medicine, and transportation. *Newsweek* magazine gushed over the prospect of a nuclear-powered utopia destined to "make the comic-strip prophecies of Buck Rogers look obsolete," a sentiment reinforced by scientists and intellectuals who anticipated atomic-powered cars and aircraft and virtually free electricity.[40] These positive reactions emerged, in part, because Americans were not yet fully informed of the bomb's true effects.[41]

At the same time, the unleashed atom also menaced the hopes of millions who sought nothing more than a return to normalcy. If—or when—America's enemies developed nuclear weapons, the argument went, the United States might have to disperse its cities and drive its population underground to avoid an atomic holocaust. Some Americans who saw danger rather than promise in nuclear power began agitating for international control of atomic energy or even a world government. In 1946, Robert Oppenheimer, the wartime head of the Los Alamos laboratory that built the atomic bomb, wrote that the development of nuclear weapons required "radical and profound changes in the politics of the world."[42] This then was the question facing Americans in the wake of Hiroshima and Nagasaki: would atomic power override centuries of faith in independence, patriotism, and national defense? Or would this new and potentially world-ending invention become simply another weapon in the arsenals of nations?

Between 1945 and 1950, American commercial comic books of-fered very mixed reactions to the revelation of atomic energy. Comics like the first issue of *Picture News in Color and Action*, dated January 1946, summarized early fears of runaway atomic power. Its cover depicts a skyscraper crumbling under atomic attack. Below, bold letters ask: "Will the Atom Blow the World Apart? George Bernard Shaw Warns: It's Likely—If We Don't Watch Our Step!" In the lead story, Shaw warns readers of the threat posed by atomic fission. An

Irish playwright, political activist, and public intellectual, he was a pessimist regarding humans and their propensity for violence. In *Man and Superman*, Shaw states, "There is nothing in man's industrial machinery but his greed and sloth: his heart is in his weapons." The advent of atomic weapons did nothing to brighten his perspective. In a *Picture News in Color and Action* story titled "Could Science Blow the World Apart?," the fictionalized Shaw suggests that human nature will likely trigger an atomic war that will destroy civilization. Shaw closes the story by cautioning Americans, "Finally, like a sorcerer's apprentice, our magic, without knowing how to stop itself, will destroy us, if we don't watch out." Shaw, along with many other people both famous and anonymous, saw a terrifying tautology in the discovery of atomic weapons: their creation guaranteed their use, whether intentional or accidental. Humans had proven themselves unable to resist the temptation to use other horrifying weapons, from the machine gun to chemical and biological agents. Following this view, it was delusional to expect any more restraint on the use of atomic weapons.[43]

Early fears of nuclear weaponry also appeared in *Air Ace*, a Street & Smith publication that had been used for propaganda purposes by the WWB. In 1944, editor William DeGrouchy cited *Air Ace* to the WWB board as an example of a title that could incorporate "real happenings" into comic book narratives.[44] The comic book did begin to blend real events into its stories, a convention that continued after the end of the war. The January 1947 cover of *Air Ace* 7 proclaims, "The Atom Bomb—Top Thrill of the Air." It purports to tell the story of the American atomic test at Bikini Atoll, but the cover art and contents are rather more sensational and racially fraught. Against a bright red background on the cover, a US Navy plane streaks skyward, the pilot peering out from the cockpit at a remarkable scene below. Beneath the plane stands a White woman tied to a pole, her dress falling off as she struggles to escape from a stereotypical dark-skinned "native" brandishing a large, colorful snake. Above her head the cover slug screams: "Caught in the Vortex from the Atomic Bomb! No Man Ever Went Through It Before!"

One of the two atomic-themed stories in this issue, "The Push-

Button War," offers a dark, lurid image of a nuclear-armed future. It depicts "the last war on earth . . . a preview of what may happen if the peoples of earth cannot learn to live together peacefully." Twelve pages of devastation follow, as men and women of all nationalities die from radiation poisoning, cities disappear under mushroom clouds, and half of earth is destroyed by nuclear detonations. Then, after forty-eight hours of combat, "The war is over! The push-button war. . . . And we won! Or did we? No! Nobody won. . . . Man has reduced himself to a level lower than that of prehistoric ape-men!"[45] This story exemplifies postwar fears that the atomic bomb was not a political and social panacea but an all-too-easy means of self-extermination.

Faced with the specter of atomic war, some comic book creators responded with dark, mocking humor. In 1947, General Mills released a series of comic book premiums as promotions for its Cheerios breakfast cereal. They were packaged in four sets, lettered W through Z, each containing four, thirty-two-page stories. Consumers across the country mailed in an order blank from a box of Cheerios, plus a dime, and received one set of four comics in return. The titles starred popular Disney characters like Mickey Mouse, Goofy, and Dumbo. Set Y featured Donald Duck in *Donald Duck's Atom Bomb*, along with *Mickey Mouse Meets the Wizard*, *Brer Rabbit's Secret*, and *Dumbo and the Circus Mystery*. It seems impossible that anyone from Disney or General Mills read *Donald Duck's Atom Bomb* before including it. Written and drawn by Carl Barks, who drew the first original Donald Duck story published in a comic book and created numerous elements of the character's world, including Scrooge McDuck and Duckburg, its subject matter is wildly inappropriate for a children's cereal premium, as is its flippant, bleak take on atomic weapons. The comic is an assault on any measured discussion of nuclear power; it ridicules not only any effort to represent the bomb as a justifiable, war-ending weapon but also other comic book attempts to debate seriously the dangers posed by a nuclear arms race.

The story opens with Donald assembling an atomic bomb made of "mashed meteors," the "juice of one lightning bolt," and "ten cat hairs," among other ingredients. Frustratingly, the bomb goes off with a fizzle rather than a boom. Irked, Donald consults his friend Professor Mollicule, an atomic scientist. Mollicule enlists the help of his foreign colleague, Professor Sleezy. Professor Sleezy appears as a stereotype of an Eastern European spy—he dresses like a dandy, speaks with an incomprehensible accent, and, at the first opportunity, steals Donald's prototype bomb and atomic formula. He gloats, "I haf here der formula—so still my guntry can haf an A-bumb." In the midst of his celebration, Professor Sleezy inadvertently sets off the bomb with his cigar. Witnessing the detonation, Donald and Professor Mollicule reach safety behind a rickety wooden fence. The other residents of Duckburg are less fortunate, and as the bomb's invisible rays sweep across the city, its residents lose all their hair. Bald poodles hide in shame, and suddenly bald women race for cover. Outraged, three of the women attack Donald and Professor Mollicule with umbrellas, bricks, and boots.

Once sheltered behind another fence, Donald renounces his new weapon. But Professor Mollicule urges him to reconsider, reminding Donald, "Think of the reward! Money! Money! Vast riches!" Donald simply laughs, telling the professor, "I've got a way picked out to make money, and lots of it."[46] The last panel of the comic reveals Donald's plan: he will sell "Prof. Duck's Atomic Hair Grower" to the hapless, irradiated citizens of Duckburg. A line of morose, bald citizens winds out of the panel, as Donald and his nephews cheerfully sell bogus hair tonic at a dollar per bottle. It is a remarkably morbid and cynical ending, even for a character as obnoxious, vengeful, and short-tempered as Donald Duck. Faced with a city poisoned by radiation, Donald Duck offers false hope to the survivors and then robs them. The entire narrative mocks the ideals of patriotism and shared responsibility so central to the American government's framing of the war between communism and capitalism. To Donald Duck, the only suitable response to atomic war is to laugh and profit from it.

The subject matter of the comic book, along with Donald Duck's cruelty toward the irradiated citizens of Duckburg, created a problem for Disney. It responded by banning the reproduction of *Donald Duck's Atom Bomb* in its original form. When the story was reprinted decades later, Disney instituted two changes. When Professor Molli-

FIGURE 3.5 In this remarkably cruel comic from 1947, Donald Duck first irradiates the residents of Duckburg with an atomic bomb, causing all their hair to fall out, then sells them bogus hair tonic. The hair tonic is reminiscent of quack medicines advertised in comic books.

cule encourages Donald to sell his hair tonic, Donald now replies, "No thanks, Professor! I've got more than money in mind." And on the final page of the comic book, the word "radiation" no longer appears, and the hair tonic is now free for anyone afflicted by the atomic bomb, with "Growth Guaranteed!"[47]

In its August 31, 1946, issue, the *New Yorker* magazine published John Hersey's account of the first atomic bombing, "Hiroshima," which followed six victims as they struggled to survive in the radiating ruins. "Hiroshima," first as an article and then as a book, captivated readers. Periodicals discussed the book, ABC Radio read the entire contents over the air, and the Book-of-the-Month Club distributed free copies to many of its more than three-quarters of a million members.[48] Yet at virtually the same time, a pair of vivid depictions of nuclear weapons appeared on newsstands—and likely reached a wider audience. Both comic books bore a cover date of October 1946, suggesting that they went on sale in August or September of that year.[49] They typify one sort of comic book reaction to the atomic bomb—a reaction couched in the government-sanctioned wartime language of international cooperation.

The first story was in the pages of *Action Comics*, the home of Superman, the most iconic and popular hero in comics. "Crime Paradise" begins with a crooked scientist's discovery of an ancient formula that, when ingested, drives the victim insane. He and a gang of criminals use the concoction on wealthy men, with the intention of extorting huge sums of money in return for the antidote. When Superman threatens their plan, the crooks force him to drink the potion as well. The Man of Steel tries to escape but, under the influence of the drug, is only able to fly backward. He loops the earth, plummeting out of the sky over a desolate Pacific atoll, the site of an atomic bomb test. Superman disappears within the ensuing "man-made holocaust," which clears his head. Once recovered, he seizes a newsreel camera from an astonished photographer and flies back toward the rising mushroom cloud, noting, "The photos will be a warning to men who talk against peace."[50] Although the story reduces the atomic bomb to a plot device, the narrative identifies the new weapon as a danger to not only Americans but everybody on earth. It is not, however, a danger to Superman, who repeatedly flies through a nuclear mushroom cloud without suffering any ill effects.

The editorial decision to make Superman invulnerable to nuclear power may have been an attempt to demonstrate that the bomb had not, in fact, changed everything. Superman remained invulnerable to all weapons but kryptonite (and the odd insanity potion). Certainly, the second atomic-themed comic narrative that appeared in February 1946 was far less optimistic. "The Atomic War" occupied the first twelve pages of *Captain Marvel Adventures* 66, a product of Fawcett Publications. Fawcett was not known as a company eager to push the boundaries of acceptable content. During World War II, Fawcett energetically cooperated with the WWB and other government agencies on comic books promoting patriotism and international cooperation.

Although Captain Marvel boasted the typical combination of superpowers and colorful tights, his adventures were very different in tone from those of other popular superheroes. Rendered by C. C. Beck in a bold, cartoonish style, Captain Marvel inhabited what Jules Feiffer called a "Disneyland of happy violence" in which even the villains often appeared more fanciful than threatening.[51] His opponents included Mr. Tawny the Talking Tiger, who stood upright and wore a sports coat, and Mr. Mind, a talking worm who wore glasses and dreamed of world domination. The other members of the Marvel family—Captain Marvel Jr. and Mary Marvel—frequently joined the captain on his adventures. Among the many hundreds of comic books on sale in the mid-1940s, *Captain Marvel Adventures* perhaps appealed to the broadest audience. Fawcett billed it as the best-selling comic book, with over one million copies sold per issue.[52] Even allowing for the inevitable inaccuracy of self-reported sales, there is little doubt that Captain Marvel was very popular, perhaps outselling Superman. Its combination of lighthearted but earnest plots, cheerful artwork, and funny, grotesque characters appealed to anyone looking for entertainment as distraction. Captain Marvel, then, was hardly an edgy or overly violent character.

Despite this, "The Atomic War" demonstrates a relatively sophisticated understanding of the dangers posed by the atomic bomb. Stylistically, "The Atomic War" is very different from Hersey's understated social realism or the mild tone of "Crime Paradise." On one of the most striking comic book covers of the early Cold War, Captain Marvel stands helplessly among the rubble of a city under atomic attack. Frozen in fear or confusion, the captain braces himself for the impact of an atomic bomb that is about to strike his chest. Standing out against a white background, the cover slug screams, "Captain Marvel Battles the Dread Atomic War!" Inside, the first panel of the story shows the superhero slumped over, unable to stop a sneak attack. At the bottom of the panel a text box warns, "Atomic war! Stark! Devastating! Ruinous! What would it mean to the world?

FIGURE 3.6 In this stark portrayal of atomic war from 1946, radiation makes it impossible even for Captain Marvel, "the World's Mightiest Mortal," to save American lives. Such images would not appear for long in postwar comic books.

Captain Marvel learns the dread truth as the most fearful holocaust of all bursts forth over the entire earth!" Although the comic contains few images of human suffering, Captain Marvel does discover a mother and child trapped in a burning house. The captain pulls the pair from the fiery wreckage but quickly realizes that they are dying from radiation poisoning. Faced with the nightmare of atomic war, Captain Marvel covers his face and says, "I'll go mad if I keep thinking about it!"

Thankfully, the war turns out to be nothing more than a simulation of atomic conflict broadcast by a local TV station with Captain Marvel's cooperation. The TV announcer reminds the audience watching at home, "We were handicapped by studio limitations from showing the horrors of an atomic war! The atomic war itself would be much worse!" A young boy then breaks the fourth wall and says to the reader, "I guess we'd all better learn to live and get along together—one nation with all other nations and one person with all other persons—so that the terrible atomic war will never occur!"

Simulation or not, the story makes clear that even Captain Marvel, "the World's Mightiest Mortal," is powerless to stop an atomic war.[53] Captain Marvel's appeal for international understanding and cooperation echoed the narratives of Fawcett's WWB-sanctioned stories. In 1946, these sentiments were still culturally acceptable, but they would not be for much longer.[54]

WEIRD SCIENCE

As Soviet-American relations worsened, and Americans learned of the first Soviet nuclear test in 1949, many of the remaining atomic-themed comic books treated the liberated atom as both controllable and relatively benign. Beginning in the early 1950s, this tamed comic book version of the bomb often incinerated communists and pulverized Soviet cities but rarely inflicted equivalent damage on the United States. In these stories, destruction remained contained, and American scientific prowess provided a means of retaliation and defense. These narratives suggested that even if communists dared to launch a nuclear sneak attack on the United States, their weapons could not completely destroy the American spirit or civilization. In one, *World War III*, an old woman lies dying in New York's Grand Central Terminal after the detonation of a "small" Soviet atomic bomb. Rebuffing offers of first aid, she gamely insists, "I'm more mad than hurt, dearie! Take care of some of the others! The cowardly Reds are striking at us from all angles and we're doing nothing in return! Why? Why?"[55] American comic book scientists ensured that these attacks did not go unanswered, shattering all of Soviet society with a massive counterattack.

Another example of controlled atomic conflict appears in 1952 in the second issue of *Atomic War*, a four-issue arc depicting a full-scale war between the United States and the Soviet bloc. The editors of *Atomic War* explain to their readers, "The purpose of this book is clear. We want everyone—friend and foe alike—to know the utter devastation that another war will bring to all, the just as well as the unjust. We hope that all who read this magazine will think about this—and pray that what you see here will never happen." But rather than depicting the destruction of "the just as well as the unjust," *Atomic War* presents the atomic bomb as a manageable weapon, a force able to defeat the Soviet Union but not the United States. Throughout the series, American soldiers use "atomic artillery" and "atomic ammo" while battling communist attackers. When the Soviet Union invades Canada, American defenders counterattack with their atomic weapons, totally destroying the Soviet offensive while suffering almost no casualties. Similarly, American soldiers swiftly repulse a Soviet attack in West Germany with the products of American scientific know-how: "atomic artillery" and a new explosive called "polytomic." The comic depicts Soviet soldiers dying from American flamethrowers and atomic artillery, but when an American soldier is machine-gunned, he survives, reassuring his comrade that "one bullet only stunned me! I just have a slight flesh wound!"[56]

The series begins with a meeting of "the Big Four" in Paris, where "Russia again delivered its message of peace . . . nothing but peace, on a fateful Sunday afternoon in May."[57] As diplomats cheer the Soviet proclamation, Americans rejoice at the prospect of an end to the Cold War. The following pages show US Air Force radar operators relaxing during "the quietest shift we've ever had!" But moments later, one of the operators notices a squadron of planes flying across Canada toward New York City. When he attempts to sound the alarm, one of his fellow radar operators pulls out a gun and shouts, "Don't anyone make a move! In twenty minutes New York will be a rubble heap! We'll all be dead, but the Soviets will conquer. For this, I give my own life!" The radar operators subdue the Soviet agent but fail to warn the rest of the United States of the sneak attack. Just before the first atomic bomb detonates above Manhattan, one of the radar operators mutters, "Peace! Yeah—this is the peace they wanted!"

The next five pages depict the destruction of New York City, but the scenes are largely limited to shattered buildings, monuments, and property. There are few images of human suffering and no pictures of burns, radiation poisoning, or death. The comic then depicts similar attacks on Chicago and Detroit but never suggests that these attacks might impede America's ability to heal and

FIGURE 3.7 In this more optimistic representation of atomic war from 1953, American pilots cheerfully exact revenge on the Soviet Union for launching a sneak attack on the United States.

launch atomic counterattacks. As an American soldier surveys the wreckage, he spies a flight of planes overhead and shouts, "This means we're not going back anymore! Only forward! And this time maybe we're not stopping at Berlin! I wanna be able to take my shoes off in what's left of the Kremlin!" Later, after destroying Sverdlovsk, Chelyabinsk, and Moscow, an American pilot draws an "X" through each city on a map and exclaims cheerfully, "We've changed the map of Russia!"

One of the few publishers that continued producing dark, challenging atomic-themed stories after 1950 was EC. Many of the most pessimistic ones appeared in *Weird Science* and *Weird Fantasy*, science fiction titles. These were elaborately drawn—and money-losing—comic books often containing stories penned by Ray Bradbury, Isaac Asimov, and other authors whose work appeared in books and middlebrow media. Neither editor Al Feldstein nor publisher Bill Gaines accepted that the United States could prevail in an atomic war. Feldstein insisted that to both men, any conflict involving atomic weapons would mean mutual "complete annihilation."[58] Unlike most other comic book publishers, EC consistently portrayed the atomic bomb as something too huge and too powerful for humans to manage. It depicted nuclear weapons and American science in a remorselessly negative light even after Cold War attitudes toward the Soviet Union hardened in the early 1950s. As discussed in chapter 4, this cynicism would soon attract the attention of army intelligence and the FBI.

EC Comics also depicted humans suffering from the effects of atomic bombs. Many of these stories suggested that atomic war would probably destroy the world because humans were hopelessly flawed and fundamentally uninterested in peace. On the cover of a 1950 issue of *Weird Science*, two robots stand amid the rubble of New York City, as a third looks down at a burnt piece of newspaper. The headline reads, "U.S. threatens to use hydrogen bomb to end atomic war," and the robot confirms, "Our observations were correct! There is no longer any life on this planet!"[59]

The cover of a 1952 issue of *Weird Fantasy* depicts New York City after a nuclear attack. Manhattan is completely destroyed, with an enormous crater running east to west across it.[60] The image is virtually identical to one from *Collier's* magazine painted by artist Chesley Bonestell and titled "Hiroshima, U.S.A.—Can Anything Be Done?" Bonestell's painting depicts one of the world's great cities on fire. At its center, midtown Manhattan burns brightly, suffused with an eerie orange glow from the unimaginable temperatures of nuclear fire.[61] Where it differs from comic book representations of atomic warfare is in its absence of human subjects. Bonestell's painting shows Manhattan from high above. Feldstein's *Weird Fantasy* cover does as well, but inside the comic book are images of burned and irradiated people. Some have their faces blasted away; others have organs spilling from their burned torsos. These were images too shocking for middlebrow magazines like *Collier's*, yet to comic book readers, they were familiar. The comic book was perfectly suited to depicting large-scale destruction and chaos.

Feldstein edited most issues of *Weird Science* and *Weird Fantasy*. Like EC's crime and horror titles discussed in chapter 2, its science fiction comic books frequently featured surprise endings. Often, Feldstein ensured that a villain about to get away with his crime was brutally killed in the final frames. At least one of Feldstein's surprise endings used an atomic bomb to punish a villain beyond the reach of conventional justice. "Atom Bomb Thief" appeared in a 1950 issue of *Weird Fantasy*, at a time when revelations of Soviet subversion and spying were rushing toward their peak. The story reads as a deliberate evocation of the spy ring that delivered crucial details of the American atomic bomb to the Soviet Union. The best-known members of the ring were Julius and Ethel Rosenberg, the husband and wife team convicted of committing espionage in 1951 and sentenced to die in the electric chair. Some of their coconspirators were convicted too. These included chemist Harry Gold and his contact at Los Alamos, machinist David Greenglass, who was Ethel Rosenberg's brother. Greenglass passed sketches of atomic bomb designs to Gold, who in turn delivered them to Soviet agents.

Greenglass was arrested in January 1950, just a few months before

"Atom Bomb Thief" was published. It seems likely that Harvey Kurtz-man, the artist and writer of the story, was thinking of Greenglass. "Atom Bomb Thief" is a tale of karmic vengeance against a man in many ways similar to Kurtzman, Feldstein, and much of the staff at EC: a young, outer-borough, Jewish New Yorker drafted into service during World War II. Greenglass, though, had betrayed his country. Not all people who shared Greenglass's background were traitors, Kurtzman seems to say.

The story opens on a summer afternoon in 1946, as young physi-cist Paul Arnold leaves his job at the Oak Ridge, Tennessee, nuclear plant. Paul furtively knocks on the door of an apartment and, once inside, exclaims to his waiting conspirator that he has stolen the final details of the atomic bomb, securing the secrets in the sweatband of his hat. Paul's partner Karl shouts, "This is the last piece in the jigsaw puzzle! We now have a complete record of the factory technique of isolating the isotope, U-235!"

Paul then reminisces about the years spent stealing data on the atomic bomb and concludes, "It's been worth it. Any other world power will pay us a million dollars at least for this information." Karl agrees, reminding Paul of the world's interest in the upcoming nuclear tests at Bikini Atoll in the Pacific Ocean. Coincidentally, the customers for Paul and Karl's atomic secrets want to meet the two spies at a rendezvous point in the middle of the Pacific. Paul and Karl then board a small plane. While in the air, Paul asks Karl what he intends to do with his share of the profits. Karl replies, "I hate to tell you this Paul, but there won't be any 'shares,'" and pulls a gun from beneath his coat. The two struggle in the cockpit, causing the plane to crash into the ocean. Paul manages to inflate a life raft and escape with his briefcase full of atomic secrets. Badly wounded, Karl pleads for mercy, begging Paul to help him onto the life raft. Paul refuses and watches gleefully as a shark graphically devours Karl.

Until this point, "Atom Bomb Thief" relies on a fairly generic espionage story line: a scientist manages to steal a formula and flees the United States to sell his information. Now, with Paul alone and adrift on the Pacific, Feldstein begins to twist the plot—"Two burning, torturous days later, as the fiery sun is just rising from the rim of the sea, Paul Arnold feels a strange sensation! His rubber boat is scraping sand!" Delirious with thirst, Paul staggers onto the island that has saved his life. After drinking some water, he explores, making some surprising discoveries. First, Paul finds goats and pigs locked in small pens all over the island. He then notices signs of modern man: "Machinery! Cameras! Recording devices! A Geiger counter!" Horrified, Paul frantically searches his briefcase for "the data on the atom bomb tests." Paul soon exclaims, "Here it is . . . diagram of the test to be held on a Pacific atoll . . . July 25 . . . 1946 . . . That's today! And this island is Biki-" The next panel shows Paul suffused with a bright yellow light as the blast from the atomic test vaporizes him along with his stolen secrets. In the final panel, a huge mushroom cloud looms over the atoll, and the caption reads, "July 25, 1946, 8:35 A.M. Baker Bomb is detonated at Bikini Atoll!"[62] The atomic bomb, acting as an instrument of vengeance, kills an American spy.

"Atom Bomb Thief" represents American scientists as flawed, vain men. Few other contemporary comic books went so far. Some publishers might have allowed Paul Arnold to steal atomic secrets, but diligent FBI or intelligence agents would have thwarted him from selling the information. Certainly, most atomic-themed comics published between 1950 and 1955 suggested that there was no need to fear communist infiltration of the American nuclear program, thanks to a veritable army of government operatives.[63] In contrast, EC refused to portray Americans as universally well intentioned and moral. CIA and FBI agents appeared within EC comics, but they often died or failed to defeat threats against the United States and the earth.

In the few years that *Weird Science* and *Weird Fantasy* appeared, practically every issue contained a reference to atomic power. Perhaps this is unsurprising, but no other comic publisher seems to have created so many stories about the atomic bomb in so short a time, and certainly no others addressed the issue with the same pessimism as EC. Gaines and his staff treated the atomic bomb as a serious topic with real consequences. EC stories never ended on

FIGURE 3.8 Within comic books published by EC, like this 1950 issue of *Weird Fantasy*, humans inevitably fail to control atomic power.

an optimistic note or suggested that humanity might learn to live without atomic war. Instead, these stories always concluded with dreadful finality; someone had foolishly dared to tamper with the atomic bomb, and now he, along with millions of others, was dead. The atomic bomb was synonymous with the End.

CRACKPOT REALISM

On January 12, 1954, less than a year after the end of the Korean War, President Eisenhower's secretary of state, John Foster Dulles, gave a speech on the global conflict between East and West. He described a new and terrifying world in which the United States would no longer contain communist expansion as it had in Korea, through multinational forces armed with conventional weapons. Instead, the United States would move more aggressively to roll back, rather than simply contain, the advance of communism. It would do so at will and perhaps at spots the Soviet Union believed were well within its defensive perimeter. "The way to deter aggression," argued Dulles, "is for the free community to be willing and able to respond vigorously at places and with means of its own choosing."[64] That last phrase was a none-too-subtle euphemism for the vast American nuclear arsenal. Should communists persist in expanding, the United States might respond with a massive nuclear spasm, and not necessarily at a specific crisis spot but wherever it wanted. This two-pronged strategy, claimed Dulles, was strategically and economically essential, as the United States could not provide indefinite aid and military support to the anticommunist world. Massive retaliation, as the policy was termed, would be both cheaper and more effective.

For American policy makers, the early postwar period was a critical one. They sought control over the public image of nuclear power and atomic weaponry, a fight whose stakes increased with America's growing commitment to long-term battle against the communist bloc, an enemy that would soon possess nuclear weapons of its own. All of this—the fear of secret weapons built without regard to morality or practicality; the creeping realization that some in American society were working to destroy it; the sheer implausibility of the

world's wealthiest nation ceding its security to a policy of genocide—
played out in popular media, and nowhere more vigorously than in
the pages of comic books. During the decade following World War
II, comic books included numerous terrifying and grotesque images
of political folly, out-of-control science, and nuclear war. None,
however, were any more chilling than the United States' declared
policy of massive retaliation or its secret radioactive experiments on
its own citizens. They were examples of what C. Wright Mills termed
"crackpot realism." "In the name of realism," Mills argues, "men are
quite mad, and precisely what they call utopian is now the condition
of human survival."[65] Americans sought knowledge and safety by
poisoning their fellow citizens with radioactive metals and promoted
national defense through the threat of a worldwide holocaust. If this
was realism, what constituted a nightmare?

THE DEVIL'S ALLY

NIGHTS OF HORROR

During the summer of 1954, a group of four teenaged boys ran wild in Brooklyn, New York. Fascinated by Nazism, they attacked young women with bullwhips and went "bum hunting"—abusing unhoused men and even setting some of them aflame.[1] One night in August, the boys assaulted a Black man sleeping on a park bench. At first, they burned his feet with cigarettes and beat him in the face. Then they marched him to the banks of the East River, forced him in, and watched him drown. Horrified by the screams of the dying man, a passerby notified police, who caught the boys before they disappeared into the short summer night.

Two of the attackers were set free due to a lack of evidence. Unsure whether the two remaining boys were mentally competent to stand trial, the court requested that they meet with a psychiatrist. Dr. Fredric Wertham duly visited the jail and, after speaking to seventeen-year-old Mel Mittman, concluded that the teen had tortured and murdered because "his ideal was Superman, and he tried to prove himself a superman by meting out the violence with which Superman solves problems."[2] Wertham spent much longer—ten

FIGURE 4.1 Images like this one from *Nights of Horror*, along with the contents of numerous other crime, horror, romance, and jungle-themed comic books, led Dr. Fredric Wertham to claim that comics contributed to violent, even murderous behavior by readers.

hours—speaking with the gang's ringleader, eighteen-year-old Jack Koslow.[3] Koslow freely admitted that he was not only an admirer of Adolf Hitler but also an enthusiastic consumer of superhero, crime, and horror comic books. Wertham tracked down copies of one of Koslow's favorite titles, *Nights of Horror*, and found them packed with images of rape, torture, bondage, nudity, and racist grotesques.

Wertham carefully tallied all these scenes, breaking them down into ten categories, including "whipping," "whipping orgy with kissing feet features," and "burning-torture."[4] He likely did not notice the eerie physical similarities between characters in *Nights of Horror* and those in Superman's early comic book adventures, but the same man—Joe Shuster, the cocreator of Superman—drew them both. Despite inventing the look of the most popular and famous character in comic book history, Shuster was impoverished and losing his sight. Unable to find work with more mainstream publishers, he was reduced to illustrating the *Nights of Horror* series. Drawing on muscle memory and instinct as darkness consumed his vision, Shuster brought his creations—Superman, Lois Lane, Lex Luthor, and Jimmy Olsen—to a new and violent world.

Wertham may have missed Shuster's handiwork, but he was familiar with comics like *Nights of Horror*. He and his staff had for many years treated children accused of various crimes and cruelties, and they spoke often of their favorite comic books. Some recalled specific images of violence; others told him how they shared and traded particular issues. Not only did Wertham suspect comic books of encouraging violence, but he also worried that comic book advertisements had furnished the costumes and weapons, including a vampire outfit, bullwhip, and switchblade knife, that Koslow used on his victims. Writing to a New York state senator curious about the case, he warned, "Fifteen years ago young people with [Koslow's] kind of mental disorder—or more serious ones—did not commit such wanton acts of cruelty for sheer enjoyment." The new and critical factor, concluded the psychiatrist, was the comic book. Koslow was an addict "steeped in horror comics, his mind filled with all the thrill of violence, murder and cruelty described in them."[5]

FIGURE 4.2 Dr. Fredric Wertham, acquainting himself with the latest comic books available at a newsstand, likely in early 1948.

Wertham was equally sure that comic books drove the boys to seek out a Black victim. "Race prejudice against colored people," he emphasized, "was part of this boy's comic book and horror literature indoctrination." To him, the case confirmed that violent mass culture negatively influenced behavior and that it also encouraged racism. With crime and horror comics so easily obtained by young readers, Wertham feared juvenile delinquency, racism, and violence were the inevitable results. Even if parents kept their child away from comics, they could not prevent exposure to other children that did read crime or horror titles. Koslow, he suggested, was merely the weakest link in this system of cultural consumption and delinquency. "As long as this type of literature is accessible to children," he pronounced, "we shall have such crimes."[6]

Wertham cleared Koslow to stand trial. But he planned to speak in Koslow's defense, in the hope that he could convince the jury to see Koslow as a victim of his comic book addiction. At the last moment, for reasons never explained to him, Wertham was not permitted to speak, and Koslow was sentenced to life in prison. This troubled Wertham, who wrote a warm and apologetic letter to Koslow, reminding him, "you were the victim of vicious outside influences over which you had no control."[7]

A CANCEROUS GROWTH

By the late 1940s, as gangster, romance, and horror titles edged more and more superheroes off the newsstand, comic book publishers could no longer coast on the patriotic goodwill earned during World War II, when they cooperated with the WWB and sold millions of antifascist titles. In 1948, these new comic books became national and international news, as newspapers and magazines reported on crimes seemingly connected to comic books. The *Chicago Defender*, a Black newspaper, reported the death of nineteen-year-old Carl Richard Brooks, who shot himself in the head with a pistol. Although there was no clear explanation for Brooks's suicide, his mother informed the newspaper, "He seemed interested in reading comic books."[8] After an eleven-year-old boy burned down an apartment building in Chicago, newspaper articles blamed a superhero comic called *The Human Torch*, although the boy's father reportedly supplied him with "at least a pack of cigarettes and a lot of 100-proof whiskey every day."[9] Such articles portrayed comic book readers as addicts at the mercy of unscrupulous publishers, lazy parents, and inattentive teachers. According to the *New York Times*, whose editors showed a newfound interest in the medium, crime, horror, and even traditional superhero comics were "a cancerous growth" that polluted the minds of readers and fostered criminality and sexual perversion.[10]

Thanks to the movements of Cold War plague carriers—soldiers, tourists, diplomats, and American corporations—Lev Gleason's crime comic books and their offspring mingled with cultures around the world. *Crime Does Not Pay, Crime and Punishment,* and *Boy Loves Girl* went to key allies like South Korea and West Germany. *Web of Evil* shipped to Egypt, a prominent member of the nonaligned movement. The Pan American International Agency sent anywhere from fifty thousand to ninety thousand copies per month of the crime comic *Accion policiaca* to "all Spanish-language countries of Latin America except Argentina." The International Comics Group sent Spanish-language versions of *Out of the Night, Forbidden Worlds, Lovelorn,* and three other horror and romance titles "to the Spanish speaking countries of the world." Ziff-Davis and the American News Company sent copies of *G.I. Joe* to thirty-five countries. In 1954, a Senate subcommittee discovered that every month many thousands of American comic books were distributed in over sixty countries, not including nations that received comic books through informal means of distribution.[11] The Cold War was dissolving whatever lines existed between domestic and global culture. Suddenly, the commercial comic book was a symbol, at home and abroad, of both popular American culture and the United States itself. This notoriety attracted increasing attention from parents, activists, and policy makers concerned that the comic book industry was out of control.

Anti–comic book sentiment coalesced around a single man and became a national movement. Fredric Wertham served as the de facto leader of the postwar anti–comic book campaign, which grew to include an array of men and women from across the political, religious, and racial spectrums. Wertham motivated and connected a network of activists, politicians, and law enforcement officials across

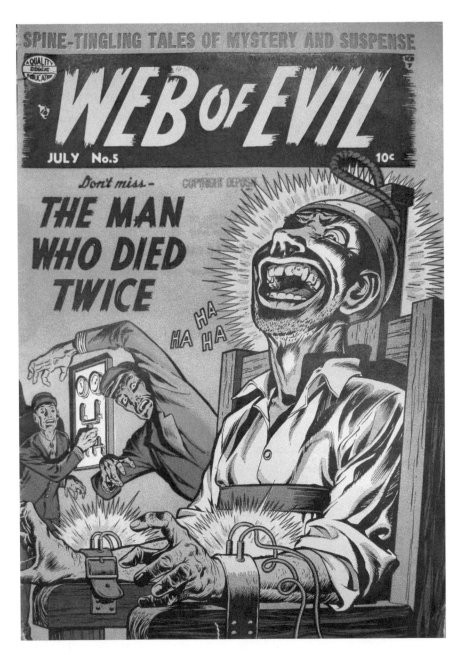

FIGURE 4.3 *Web of Evil* was distributed throughout the decolonizing world, to countries as far afield as Egypt. Policy makers and propagandists feared that brutal images like this one, from a 1953 issue, generated anti-American sentiment among potential Cold War allies.

the country, many of whom wrote to him seeking advice on how best to combat the comic book menace. Simultaneously, the FBI and army intelligence initiated long-term, covert investigations of the industry, focusing on two publishers of crime and horror titles. These agencies understood that comics contained dangers beyond simple violence: skepticism regarding the Korean War, cynicism toward government, racist and pro–civil rights imagery, and vicious misogyny were all potentially devastating to domestic stability and foreign relations. This combination of civic and covert pressure led in 1954 to a very public investigation of the comic book industry by a senate subcommittee on juvenile delinquency. The result, just a year later, was a broken and neutered comic book—a cultural form infantilized and bent to prevailing public and political tastes.

In his best-known work, *Seduction of the Innocent*, Wertham offered a powerful critique of the relationship among comic books, race, foreign policy, and international perceptions of the United States. He cautioned that the ceaseless torrent of racist and violent comics caused real harm to consumers at home and abroad. Wertham also warned that these images would inevitably weaken America's global stature, framing the nation as obsessed with crime and White supremacy at a time when earning friends in the global south was among the highest national priorities. Wertham also understood that worldwide awareness of America's shameful history of White supremacy could translate into pressure on the nation's policy makers. This was significant because he saw federal legislation as the only means of regulating the comic book industry. And if the idea that comics weakened America's efforts in the global south convinced domestic policy makers to act, Wertham would be closer to reining in the industry he blamed for so many domestic and international ills.

Publicly, the anti–comic book campaign focused overwhelmingly on the perceived links between comic books and juvenile delinquency. In private, federal propagandists and policy makers fretted over the damage done to their efforts by racist and antiwar comic books. Their fears received little attention until the 1954 Senate subcommittee investigation of the comic industry, when Wertham

FIGURE 4.4 Publishers translated horror and jungle-themed comics into a variety of languages, including Spanish, for international distribution. These are some of the sample comic books submitted to the Senate subcommittee tasked with investigating the comic book industry.

and representatives of the foreign policy establishment spoke about the effects of comic book racism on global audiences. On the one hand, policy makers worried that grotesque representations of non-White characters would cause diplomatic and economic problems for American officials and corporations. On the other, anti-racist narratives seemed equally troubling, as they might lead American readers to question whether their country really was justified in the Cold War. If American soldiers believed they were fighting for a racist society that valued White citizens above all others, they might be more susceptible to communist propaganda or even refuse to fight against non-White communist forces in battlegrounds like Korea. Above all, federal agencies feared a comic book industry able to publish and distribute without external supervision and censorship. Activism of any sort was dangerous; it gave the comic book too much unchecked power within a fraught and fluid international system.

J. EDGAR HOOVER GOES TO THE NEWSSTAND

By the late 1930s, comic book publisher Lev Gleason was, according to the FBI, a member of the Communist Party USA.[12] Certainly Gleason was a leftist, and his political outlook influenced not only the contents of his publications but also his relationships with writers and artists.[13] Artist Jerry Robinson remembered Gleason as "a very clever businessman and a social idealist."[14] Gleason, who, according to artist Joe Simon, "hustled like a proud capitalist and talked like a frustrated socialist," reportedly shared the profits from *Crime Does Not Pay* with the two editors of the title, Charles Biro and Bob Wood.[15]

Although in his forties when the United States entered World War II, Gleason reenlisted in the army in 1942 and served until mid-1943. By that time, he was also under FBI surveillance. In 1944, the bureau identified Gleason as "a key figure in Communist activities in the New York area," and he was soon caught up in a larger federal effort to identify and punish suspected communists.[16] In March 1946, the House Un-American Activities Committee (HUAC) voted to hold in contempt seventeen members of the executive board of the Joint Anti-Fascist Refugee Committee (JAFRC), including Gleason. The committee charged Gleason and his fellow members with refusing to supply subpoenaed JAFRC records.[17] In May, the House upheld HUAC's decision and voted to cite the executive committee.[18] Later that year, according to an FBI informant "of known reliability," Gleason attended a fundraiser sponsored by the Civil Rights Congress and contributed money to a program intended to remove from office Theodore Bilbo, the openly racist senator from Mississippi.[19] Then in 1947, a bureau memorandum cited an unnamed source that described Gleason as "pro-Red" and a "Communist fellow traveler."[20] He had been marked as a potential threat to national security.

Gleason's public relationship with left-wing causes and organizations occurred at a time when the Soviet Union was transitioning from an ally of necessity into a dangerous enemy. In March 1947, President Truman gave a major speech on US foreign relations that warned of a potential communist takeover in Greece. He pledged American support to Greece and other nations that resisted "attempted subjugation by armed minorities or by outside pressures." The Truman Doctrine, as the policy of active intervention against communism become known, announced America's intention to challenge Soviet expansion. Truman's speech conspicuously omitted any reference to one of the most significant and fraught issues in the rapidly polarizing postwar world: decolonization. For the United States, with its long and brutal history of chattel slavery and Jim Crow segregation, race was simply too dangerous to discuss; it served only to remind populations in the decolonizing world as well as communist propagandists of the nation's failure to treat its own citizens with the respect it called for abroad.[21]

At the time, Gleason published the *New Castle News*, a newspaper in suburban Westchester County, New York. It responded to Truman's speech with an editorial asking, "Are we going to police the whole world, attempt to shove our ideas down the throats of smaller peoples everywhere by force of arms?" Just days later, President Truman signed Executive Order 9835, instituting a loyalty oath for federal employees. At a stroke, men and women unwilling to denounce communism and pledge fealty to the United States were no longer welcome as federal employees. It was a step not taken even during the existential war against fascism. Once again, the *New Castle News* pounced, warning, "Some of the deep and hidden elements behind this witch hunt are themselves the disloyal ones for it is they who are developing a pattern of potential fascism in the United States."[22] These were increasingly heretical opinions.

Gleason's open affiliation with the JAFRC reinforced fears that comic books were generally subversive, unwholesome, and un-American. The FBI shared this view, noting that he published *Crime Does Not Pay* and that "the publishing of the cheap pulp paper type comic booklets is a common practice and is considered a racket in the publishing fraternity in New York as little capital is needed to engage in this type of business, which is not highly regarded by reputable publishers."[23] When in 1947 the New York FBI office temporarily stopped submitting reports on Gleason, it received terse instructions from Director J. Edgar Hoover to resume regular updates on the publisher's activities. Hoover reminded the special agent in charge (SAC) that "in view of the tense international situation at the present time, a new report should be submitted setting forth the extent of the subject's present activities in connection with the Communist Party and related groups."[24] Three months later, the New York office notified Associate Director Clyde Tolson that the bureau possessed evidence of Gleason's "deep involvement in the Communist movement."[25]

Indeed, Gleason posed a dual threat to domestic stability as both a publisher and an accused communist. While the FBI investigated Gleason, sales of his *Crime Does Not Pay* climbed toward one million copies per issue and fueled a wave of crime-themed titles. In 1946, 3 percent of comic books were crime-themed; by 1948, the percentage had more than quadrupled. That year alone, thirty new crime comic books went on sale.[26] Suddenly, Gleason was helping to define the culture of postwar America. Within *Crime Does Not Pay* and its imitators, American society was synonymous with violence, chaos, and utter disrespect for authority. Whether these images represented Gleason's personal or political views or were a result of commercial calculations, their popularity doubtless heightened the bureau's case for surveillance.

Like Gleason, Bill Gaines was an anomaly in the comic industry. He had hoped to be a chemistry teacher, rather than follow his father, Max Gaines, into the publishing business. Max ran a small, foundering company named Educational Comics, publisher of *Picture Stories from the Bible*, *Animal Fables*, and other similarly tame titles. But after Max died in 1947, Bill unexpectedly found himself running his father's failing firm. Working with editor Al Feldstein, Gaines replaced the company's offerings with bold, new crime-, horror-, and war-themed titles. In 1950, he renamed the company Entertaining Comics and advertised its fresh titles as a "new trend" in comic books.[27] As the comic book industry had no official production code, Gaines and Feldstein spurred each other to create comics boasting original and shocking images and stories.[28] They produced crime and horror titles, including *Tales from the Crypt*, *Crime SuspenStories*, and *Shock SuspenStories*, packed with murder, dismemberment, and torture committed by—and against—very average-looking American men, women, and children. Readers responded eagerly, and soon, Entertaining Comics—better known as EC—was a thriving business.[29]

Covert government interest in publisher Bill Gaines and EC Comics began in late 1951, when army intelligence began receiving copies of EC's war-themed titles from various commands in the United States and abroad. Stories in EC Comics portrayed army officers in an unflattering light and presented "a picture of the inevitability of personal disaster in combat."[30] In April 1952, army intelligence advised the FBI that EC titles contained politically questionable material yet were readily available to American servicemen at home and overseas. Worse still, the two most troublesome titles, both edited and painstakingly researched by Harvey Kurtzman—*Two-Fisted Tales* and *Frontline Combat*—were military-themed.

Concern on the part of the FBI and army intelligence stemmed from not only the contents of specific EC comic books but also the ubiquity of comics in military life. Just as comics were virtually omnipresent in the civilian sphere, so, too, were they an integral part of the military experience, both within the United States and internationally. They circulated on bases, in airplanes, even in submarines—comics lurked anywhere soldiers sought distraction. This meant that comics had real implications for military morale, especially among American troops fighting communism in Korea.

Although *Two-Fisted Tales* and *Frontline Combat* appeared superficially similar to conventional, patriotic combat-themed titles, army intelligence warned that EC's versions menaced American security by highlighting "the horrors, hardships, and futility of war," as well as "blunders on the part of officers." EC's war-themed titles were politically subversive "because they tend to discredit the army and undermine troop morale by presenting a picture of the inevitability of personal disaster in combat."[31] *Two-Fisted Tales* and *Frontline Combat* also challenged core tenets of the Truman Doctrine, like the merit of containing communism through military power. Editor

Harvey Kurtzman was not a communist and resisted romanticizing the Soviet bloc. Rather, he and his staff of artists and writers simply brought a gritty, realistic—if not fatalistic—perspective to military comics. Some of them had served during World War II, and they drew on their experiences and fears.[32] While many military comics treated the Korean War as nothing more than a continuation of World War II, with communist Asians substituted for the Japanese, EC's war comics emphasized the brutality and senselessness of combat in Korea. Some stories even encouraged sympathy for the communist North Koreans.

As in many crime and horror comics, *Two-Fisted Tales* and *Frontline Combat* contained scenes of intimate, highly personal violence. Soldiers died on the ends of bayonets, with hands about their throats, and in the arms of comrades. These images not only emphasized the brutality of combat for American troops but also humanized their enemies by depicting them as individuals. North Koreans were not simply World War II–era caricatures of Japanese soldiers in communist uniforms. They were people with friends and families, who feared American military power and wanted only to survive. Kurtzman and his staff portrayed all combatants as weary men, pushed beyond their limits in a world outside of their control.

A 1952 story from *Two-Fisted Tales*, "Corpse on the Imjin!," opens with four wordless panels depicting the corpse of a North Korean soldier slowly drifting down the Imjin River in Korea. An impassive American soldier sitting on the riverbank watches the body and wonders, "We must have killed thousands of them in this offensive! Wonder how this one got it?" As he rests, a North Korean soldier, "wet and scared and hungry," sneaks up on him. The two men fight hand-to-hand, beating and tearing at each other with any available weapon. They tumble into the river, and the American soldier ends up on top. Slowly, across seven panels, the American drowns his opponent, who desperately kicks and scratches. After the Korean soldier dies, the American stares into the water, as the narrator intones, "You're tired. Your body is gasping and shaking and weak. And you're ashamed." He flees up the riverbank, and the corpse of

FIGURE 4.5 "Corpse on the Imjin" appeared in a 1952 issue of EC's *Two-Fisted Tales*. Stories like this one, which humanized communist North Koreans, led the FBI and army intelligence to worry that EC comics might cause American soldiers to question why they were fighting in Korea, or even reject orders to kill communists.

the Korean soldier drifts out to sea. The narrator begs the reader, "Have pity! Have pity for a dead man! For he is now not rich or poor, right or wrong, bad or good! Don't hate him. Have pity, for he has lost that most precious possession that we all treasure above everything. He has lost his life!"[33]

Alarmed by such narratives and the concept that the lives of non-White communists might be equivalent in value to those of Americans, the FBI contacted Assistant Attorney General Charles Murray to inquire whether EC's war comics merited prosecution.[34] Although the Department of Justice agreed that the comics were excessively violent, they were not convinced that the titles promoted disloyalty or refusal of duty. In March 1953, Murray duly notified the bureau that prosecution was impossible.[35]

This ruling did not mark the end of the FBI's interest in the EC staff. Gaines's bureau file contains a memorandum from 1967 concerning another investigation. After criticizing Kurtzman's lack of respect for the United States, the memorandum recounts the artist's earlier efforts on *Two-Fisted Tales* and *Frontline Combat*. The bureau had not forgotten the comics it deemed "so brutal and blood thirsty that they appeared to border upon sedition."[36]

I WANT TO BE A SEX MANIAC

All of this, however, took place in secret. But while the FBI covertly monitored members of the comic book industry, a very public anti-comic book campaign was coalescing. It began soon after World War II and became much more visible in 1948. Within the millions of comic books printed each month, critics found evidence of whatever depravity or subversion they sought. Such comic books, they argued, were breaking down traditional family and social bonds and fueling a supposed surge in juvenile delinquency. Individuals and groups circulated lists of "unacceptable" titles, fought for local bans on crime and horror comics, and advocated for state and federal oversight of the comic book industry. The anti–comic book campaign was neither reactionary nor inherently anticommunist; it was remarkable for its inclusion of men and women from across the political, religious, and racial spectrums. With distinct motivations and citing different evidence, conservatives, centrists, liberals, and American communists alike argued that the contents and sheer availability of commercial comic books were harmful to society. At the head of this diverse and disparate movement was psychiatrist Fredric Wertham.

Born and raised in Germany by Jewish parents, Wertham made his way in 1921 to Baltimore. Five years later, Wertham became an American citizen, and in 1934, he settled in New York City. He was for a time the senior psychiatrist at Bellevue Hospital's children's ward and director of the hospital's Mental Hygiene Clinic, a position he left in 1940 to become the director of psychiatric services at Queens Hospital Center. He also worked as a forensic psychiatrist, participating in several high-profile murder cases. An outspoken opponent of segregation, Wertham helped establish the Lafargue Clinic in 1946, the first mental health facility in Harlem. Staffed by volunteers, the clinic charged a fee of twenty-five cents per visit, which was waived if patients were unable to pay. Five years later, Wertham conducted a study on the harmful effects of segregation on Black schoolchildren in Delaware, and his testimony on this topic was cited in *Brown v. Board of Education*, the 1954 Supreme Court decision that mandated the desegregation of public school systems. NAACP director Thurgood Marshall sent Wertham a warm letter thanking him for his assistance "not only in this case, but whenever we have called on you."[37]

Wertham rose to public prominence as an anti–comic book crusader in 1948, when the *Saturday Review of Literature* published his article "The Comics . . . Very Funny." It opened with a harrowing description of the abuse suffered by a four-year-old girl living in an apartment building: "Whenever they get a chance the boys in the building, ranging in age from three to nine years, beat her with toy guns, tie her up with rope. They manacle her with handcuffs bought with coupons from comic books. They take her to a vacant lot and use her as a target for bow and arrows. Once they pulled off her panties to torture her (as they put it)." What factor, Wertham asked, could connect this ghastly array of physical, sexual, and emotional cruelties? "The common denominator," he answered, "is comic books." Wertham followed with more descriptions of vicious acts committed by children, as told to him by his young patients or their parents. A thirteen-year-old boy acted out at home and school; he deemed the child as "a real comic-book addict." A fourteen-year-old boy, referred to Wertham for stealing, denied that comic books influenced his bad behavior because "in the comic books it is mostly murder." Another young boy, when asked what he wants to be, shouted, "I want to be a sex maniac!" A violent gang, led by a fifteen-year-old girl, acted like "bandits."[38] Again, the common factor was the comic book. Children that acted violently, Wertham suggested, read violent comic books.

This claim likely emerged from clinical sessions Wertham and his staff held with troubled New York City children.[39] In one session, a clinician spoke to a nine-year-old boy who had been witness to older children having sex in abandoned buildings, thrown out of six different schools, and told repeatedly that he was not wanted by his mother and stepfather. The boy also read comic books, explaining, "A couple of tricks I found out in comic books—that's why I keep buying them. Like when we were playing guns—a guy would get me covered—got my hands up like this—I'd get behind him like this (turns fast and punches) then I grab his gun and then I shoot him." Accompanying notes described the explanation as "one of the best cases showing direct influence of comic books: he learns tricks, that is how to attack others with and without weapons, he buys guns from c.b. [comic book] ads, he makes guns using what he learned in comic books. He is retarded in reading due to comic book pictures gazing. He likes Wonder Woman because she is an active and cruel woman just like his mother."[40] Of a session with a different nine-year-old patient Wertham or one of his staff noted, "Mother is divorced from patient's father for the past 4 years. One time the patient hit his grandmother and said he would kill his sister. 'If he can't have his own way, he raises hell.' Patient reads comic books."[41] From such sessions and his experiences, Wertham concluded it was "inescapable" that violent comic books taught violent behavior.[42]

He did not limit his criticism to violent titles. Yes, violent comic books were particularly harmful to young minds, but any comic book, no matter how benign it seemed, was dangerous.[43] There were no good comics, Wertham charged, because the medium itself was poisonous. The artwork was rough, the language crude, and the advertisements deceptive and dangerous. Even adaptations of classic literature, like a comic book version of Charles Dickens's *Great Expectations*, were full of vicious images, like a character screaming, "Oh, don't cut my throat, sir!" Was this Dickens's sentiment, Wertham wondered, or that of the circulation manager at a comic book company? Even public service and antidrug comic books, he argued in a later work, could not do any good in minds conditioned to associate comics with erotically charged images of "murder and morphine." Political comic books like *The Story of Harry S. Truman* were unacceptable because they whitewashed the true, crime-soaked reality of American politics, omitting "characters who might well be featured in a crime comic book," like local party bosses.[44]

Comics could not even promote reading, Wertham argued, since children focused overwhelmingly on the pictures. Teachers, he stated, knew this so well that they had to dispose of all comic books in the classroom before convincing children to read "real books." Wertham listed seventeen potential reasons parents might think comic books are good, before shattering each one in turn. They were, he determined, "the marijuana of the nursery." He closed with a claim, "pretty well established," that 75 percent of American parents were opposed to comics, while the remaining 25 percent were either indifferent or deceived by research funded by the comic book industry. Wertham saw comic book publishers as powerful, wealthy, and organized to exert significant influence on children and unsuspecting parents. "Crime does not pay," he warns, "but crime comics do."[45]

"The Comics . . . Very Funny" touched on the realities and results of child abuse, sexual assault, bullying, and economic inequality, treating them all as expressions of juvenile delinquency and implying that their complex causes might be reduced to a single, simple truth: comic books contributed to vicious behavior in children.

Anywhere that Wertham discovered children or young adults committing acts of violence or cruelty, there, too, were comic books. It was impossible to understand violent behavior, Wertham asserted, without accounting for the influence of comic books and "the way in which they cause trouble or determine the form that trouble takes."[46] The article did not propose that comic books were the primary cause of juvenile violence, but it implied numerous benefits to taming the comic book industry.

Reader's Digest, one of the most widely read periodicals in the country, published a condensed version of "The Comics . . . Very Funny" in August 1948, which it then reprinted in five of its thirteen international editions. Fredric Wertham became the most visible anti–comic book advocate in the world.[47] He was invited to talk before concerned parents, academics, and politicians. He appeared on national radio shows, published articles in magazines, and even participated in early television panels—in one case, alongside Lev Gleason.[48] Wertham later testified before the Senate Subcommittee on Organized Crime in 1950, the New York Joint Legislative Committee to Study the Publication of Comics in 1951, and the Senate Subcommittee on Juvenile Delinquency in 1954.

Although Wertham loathed the comic book industry, he acknowledged its output as a potent form of mass media, rather than dismissing comics as meaningless entertainment. His research files contain clinical notes for a young adult man that worked as a comic book illustrator. The heavily highlighted pages make clear that Wertham and his staff viewed even proximity to comic book production, as well as consumption, as a potential cause of violent behavior. The artist voluntarily admitted himself for observation at Bellevue Hospital and showed up for a therapy session bearing instructions from his supervisor for drawings to be made "as sexy as possible." They specified an image of two women fighting, "thighs showing, seductive poses, cruel faces, and one or both flailing the air with a long blunt club." The artist was disturbed by such requests and despondent over criticism that his drawings were "not sexy enough." The artist further told his doctors that the boldest and most sexual images were not just used in comic books but also reproduced and cataloged, then sold to individuals with "strange erotic desires."[49] Despite these allegations, the artist was deemed "not psychotic" and released. Wertham, though, took his claims seriously.

In addition to causing harm on an individual level, Wertham argued that comic books were powerful enough to trigger serious anti-American sentiments around the world. As an example of the sort of imagery that hardened international opinions of the United States, he cited a panel from an issue of T-Man, whose publisher boasted that it distributed the title in over twenty-five countries. In it, Treasury agent Pete Trask, who has traveled to Central America to investigate a communist plot against the Panama Canal, savagely attacks a Soviet spy with the butt of a rifle while exclaiming, "Boy, that's the sweetest sound on earth!" The image of a US federal agent operating abroad and engaging in such gleeful brutality against a non-American was too much for Wertham. "It is a fair statement to make," he concluded in Seduction of the Innocent, "that most civilized nations feel threatened by [such comic books] in their most holy possession, their children."[50]

He also suggested that comic books contained coded text and images comprehensible to children and compelling enough to override instructions from traditional authority figures. Their addictive combination of images, text, and hidden messages also encouraged racism. Violence and racism, Wertham believed, were linked. If comic books promoted violence, they were an impediment to social progress in general and the elimination of racial prejudice in particular. He viewed comic books as a contributing factor to delinquency, which was linked to racism, which in turn worked to perpetuate crimes against humanity like segregation. Wertham thus believed that comic books could teach consumers to hate from an early age.[51] His copy of a 1951 issue of Howdy Doody bears signs of his frustration. The cover depicts Howdy Doody, a freckled, wooden marionette, in a cauldron of boiling water, surrounded by stereotyped Black cannibals. Across the image, Wertham scrawled, "Even Howdy Doody has race hatred. What does it mean to children? Race hatred has become

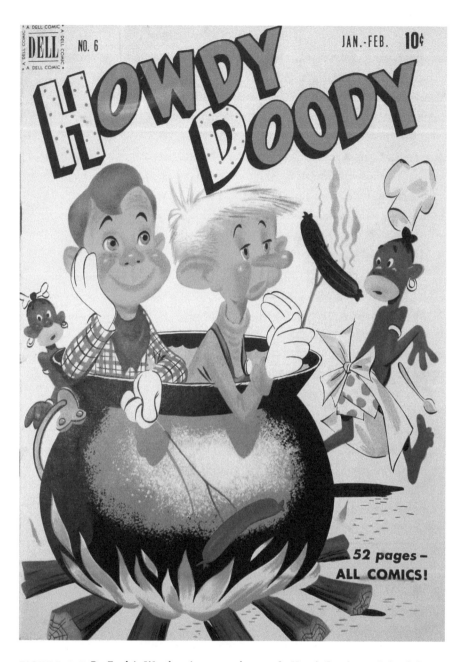

FIGURE 4.6 Dr. Fredric Wertham's personal copy of a *Howdy Doody* comic book from 1951. It includes his handwritten notes, like the claim, "Race prejudice has become 2nd nature to American bourgeois, even liberal ones."

second nature to American bourgeois, even liberal ones."[52] Because comic books were so powerful and pervasive, Wertham feared, parents and educators stood little chance of countering their insidious influence.

Comic book publishers had no financial incentive to censor or otherwise modify their products and would have to be forced to change through protests and bad publicity. Wertham's proposed solution was a federal law banning the sale of adult or crime-themed comic books to children under the age of fifteen. In a letter to a concerned parent, he defined crime comic books as "all comic books depicting crime, whether or not they are disguised as science fiction, jungle, Superman, Western, horror, or whatnot."[53] Local bans on comic sales were fine but could not tame the endless stream of comic books flooding the country every month. Only a national ban would do. This was a bold solution that required policy makers to view comics as analogous to narcotics or machine guns. Enacting such legislation would require the participation, at the local, state, and national levels, of many dedicated parents, activists, and politicians. To motivate demands for federal regulation, Wertham offered his supporters a stark choice between a society in which parents and teachers exerted an appropriate level of influence over young people or one in which a torrent of uncensored, violent comic books molded the morals of the nation's children. The price of inaction, Wertham warned, was a generation of Americans roused to violence and racism by crime comics, militarized by fascist superheroes, and enfeebled by the coarse language laced throughout all comic books.

Although compelling and passionately argued, Wertham's proposed connection between comic books and violence was not easily verified. When supporters asked for specific titles to keep away from their children, he would not provide any. It was impossible, he wrote, because new comics appeared so often, while existing titles changed their names. In a letter to *The Times* of London, he warned that a "shocking number" of American children who hanged themselves were found with comics depicting identical scenes beneath their dead bodies. But there were no references to specific cases and no citations of the relevant comics.[54] Josette Frank, an educational associate at the Child Study Association of America, wrote him to ask for evidence for his argument that comic book consumption contributed to violent behavior. Wertham's secretary replied tersely, noting only that the doctor's data had not yet been released.[55]

In 1950, the Committee to Investigate Organized Crime in Interstate Commerce, a subcommittee of the Senate Judiciary Committee, sent out questionnaires to law enforcement officers across the United States. The committee hoped to better understand the causes and scope of juvenile delinquency. Some of its questions concerned the possible connection between comic books and delinquent behavior. Although anecdotal, the responses did not generally support Wertham's hypothesis. A juvenile probation officer from North Carolina replied, "Reading crime comic books may affect a small percentage of the cases that come before this court." A warden in New York dismissed the question, stressing, "In our opinion, the radio, movies and newspapers are a far greater factor in delinquency than comic books." A New York judge similarly rejected the idea, writing, "I never came across a single case where the delinquent or criminal act would be attributed to the reading of comic books."[56]

Still, the argument that comic books contributed to juvenile delinquency went largely unchallenged outside the pages of academic journals. In a 1949 article published in the *Journal of Educational Sociology*, Dr. Frederic Thrasher dismissed Wertham's methodology and conclusions as "not supported by research data." Wertham included no statistical summary of his research, refused to clarify the composition of his control groups (i.e., nondelinquents), yet treated comic books as the primary cause of delinquency. By treating anecdotes as facts, Wertham failed to meet criteria for a scientific study. "Unless and until Wertham's methods of investigation are described, and demonstrated to be valid and reliable," Thrasher concluded, "the scientific worker in this field can place no credence in his results."[57] The *Journal of Educational Sociology*, however, enjoyed substantially smaller circulation numbers than *Ladies' Home Journal* and *Reader's Digest*. As far as most readers knew, Wertham's claims remained valid.

NIETZSCHE IN THE NURSERY

Wertham was not alone in sounding the alarm over comic books. In postwar America, they presented an equally tempting target to cultural critics from across the ideological spectrum. Local anti–comic book organizations formed around parent-teacher associations, American Legion posts, and religious groups. Their members hailed from cities, suburbs, and rural areas.[58] Schools hosted comic book burnings, and churches and synagogues organized committees to safeguard the young. National groups appeared as well, including the anti–comic book wing of the National Organization for Decent Literature (NODL), which published a "blacklist" of comic books that failed to meet its standards. The organization also distributed a pocket-size booklet, *The NODL Code and Its Interpretation*, which included instructions on how to organize local watchdog groups. Members were encouraged to send local lawmakers an attached sample ordinance prohibiting the sale, display, and production of comic books.

To critics on the left, violent comic books were symptomatic of the increasing militarization of American society after 1945. They found an ally in Wertham, who interpreted superheroes as fascist. Muscular, uniformed comic book heroes dressed like "S.S. men, divers, and robots" and solved every problem with brute force, he argued. "How," he wondered, "did Nietzsche get into the nursery?"[59] Jewish anti–comic book activists worried that comic book villains were often represented as dark-skinned or Jewish.[60] Writing in the *New Republic*, Marya Mannes echoed these concerns, denouncing comics as fascist and warning that they produced the same sort of intellectual and spiritual void that led Germans to embrace Nazism.[61] The communist *Daily Worker* also attacked comic books as racist, anti-Semitic, and emblematic of the postwar "culture of death."[62] *Masses & Mainstream* decried comic books as militaristic, going beyond Wertham's critique to argue that they "fit the needs of the Cold War, since they have been accustoming millions upon millions of young Americans to concepts of violence, savagery, and sudden death."[63]

African American writers were among the few who highlighted

the absence of positive Black characters in postwar comic books. In 1949, the *Chicago Defender* applauded Wertham's argument that publishers' viciously stereotyped depictions of the small number of remaining Black characters bred racial prejudice.[64] In a warm review of *Seduction of the Innocent*, *Jet* magazine similarly supported Wertham's claim that comic book consumption negatively influenced perceptions of race.[65] These publications generally embraced Wertham's larger claims as well. A 1951 article in the *Chicago Defender* emphasized that a young heroin dealer had been reading a copy of *Crime Does Not Pay* when apprehended by police.[66] Referring to sources of juvenile delinquency, *Jet* pointed "the accusing finger of causation" at not only parents and community members but also comic book publishers eager to depict crime and violence. The magazine praised Wertham's effort to halt the "shocking demoralization" of young Americans by the comic book industry.[67]

Conservative observers, by contrast, interpreted comic books as tools of the far left. A 1946 article in the *Los Angeles Times* cited Jack Tenney, California state senator, who warned that comics made appealing such concepts as "class and racial consciousness" and suggested that atomic secrets be made public. Comic books, Tenney further claimed, promoted the idea that "parental advice may be well questioned by teen-agers, that jazz music is great and good music the bunk . . . and that employers are greedy wage-cutters to be handled by the government."[68] A year later, J. Edgar Hoover cited crime comic books as a contributor to juvenile delinquency, since they were "crammed with anti-social and criminal acts, the glorification of un-American vigilante action and the deification of the criminal."[69] In 1948, the American Legion criticized the comic book industry for its violent and subversive contents and for failing to embrace a system of self-regulation, such as the Hays Code adopted by Hollywood film studios.[70]

Critics agreed on a few core factors. They saw comics as a cheap, industrialized distraction made by dull and irresponsible adults and intended for children, with the power to poison young minds and blot out more positive influences like parents, teachers, and friends. They also understood comics as a specifically American form of

entertainment. Wertham took this critique further, seeing the
comic book as a national disgrace with international implications;
it was an American artifact capable of poisoning the nation's global
relationships.

The doctor used his newfound visibility to serve as a conduit
between private activists and public officials, working to channel
local outrage into legislation. As early as 1948, Wertham coordinated
efforts between local activists and the city government in Los Angeles.[71] Comic book opponents sought a ban on the production and sale
of crime comic books within the city. As part of this effort, in July
1948, the Christian Churches of Southern California, representing
130 churches, passed a resolution condemning violent comic books.
Two months later, the California Congress of PTAs demanded that
the publishing industry clean up comics.[72] Wertham encouraged the
campaign and placed activists in touch with county lawyer Harold W.
Kennedy.

Both activists and lawmakers kept Wertham updated on the effort
and sought his advice. Kennedy even asked Wertham for assistance
in formulating and phrasing the ban.[73] Although lawyers for the city
feared that any ban would run afoul of the First Amendment, Kennedy hoped that Wertham's findings on the link between comics and
delinquency could form the basis of a successful legal challenge.[74]
Wertham responded by sending more of his writings and findings
to Kennedy, along with a gloomy warning that the campaign would
meet stiff opposition from publishers and wood pulp manufacturers
in the United States and Canada.

Ultimately, it was a court case that stalled efforts to legislate the
sale of comic books. Years earlier, a New Yorker named Murray
Winters had been arrested for the possession and intent to sell a
copy of *Headquarters Detective*, a crime-themed magazine. Police
claimed the magazine violated a New York State anti-obscenity
statute.[75] Winters was convicted and lost his appeals. Then in 1948,
the Supreme Court declared the New York statute to be uncon-
stitutional. The Supreme Court further rejected the claim by the
New York Court of Appeals that crime magazines were indecent or
obscene. "Though we see nothing of value in these magazines," it

declared, "they are as much entitled to the protection of free speech as is the best of literature."[76] One of Wertham's core arguments— that comic books required unique regulation because they exerted an outsized influence on children and therefore on society—had been shattered. Although other cities and states tried to implement anti–comic book ordinances, hopes for federal legislation faded. Federal investigations into the comic book industry, however, persisted, as did Wertham.

Six years after *Winters v. New York*, Wertham published *Seduction of the Innocent*, a book-length critique of the comic book. It framed the American commercial comic as a global problem, connecting comic books, violence, race, and diplomacy as inseparable factors in the Cold War. Wertham described the international distribution of American comics as akin to the spread of harmful drugs, writing, "The more I followed the reactions abroad, the more I realized that, like the export of narcotics, crime comic books have become an international problem." Fusing the domestic with the diplomatic, Wertham further warned that at home, comic books provided a space for the darkest, most primitive expressions of racism, sexism, and xenophobia while also serving as "our ill-will ambassadors abroad."[77] At a time when the United States presented itself as a modern and sophisticated society, comic books showed global consumers its most crude and violent elements. "Whatever differences there are between the Eastern and Western countries of Europe," he wrote, "they are united in their condemnation of American crime comic books."[78] Long-standing allies like Canada and Britain would be horrified by violence in comic books, while potential friends in the decolonizing world would be repelled by the racism in them. Without a political solution to the comic book problem, Wertham argued, domestic society and diplomacy would founder.

The fact that the United States subjected its own citizens to brutalities and indignities raised real doubts about its commitment to global civil rights. After fighting fascism overseas, veterans of color returned home to a society still built on the premise of White supremacy. In 1946, Isaac Woodard, a recently discharged Black sergeant, was dragged off a bus and beaten by police in South Carolina, who then arrested him for disorderly conduct. In jail, Woodard was attacked so severely he was left permanently blind. After local authorities refused to investigate, President Truman ordered a federal inquiry. At trial, the police chief admitted to hitting Woodard in the eyes; an all-White jury acquitted him and his officers. In 1951, about three thousand protesters and police in Cicero, Illinois, rioted when a Black veteran, Harvey Clark, moved his family into a previously all-White building.[79] It took troops from the National Guard to disperse the rioters, and this explosion of intolerance and violence was international news.

A few months after the rioting in Cicero, Avon Periodicals launched a new comic book title, *White Princess of the Jungle*. In addition to a number of stories featuring a White woman who alternately slaughtered and coddled African men, it included a reprint from another Avon comic, *Slave Girl*. This was a racist caricature of the Middle East, a space in which cruel men of color owned and abused brave and beautiful White men and women. Malu, the titular slave girl, is variously abducted, assaulted, and tortured by an array of bloodthirsty rulers and thieves. Garth, her White lover and protector, is always close behind, ready to stab anyone that has wronged Malu. Together, the two hack a path through one mystical city after another, fomenting slave revolts and killing enslavers wherever possible. They encounter Taanda, a White princess, who forces an African male to kneel before her and, with a knife at his throat, demands, "Talk! Or you will never see tomorrow's sun!" He pleads, "Great one, gladly!" Another towering White woman, Zaleen, commands a group of African warriors to attack a neighboring village ruled by Taanda. In the midst of battle, a man screams, "Kill the swine!" while two other warriors gloat, "We have killed hundreds! This is a great day!" At the end of the fight, neither group of Africans has been able to defeat the other. So the two White women dismiss the remaining men and resolve things themselves, fighting hand-to-hand until Taanda the White princess kicks the gigantic Zaleen to death.[80] Comic books like *White Princess of the Jungle* and *Slave Girl* were cultural constants; millions appeared every month, even as older issues were passed from reader to reader.

FIGURE 4.7 Images like this one from a 1948 issue of *Dagar*, combining racism, sexuality, and violence, presented the United States as culturally insensitive and oblivious to the true history, cost, and legacy of chattel slavery. Federal policy makers feared that such images complicated efforts to win hearts and minds in the decolonizing world.

In the first chapter of *Seduction of the Innocent*, Wertham describes a comic book owned by Willie, a young Black boy in his care who had been accused of shooting a man with pistol: "Here is one man mugging another and graphic pictures of the white man shooting colored natives as though they were animals." Once again connecting the domestic to the global, Wertham called out the vicious racism in jungle-themed comics as particularly problematic. He devoted an entire chapter of *Seduction of the Innocent* to the harmful effects of racist imagery in comic books. In it, he emphasized that jungle titles, sold internationally after the war, sapped self-respect from readers of color in the United States and bolstered feelings of superiority in White consumers. "While the white people in jungle books are blonde and athletic and shapely," Wertham wrote, "the idea conveyed about the natives is that there are fleeting transitions between apes and humans. This characterization of colored peoples as subhuman, in conjunction with depiction of forceful heroes as blond Nordic supermen, has made a deep—and I believe lasting—impression" on young and adult readers. "The brunt of this imputed inferiority in whole groups of people is directed against colored people and 'foreign born,'" argued Wertham.[81]

In a clinical interview with a fifteen-year-old subject, Wertham asked "whether jungle comics create race hatred." In the subject's much highlighted reply, he told the doctor, "In the funny books it is understood the Negroes are slaves, more or less. . . . There are Negroes who try to rape white people in funny books. The white people feel they are superior to the Negroes. Negroes are not much use to them, just to do their bidding. It could be the kids are influenced by the funny books. There are too many sexy pictures in the funny jungle books. . . . It is like a Negro goddess I read about. The pictures I had of her, they might as well be bare." The subject also told Wertham that knives purchased from comic books—disguised as kitchen tools—enabled brutal fights between White and Black kids in New York City. Even though the subject detailed his friendship with a Black peer, he also stressed, "The Colored kids get into arguments with the Whites and stab somebody. Say they are losing in a fight.

The first thing they pull out is a knife." The interview subject further claimed that comic books incited girls to have sex with multiple partners of different races.[82] Wertham was horrified by these stories and took them as more evidence that comic books fueled violence, race hatred, and sex. As detailed in chapter 6, elements of the federal government agreed with Wertham and worked to transform the comic book from a highly visible example of racist culture into a means of reaching potential allies in the decolonizing world.

THE SEVERED HEAD

If 1948 was the year that the anti–comic book movement really took off, 1953 was the beginning of the end for the industry as it had existed since the 1930s. That year, the Senate Subcommittee on Juvenile Delinquency began a series of hearings on the causes of juvenile delinquency. It did not take long for its members to zero in on the comic book. The subcommittee chairman, Senator Robert Hendrickson of New Jersey, already suspected that mass culture might be a primary cause and noted that the subcommittee had received over seven thousand letters from citizens worried about juvenile crime. Of these, said Hendrickson, 90 percent blamed an increase in sex and violence in entertainment. His committee soon received many thousands more letters, over half of which faulted comic books as potential sources of criminal behavior in children.[83]

In early 1954, Hendrickson announced that due to "significant public concern over the possible harmful effects of comic books on the young mind," his subcommittee would hold hearings on the comic book industry.[84] Although the issue of delinquency attracted the most attention, the committee also heeded Wertham's warning that commercial comic books were damaging American cultural outreach and diplomacy (see chapter 5). Held over three days in April in New York City, the heart of the comic book industry, the hearings were a public event covered by the popular press, debated in the pages of comic books, and even transmitted live on a new medium that would greatly stifle the popularity of the comic book: television. Senators heard testimony from twenty-two witnesses. Wertham, along with two other experts on juvenile delinquency, was invited to testify as a friendly expert witness. Although the committee invited two comic strip artists—Walt Kelly and Milton Caniff, the creators of *Pogo* and *Terry and the Pirates*—it did not call a single comic book artist or writer. Initially, the publishers most focused on crime and horror comic books were to be left unrepresented as well, although the committee heard from representatives from Timely and Dell Comics. Ultimately, Bill Gaines of EC Comics requested and was granted a chance to speak before the committee on the same day as Wertham.

Just days before the hearings, *Seduction of the Innocent* received an effusive review in the *New York Times* from sociologist C. Wright Mills, who declared that "all parents should be grateful to Dr. Fredric Wertham." In an advertisement for the book, critic Sterling North, one of the earliest opponents of comics, christened *Seduction of the Innocent* "the most important book of the year." In private correspondence, even author Clifton Fadiman, who had worked to spread propaganda through comic books at the WWB, complimented Wertham on his work, assuring him, "the book will do a lot of good." *Seduction of the Innocent* was on its way to selling sixteen thousand copies in six months, doubtless propelled by its author's scheduled appearance at the subcommittee hearings.[85]

Wertham launched into a familiar attack. He singled out an EC story for promoting racism and commented, "I think Hitler was a beginner compared to the comic-book industry. They get the children much younger. They teach them race hatred at the age of four, before they can read."[86] Gaines spoke after Wertham and after the members witnessed a presentation of "The Orphan," from EC's *Shock SuspenStories*, in which a little girl murders her father and ensures that her mother and a boyfriend take the blame and then die in the electric chair. Undeterred—and fortified by amphetamines—Gaines reminded the subcommittee that millions of Americans derived a harmless thrill from lurid entertainment without committing crimes and urged them to reject censorship. He foundered, though, when the subcommittee questioned him about the cover art of a *Crime SuspenStories* issue, featuring a blonde woman's decapitated head and a bloody axe.[87] Newspaper reports made much of an exchange among

Gaines, Senator Estes Kefauver, and Chief Counsel Herbert Beaser in which Gaines claimed the cover was in good taste "for the cover of a horror comic." A cover in bad taste, he suggested, "might be defined as holding the head a little higher so that the neck could be seen dripping blood from it, and moving the body over a little further so that the neck of the body could be seen to be bloody."[88] His response was a disaster for the comic book industry.

The Senate subcommittee investigation, along with parallel efforts by policy makers and activists at the state and local levels, drove the comic book industry to accept a system of self-censorship in late 1954. Publishers agreed to fund the creation and maintenance of the Comics Magazine Association of America (CMAA), an organization tasked with reviewing and approving the contents of all comic books sold through major distributors. The centerpiece of this new system was a censorship code. It demanded that comic book publishers depict crime as "a sordid and unpleasant activity," required that "good shall triumph over evil," and banned representations of "horror, excessive bloodshed, gory or gruesome crimes, depravity, lust, sadism [and] masochism." It forbade depictions of cannibalism, torture, the "walking dead," and even werewolves and vampires. The code pressed publishers to use good grammar wherever possible and dress all characters in clothes "reasonably acceptable to society" and banned exaggerated images of the female body. Unspecified "sexual abnormalities" were deemed unacceptable, as were any stories or pictures that might "stimulate the lower or baser emotions." Police officers, judges, and elected officials could no longer be shown in ways that generated disrespect for their authority. Criminals could not kill law enforcement officers. Comic book advertisements, the cultural camouflage that initially drew propagandists to the medium, were subject to restrictions as well. Publishers could no longer run advertisements for weapons, fireworks, "sex or sex instruction books," or "art studies" and were told, "Good taste shall be the guiding principle in the acceptance of advertising."[89]

After nearly twenty years of relative freedom, the comic book industry had been tamed. Millions, perhaps even billions, of issues published before the code still circulated the world. From the mo-

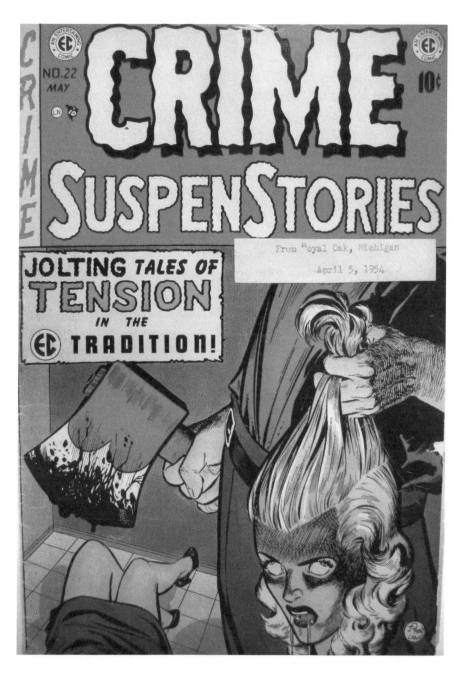

FIGURE 4.8 The copy of *Crime SuspenStories* submitted to the Senate subcommittee that investigated the comic book industry in 1954. The image of an average-looking, White American man holding a woman's severed head outraged senators and helped end the first, freewheeling phase of the American comic book industry.

ment the code went into effect, though, there would be vastly fewer problematic representations of race, violence, sexuality, and drug use to plague federal policy makers. Many companies responsible for the most challenging and confrontational titles simply disappeared, unwilling or unable to compete in a business now commonly understood to be a national embarrassment. Those that remained recognized that there were limits to what the government would tolerate from the comic book industry. Legislators, policy makers, and propagandists saw comic books as powerful, charged media, and they were no longer willing to stand by as publishers valued adult themes and profits above the nation's Cold War project. The newly constrained comic book industry now operated under the supervision of the CMAA and the federal government. Those that caused trouble for either entity might face repercussions. This clarity, perhaps as much as the code itself, constrained the contents of post-code comics. The comic book medium would still be identified with the United States and continue to be a source of embarrassment. But it would not, policy makers hoped, offer the sort of contents that hurt or outraged so many potential allies in the global south.

Still, the code did not solve the problem of racism in comic books. Surviving publishers responded to it not with more positive imagery but by virtually eliminating whatever non-White characters had outlasted the war. And as Bill Gaines learned, the CMAA also used the code to restrict even constructive representations of non-White characters. He submitted a story for review called "Judgment Day," in which a human astronaut, garbed in an opaque space helmet, attempts to mediate a dispute among a society of robots segregated by color. The protagonist eventually decides that the robot society is too primitive to solve its problem and cannot join the larger group of civilized planets. In the last panel, he removes his helmet and reveals himself to be Black. He appears with beads of perspiration on his face, presumably due to his confinement in the space suit. Gaines claimed that the code reviewers rejected the story based on the beads of sweat, which they believed violated the code's ban on "ridicule or attack on any religious or racial group."[90] It was too much. He abandoned comic book publishing to focus on his new venture:

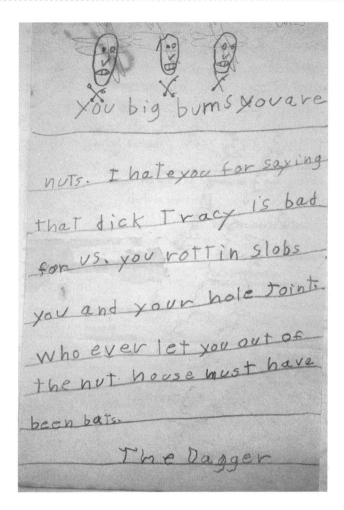

FIGURE 4.9 An anonymous letter, signed "The Dagger," sent to Dr. Fredric Wertham by an angry comic book fan.

transforming one of his most successful comic books, *Mad*, into a magazine.

To Wertham, the code was a capitulation. It symbolized the unwillingness of politicians to do what was necessary in order to protect American children from the real dangers of the comic book form. And Wertham was outraged that the new head of the CMAA, Judge Charles Murphy, publicly stated that in all his years on the bench, he had never encountered a crime connected in any way to a comic book.[91] In correspondence with Senator Estes Kefauver, the doctor argued that comics published after the code were even worse than those that had preceded it, as the CMAA stamp implied some sort of official approval. This, Wertham felt, might induce parents to permit children to read even more comic books. He felt betrayed by politicians, activists, and everyone who had abandoned the effort to pass national legislation regulating the sale of comic books. They had been seduced by assurances that the CMAA would cleanse the industry. "Neutrality," he raged, "that is the devil's ally."[92]

Wertham thought about popular culture in global terms and treated it as equivalent to military or diplomatic power. At a time of national panic over left-wing subversion, he did not blame communists for crime comic books; he faulted what he claimed were national obsessions with violence, racism, and elements of fascism. This ensured that no one political party or philosophy laid claim to the issue of opposing violence in comic books. Instead, average Americans created a loose-knit collection of local anti–comic book organizations. Fighting against violent comic books provided a means for civilian men and women to participate in the great issues of the day. By attacking uncensored comics, they could believe they were defending America's children and the comforting embrace of family. In a society seemingly menaced by external and internal enemies, these were valuable and vulnerable resources indeed.

CHAPTER FIVE

AMERICAN CIVILIZATION MEANS AIRSTRIPS AND COMIC STRIPS

RED BLOOD SPILLS OVER WHITE SKINS

Many contemporary reports distilled the 1954 Senate subcommittee hearings on comic books down to a face-off between Wertham and Gaines, who became a stand-in for all that was troubling about the medium. The comic book threat seemed neutralized; a censorship code drove many of the most daring publishers out of business and promised to regulate those that remained. If there was a connection between comic book violence and juvenile delinquency, the code would sever it. The focus on Wertham, Gaines, and delinquency, however, obscured a significant piece of the subcommittee's investigation and hearings. The subcommittee also explored reactions to American comic books in Western Europe, the decolonizing world, and the Soviet bloc. Materials and witnesses emphasized that the sheer quantity, diversity, and availability of American comics created problems for the nation's image abroad as well as for its diplomats and businesses. As the committee emphasized, "Comic books are distributed in many countries where the population is other than Caucasian. This introduces complications probably quite unforeseen by writers and artists who compose the format of these books in the

United States."[1] These findings suggested that even with the implementation of a censorship code, the many millions of issues already
in circulation around the world would continue to attract readers
and influence global perceptions of American society, culture, and
power. For as long as consumers bought, borrowed, read, and shared
problematic comic books, they would complicate federal efforts to
depict the country as a more humane, sophisticated alternative to
communism.

Comic books retained this power, despite the new censorship
code, because they were inseparable from the physical machinery
of the battle against communism: they traveled abroad through
a variety of means, official and unofficial, and respected neither
borders nor local tastes. To critics, they seemed capable of infecting
consumers with the ills of American society. The Senate subcommittee learned that Chinese communists cited comic books as evidence
of American "degeneracy" and that comics reinforced standard
Chinese propaganda regarding the "'degraded' state of U.S. culture."[2]
The news was much the same in South Asia and Africa. Regional
communist parties seized on American comics as evidence of the
"depravity" and racism in American life and as a local contributor
to crime and delinquency. The potentially negative effects of comic
books in South Asia and Africa were compounded by their delivery
systems—namely, American military personnel. Communist
propagandists could make much of the image of American soldiers
littering the decolonizing world with violent and racist narratives,
particularly because comic books were widely seen as entertainment
for children.[3]

The subcommittee also reviewed propaganda that used American
comic books as the source material for attacks on the United States
and its efforts to win new allies. The documents—from countries
as varied as Romania, Iran, and Czechoslovakia—made clear that
uncensored comic books were a rich and renewable resource for
anti-American propaganda.[4] Whether the charge was militarization,
a lack of cultural sophistication, racism, or a fascination with violence, comics provided an unending stream of supporting material.
The issue was with not simply the contents of commercial comic

books but also the quantities available. For every Black dancer or musician the State Department sent abroad, there were a thousand comic books full of racist or violent imagery.

The subcommittee reached four conclusions. First, there was growing concern in many countries over the rising popularity of American crime and horror comic books. The subcommittee had solicited the State Department for information regarding international reactions to American comics, and the department confirmed "public concern has been expressed in almost every European country over the problem posed by American comics."[5] Second, violent comic books exposed foreign readers to "a hardened version of killing, robbery and sadism which is not only an undesirable pattern to emulate but is also a negative version of the American way of life." Third, uncensored American comic books additionally created particular problems in countries with non-White citizens. Finally, the committee found substantial evidence that Soviet propagandists used comics as prime examples of depraved American culture.[6] In whatever way an anti-American propagandist might want to present the United States as backward—racially, culturally, ethically, or sexually—there were comics that supported it. Just as Wertham had warned.

Uncensored comics also provided fodder for elements of the anti-colonial movement that remained skeptical of America's troubled racial history. The subcommittee emphasized the damage to America's image in countries like Iran and India. It cited a passage from *Ambassador's Report* by Chester Bowles, former US ambassador to India. Bowles recounted a racist comic book story that horrified and offended an Indian friend. In it, a White hero fights against Mongolian villains who, at the behest of communists, drink plasma intended for American soldiers wounded in Korea. The leader of the Mongolians then orders the "blood-drinkers of Mongolia" to attack American soldiers. A vampire pounces on an American, screaming, "One rip at the throat, red blood spills over white skins. And we drink deep." Such grotesque Asian characters, Bowles noted, hampered efforts to win friends in the decolonizing world. Communist propagandists, he warned, "could not possibly devise a more persuasive way to convince color sensitive Indians that Americans believe in the superior civilization of people with white skins, and that we are indoctrinating our children with bitter racial prejudice from the time they learn to read."[7]

The source of the story Bowles described was as worrisome as its contents. "The Mongol Blood-Drinkers" appeared not in a crime or horror comic book but in a 1953 issue of *Captain Marvel Adventures*. If such a seemingly benign title contained violent, racist stories like this one, similar narratives doubtless appeared in others. In the very first panel of "The Mongol Blood-Drinkers," a grotesque vampire with stereotypically Asian features looms over a trench filled with American soldiers fighting in Korea. With red wings spread and fangs bared, the vampire screams, "Blood! Blood! I want rich, American blood!" The action then shifts to a blood drive in the United States, where Captain Marvel volunteers to fly the blood to soldiers in Korea. Within minutes of his arrival, a band of vampires discover the "Yankee pigs" have a fresh supply of blood. As a vampire attacks an American nurse, the leader of the vampires exults, "Blood! Food for the Scarlet Vampire and his Mongol blood-drinkers! Gorge yourselves!" After scattering the vampires, Captain Marvel learns that the communists have struck a deal with the "Mongol blood-drinkers": all the American blood they can drink in return for fighting against the United Nations troops in Korea. Believing that Captain Marvel has left the combat zone, the vampires then attack a large number of American soldiers, hoping to feed and secure a victory for the communists. "We will laugh at their bullets," screams the leader of the vampires, "drink their blood, and toss away their withered corpses." Captain Marvel eventually grabs an enormous wooden stake and uses it to skewer the gang of blood-drinkers. He then turns to the lead vampire and impales him, shouting, "Goodbye forever!"[8]

Bowles's comments made clear that all sorts of comic books—not just crime and horror titles—influenced global perceptions of the United States and that pre-code comics would continue causing problems abroad long after they were published.

THE STRUGGLE FOR FREEDOM

In August 1949, *Life* magazine published a profile of American modernist painter Jackson Pollock. The article dismissed Pollock's jazz-inspired painting technique as "dribbling" and noted that some critics wrote off Pollock as a "degenerate" and his work as "unpalatable as yesterday's macaroni." Still, *Life* conceded, Pollock was likely brilliant, as he not only sold twelve paintings at a Manhattan exhibition but also received an enthusiastic response from Parisian critics.[9] Thus, Pollock's abstract art met two essential criteria for American observers: it generated money—a testament to American elites' approval—and appealed to the French, the reigning arbiters of Western artistic taste.[10] Pollock's stature in the old and new worlds was particularly important at a time when the United States sought to replace Western Europe and France, in particular, as the center of liberal-democratic culture. Abstract expressionism, along with other modern cultural forms like jazz music, burnished America's international cultural credibility and contrasted with the dull, state-sponsored socialist realism imposed on Soviet artists. Even *Life*, in spite of its skepticism, emphasized that the process of creating modern paintings was, at its core, "the struggle for freedom."[11]

Appropriating the theme of unfettered personal expression, American foreign policy experts embarked on an unprecedented international rebranding campaign. Through glossy publications and traveling exhibitions of "elite" American music and visual culture, policy makers at the State Department and the United States Information Agency (USIA) promoted the United States as egalitarian, racially tolerant, and culturally diverse—a compelling example of modernity worthy of emulation abroad.[12] At the same time, the United States flooded Western Europe with financial aid, products, and propaganda through the European Recovery Program (ERP), better known as the Marshall Plan. Launched in 1948, the Marshall Plan blended American altruism, capitalism, and cold realism into an effort to rebuild Western Europe, halt the spread of communism, and strengthen the American economy.[13] Under the ERP, the United

States subsidized Europe's postwar recovery, providing war-ravaged countries with food, economic assistance, and technical expertise. In return, the United States received markets open to its products and culture. The United States also enjoyed improved security, as a healthy Western Europe provided a political, economic, and military bulwark against Soviet expansion on the continent.

Western Europeans viewed the Marshall Plan with some ambivalence. America's allies desperately needed external assistance. But permitting American intrusion into all aspects of political, economic, and military matters carried very high costs. Critics charged that the American-style pursuit of evermore efficient production processes steamrolled over individual dignity, local traditions, and intellectual diversity. Western Europeans from a variety of political backgrounds feared American cultural power and recoiled at breezy pronouncements from political commentators like Walter Lippmann, who wrote, "Fate has willed it that America is from now on to be at the center of Western Civilization rather than on the periphery."[14] Some in Europe also worried about the political and military ramifications of the Marshall Plan. Its acceptance seemed to guarantee a Europe polarized between the United States and the Soviet Union, an unpalatable prospect to those not enamored with either superpower.

Cultural outreach offered a means of building support for both the Marshall Plan and America's growing presence in Europe. But the American government did not enjoy a monopoly on cultural transmission. American aid moreover carried with it a nonnegotiable cost: a plague of uncensored and unregulated comic books. As citizens and policy makers in North America and Europe alike fought to reassert control over their domestic spheres, they sought a political solution to a cultural infection. Between 1945 and 1955, average citizens, activists, and policy makers in at least ten nations on three continents protested against American comic books. In the midst of the Marshall Plan and a series of Cold War crises, this transnational crusade united nationalists, communists, and centrists against a quintessentially American form of popular culture.

Why were citizens of other countries so afraid of American comic books? Domestically, the anti–comic book crusade focused on the dangers posed by crime and horror titles, due to fears that they contributed significantly to deviant behavior. In Western Europe, deviancy was defined differently. There, the characteristics of a delinquent overlapped significantly with the stereotypical behavior of American tourists, service members, and government employees. In *Seduction of the Innocent*, Fredric Wertham warned, "People all over the world believe that American civilization means airstrips and comic strips."[15] To be a delinquent in Western Europe was, in essence, to act like an American character from a crime, horror, romance, or jungle comic book. From this perspective, American comic books served as blueprints for negative or American behavior. American comics taught American-style violence, racism, greed, and sexuality. Men and women in ravaged countries were not in a position to refuse all American aid or an American military presence, but they could try to limit their exposure to what they perceived as the very worst of American culture: the comic book.

The protest against American comics was a critique of not only a specific medium but also the American military and the economic power that disseminated it around the world. Anti–comic book advocates first succeeded in France, where in 1949 the National Assembly instituted a system of regulation over juvenile literature. That same year the Canadian Senate held hearings on the effects of comic book consumption and subsequently passed a bill outlawing the reproduction or importation of horror and crime titles.[16] In 1955, the British Parliament passed the Children and Young Persons (Harmful Publications) Bill. Germans, too, questioned whether to regulate or ban so-called American-style comic books.[17] Whether any of these decrees eliminated or meaningfully slowed the importation of American comic books is nearly impossible to assess, but in the moment, authorities believed them necessary and effective.

SANCTIONED AND UNSANCTIONED CULTURE

Between 1945 and 1955, when the American comic book industry implemented a system of self-regulation, the transnational campaign against comic books complicated American diplomacy, weakened government-sanctioned intercultural programs, and challenged the image of an enlightened, egalitarian United States. In support of this campaign, Fredric Wertham corresponded with and lent his support to activists in Europe and Asia, and his works appeared in Britain and France as well as in periodicals distributed around the globe. As in America, the crusade flourished even in the absence of scientific support for the claim that comic book consumption contributed to degenerate behavior. For American policy makers and propagandists, though, an absence of evidence became far less important than the fact that people believed in this correlation. Vital American allies saw commercial American comic books as dangerous; therefore, the comic book threatened American diplomatic policy making. But because controlling the circulation of comics was nearly impossible, something had to be done about their contents.

By the late 1940s, embarrassed Marshall Plan administrators were scrambling to stop shipments of comics to Germany, where the newsstands were "a clutter of comic books."[18] By 1954, the State Department confirmed that "public concern has been expressed in almost every European country over the problem posed by American comics."[19] The dynamic between sanctioned and unsanctioned American culture raises two questions: Did contemporary policy makers, on both sides of the Atlantic, view American elite culture as more influential than low culture? Or did they believe that comic books would overwhelm state-sanctioned efforts to depict the United States as a sophisticated and modern society? Certainly, the sheer quantity of comic books shipped abroad dwarfed the number of concerts, performances, and fairs hosted by American federal agencies and corporations. Between 1945 and 1955, millions of uncensored comic books reached readers in Europe, Latin America, South Asia, and the Middle East. The very reasons that governments feared American commercial comics—portability, comprehensibility, and affordability—granted real significance to the medium.

ADVANCING AMERICAN ART

In the years after World War II, the United States alone possessed nuclear weapons, and its factories and farms, strengthened and honed by wartime production, stood prepared to meet the demands of millions of global consumers. The nation's technological achievements and economic might connected it with progress, purchasing power, and peace.[20] Yet American policy makers turned to intercultural relations to achieve three policy goals: (1) to win respect for the nation's noncommercial and artistic achievements, (2) to de-emphasize the racial divisions and tensions in American society, and (3) to contrast the creative freedom accorded Western artists with the artistic repression practiced in the Soviet bloc. To win allies among the communists, socialists, nationalists, and conservatives of postwar Europe, the United States had to earn cultural legitimacy there.[21] This would not be easy, particularly in postwar France, where a populace divided by war, occupation, and collaboration agreed that "Parisian art must be the best in the world."[22]

In tackling their second objective, policy makers realized that confronting the nation's historical and contemporary embrace of enslavement and segregation was inseparable from its Cold War foreign policy initiatives.[23] The skillful promotion of specific, American-branded cultural products thus highlighted the freedoms American society accorded to Blacks, intellectuals, and artists. Policy makers quickly identified avant-garde artwork as a useful medium. Bold, abstract modernist paintings were challenging and fresh; avant-garde art was a nominally apolitical expression of emotion, a counterpoint to realist art harnessed to the needs of the state. A *Life* magazine article concluded that the modern artist engaged in "a struggle to discover and to assert and to express him*self*"—a uniquely private experience available only in an open society.[24] Policy makers paraded modern art before the world as evidence that forward-looking Americans appreciated sophistication as much as brute industrialization and mass production.[25] Although the abstract expressionists were artistic outsiders at home, their philosophy and work became integral components of American foreign policy.

Accordingly, in late 1946, the Metropolitan Museum of Art announced plans to send seventy-nine paintings on an international tour under the auspices of the State Department. Yet the show, *Advancing American Art*, soon generated domestic controversy. *Look* magazine dismissed the paintings as degenerate and the exhibition as a waste of taxpayer money. The State Department also came under attack for including works by a number of artists, such as Ben Shahn and Milton Avery, with left-wing sympathies. In response, the department recalled the exhibit, and Secretary of State George Marshall announced that the department would no longer spend money on avant-garde artwork. Such outrage only served to highlight closed-minded attitudes toward avant-garde paintings and likely destroyed any international goodwill created by the exhibit. But it received favorable reviews from international observers, and the Soviet Union responded with a hastily assembled exhibition of its own in Prague.[26]

Then in January 1948, after lengthy and acrimonious debate between isolationists and internationalists, the Senate unanimously approved the Smith-Mundt Act, intended "to promote a better understanding of the United States in other countries."[27] The bill enshrined the policy of propaganda and cultural diplomacy during peacetime, a significant step for a nation still debating between a return to prewar isolationism and international engagement.[28]

In 1951, the American government hosted another display of modern art at a cultural festival in West Berlin. During the subsequent decade, American modern art traveled to Europe, Africa, Asia, Latin America, and the Middle East and hung in American embassies and consulates.[29] Despite these efforts, the *New York Times* ran a scathing editorial cautioning that the United States was losing the global battle for hearts and minds.[30] It emphasized the importance of nonmilitary power and warned that this factor was well understood in Moscow. American cultural outreach was tame and limited; more needed to be done, and quickly, if the United States hoped to fend off communist programs throughout the world. Any hesitation played into the hands of the Kremlin, as the United States also had to overcome its image as a nation infatuated by cruder entertainments. As if in response, the new Eisenhower administration soon accelerated America's cultural offensive.

Intercultural relations and covert political warfare flourished under Eisenhower. The president oversaw the establishment of the USIA in 1953, which became the organization most responsible for "informational diplomacy."[31] Though it acted on policy suggestions from the State Department, agency officials stressed that the USIA disseminated news and information, in contrast to communist organizations that spread propaganda.[32] But creating and circulating propaganda was a priority. A classified explanation of the USIA's mission bluntly acknowledged the organization's focus on "political warfare" aimed at burnishing the image of the United States and critiquing communist policies, philosophy, and culture. Its primary audience lay outside the Soviet bloc, particularly among those peoples "not fully committed to opposition to Soviet communism."[33]

Under Eisenhower, the State Department identified jazz as another useful intercultural tool.[34] Jazz was not only American but uniquely African American: a complex and deeply personal musical form influenced by centuries of racial and cultural divisions within American society. But in the hands of American diplomats, jazz functioned as an example of personal expression made possible by the freedoms American society accorded to outsiders.[35] The State Department's first international jazz tour, starring Dizzy Gillespie, left the United States in 1956. The tour, and many subsequent jazz exhibitions, was met with enormous success, entertaining large numbers of people in strategically important areas of the world, including the Soviet bloc, Africa, and Europe. By highlighting the contributions of avant-garde artists and Black musicians, these cultural outreach programs rebranded the United States as the center of modern culture.

Which cultural object wields the most power over its consumer? What is clear from the intertwined postwar histories of US foreign policy and the comic book is that despite the comic book's status as dark, low culture, it was imbued with the same sort of weight granted to elite culture like jazz or modern sculpture. Despite a military backed by the most powerful weapons in history, American policy makers worried that culture—even in the form of the humble comic book—could bring down their efforts to promote American-style democracy and capitalism. As the federal government embarked on a long-term campaign to promote American culture, comics were an embarrassing and troublesome reminder of the darker side of American society.

AMERICAN COMIC BOOKS IN FRANCE

Fear of American power ran particularly high in postwar France. A combination of practical and philosophical concerns fostered anti-American sentiment among French intellectuals, nationalists, and communists then at the peak of their influence in French society. Many of them believed that American-style "productivity mania, Coca-Cola, and the *Reader's Digest*" threatened France's status as the arbiter of Western taste.[36] French leaders thus faced a problem: how to modernize the nation's political system, economy, and culture without succumbing to the American contagion of mass-produced culture.[37]

France was integral to postwar American military and economic planning. In 1948, Acting Secretary of State Robert Lovett proclaimed France the "keystone of continental Western Europe."[38] France was a major economic and military power, a traditionally democratic society, and the home of modern culture. These factors, along with the considerable clout wielded by communist intellectuals and politicians there, made France a hotly contested space in the cultural Cold War. The challenge facing American leaders was how to bind France to the Western anticommunist alliance and open its markets to American goods without arousing anti-American and procommunist sentiment.[39]

The State Department, under the auspices of the Marshall Plan, launched a full-scale cultural offensive in France. William Tyler, the American cultural attaché in Paris, urged the use of elite and middle-brow cultural products to refute the "cultural barbarian myth"—the suspicion that Americans were nothing more than a nation of pinup-ogling McCarthyites.[40] In 1950, the cultural attaché and Mission France (the Marshall Plan administration agency) organized exhibits promoting America's accomplishments in painting, printmaking, and architecture, and in 1951, the American Embassy in Paris displayed sixty-eight prints from the Museum of Modern Art, many of which were abstract or modernist. Perhaps because the centrality of culture to the Cold War was clearer than it had been just a few years earlier, this exhibit did not trigger the same domestic outrage as *Advancing American Art*. The following year, architect Frank Lloyd Wright traveled to France to open an exhibit of his works. The cultural attaché interpreted Wright's enthusiastic reception as confirmation that the French were receptive to elite American culture.[41]

Significant numbers of French citizens also embraced lower sorts of American culture. American and American-style comic books and comic strips enjoyed enormous popularity in postwar France. *Le journal de Mickey*, a Mickey Mouse–themed comic book, sold hundreds of thousands of copies per issue, at times more than middlebrow periodicals like *Le Figaro* and *Le Monde*.[42] The availability and popularity of American and American-style comic art altered the reading habits of French children and adults. Historically, the children of middle-class French parents purchased and consumed novels, but postwar austerity meant they were less able to afford such titles. Comics were designed as cheap, short-lived entertainment prone to literal disintegration. Children's books—even inexpensive ones—were simply more costly and durable objects. Thus, middle- and working-class children and adults purchased hundreds of thousands of American comics in English and translation. A new comic cost the equivalent of ten cents; a well-worn copy might sell for less. American soldiers arrived in France "abundantly stocked with their favorite form of reading," a correspondent for the *New York Times* lamented.[43] Parisian booksellers did a brisk business in secondhand comic books, selling copies to young French readers and American adults.[44]

By the late 1940s, comic books in France, as in the United States, seemingly threatened the youngest and most vulnerable members of society. The French political Left and Right united in opposition to the torrent of American comic books and comic strips.[45] Communists attacked comics as symbols of American imperialism and the brutality of mass culture. In November 1951, an official at the American Embassy in Paris wrote despairingly of a French communist publication, *Beautés Américaines*. It warned the French against American plans to flood Europe with "their canned meats, their chewing gum, their opium cigarettes, their pin-ups, their supermen and their atomic bombs." The embassy official emphasized that French communists took particular offense at popular American publications, lashing out with a "sweeping round-house at comics, pin-up magazines, deodorant advertisements, publishing monopolies and censorship."[46] Centrists and Rightists feared that imported comics undermined the creation of a new French national identity as the country grappled with the aftershocks of defeat and occupation.

As in the United States, French critics decried the violence and sexuality coursing through American comics.[47] They appropriated the American argument that comic books contributed to antisocial behavior and displayed a similar disregard for the lack of scientific evidence behind this assertion. French activists also integrated American critiques into their assault on comic art. In 1949, *Les temps modernes* published a translation of an attack on the "psychopathology" of comics by American critic Gershon Legman. In 1955, the periodical also translated excerpts from Wertham's *Seduction of the Innocent*.[48]

Despite these similarities, the French effort was more politicized and ultimately more successful. French critics objected to American comic art on the grounds that it was fundamentally foreign.[49] Comics complicated the national effort to reimagine and rebuild France in the shadow of an ascendant United States. They were more than a moral or artistic problem; they posed a clear political and social threat. The onslaught of American comics ate away at the nation's faith in its cultural relevance and the health of its youngest citizens. A France narcotized by American mass media could never regain its former political or cultural relevance.[50] Facing down the comic book scourge presented France with an opportunity to exert control over its own society and culture.

Like Wertham, the French National Assembly sought a political solution to the challenge of comics. In July 1949, it enacted a law making it illegal "to promote, to give, or to sell to minors under eighteen, publications of a nature dangerous for youth, by reason of their licentious or pornographic character, of their immoral character, or of their criminal character."[51] The law also established the Commission for the Oversight and Control of Publications for Children and Adolescents to investigate juvenile publications and recommend prosecution of publishers who violated the new law. Proponents from across the political spectrum promoted the legislation as a means of shielding young French readers from corrupting influences and forestalling delinquency. Communist delegates went further, framing the bill as an explicitly anti-American measure. Americans, they warned, exerted an unhealthy level of influence over juvenile publications sold in France.[52]

The complexity of France's new relationship with the United States seems to have led legislators to avoid singling out American publications for criticism in the law's language, as the communists had wanted. Such a direct attack might have antagonized the larger relationship.[53] Still, the law had an immediate effect on American comic strips published in French newspapers and periodicals. For example, the newly established commission attacked the enormously popular *Tarzan*, which sold three hundred thousand copies per week during the early 1950s, the largest circulation of any comic book in France.[54] It frequently featured male and female characters in various states of undress but was quite tame in comparison with jungle-themed comic books. Nevertheless, the commission condemned the violence and near-nudity in *Tarzan*. He was, in short, an uncultured brute—as were, by implication, his American creators, publishers, and advocates. The commission requested that *Tarzan*'s publisher withdraw the title from circulation.

From the outset, elements of the American government found themselves embroiled in this controversy. A manager at *Tarzan*'s American publisher notified the State Department of the threatened ban. The manager believed this presaged future attacks on all American magazines, books, and films.[55] The State Department took these concerns seriously. Secretary of State Dean Acheson asked that the Paris embassy investigate and notify the French government that imposing a ban on the comic would be a "mistake."[56] When in early 1951 deputies in the National Assembly proposed restricting the quantity of foreign (that is, American) material permitted in French juvenile publications, the American Embassy in Paris contacted the French Ministry of Foreign Affairs. Any such restriction, warned the embassy, "would in effect result in discrimination against material of this nature coming from the United States."[57] The embassy continued monitoring the debate over foreign content in juvenile publications and remained in contact with French officials until the issue sputtered out in February 1951.[58] Regardless, *Tarzan*'s French publisher canceled the title in 1952. Tarzan, the survivor of a thousand jungle adventures, succumbed to the French Commission for the Oversight and Control of Publications for Children and Adolescents.

AMERICAN COMIC BOOKS IN BRITAIN

Unsanctioned American comic books also generated diplomatic friction in Britain, another nation integral to the postwar anticommunist alliance. Comic books first landed in Britain before World War II and found a ready audience there. The war ended imports of American comics for British audiences, although American soldiers brought with them a steady supply. Between 1945 and 1949, British companies imported large quantities of American comics of all kinds. Direct purchases virtually ended by 1950, when postwar austerity measures restricted the importation of numerous products, including comic books. British publishers circumvented the restriction by reproducing American comics locally under license.[59] And British austerity measures had no influence on American soldiers, whose appetite for comics was unabated.

As in the United States, the British anti–comic book campaign began at the local level in the late 1940s. However, the first wave of crusaders did not identify comics as dangerous to children or as a contributor to juvenile delinquency. Rather, the British movement criticized comic books as quintessentially American—a particularly loathsome example of cultural imperialism. Critics, as Martin Barker emphasizes, explicitly referred to the offending publications as "American" or "American-style comic books."[60] A 1952 pamphlet, *The Lure of the Comics*, published by the International Women's Day Committee, opened with the question, "What's all this fuss about American Comics?" There could be only one response: "Have you ever read an American so-called comic? You will never again ask 'What's the difference?' or 'Where's the harm?'"[61] The same year, *Picture Post* ran an article on American comics by Peter Mauger, a member of the National Union of Teachers (NUT) and a communist. Both Mauger's article and *The Lure of the Comics* condemned comic books as crude, undesirable, and violent: that is, as uniquely American.

The early British campaign deviated from its American analogue in another significant respect: its core members were communists. When this fact became public, British activists changed tactics (although communists remained central to the campaign).[62] Beginning around 1954, members of the newly formed Comics Campaign Council (CCC) no longer referred to "American comics" but to "crime and horror comics."[63] Rather than attacking comic books as artifacts of militarized American culture, critics warned that comics posed a clear danger to young readers.[64] As did their peers in the United States and France, British activists leveled this charge despite a total lack of supporting evidence and in spite of indications that working-class men and women, as much children, consumed comic books.[65]

Like Fredric Wertham and the French activists, the CCC sought a political solution.[66] They were aided in this effort by the NUT.[67] As in the United States, members of the groups presented comic books as harmful stimulants and contributors to antisocial behavior. With the campaign now free from overt associations with the Communist Party, politicians and activists from both the political Left and Right embraced the call for legislation. "The most sinister thing about these publications," cautioned a Labour MP, "is that they introduce the element of pleasure into violence. They encourage sadism; and they encourage sadism in association with an unhealthy sexual stimulation."[68] The Church of England denounced American comics as "a torrent of poison," while the *Tribune* condemned the comic book industry as a "steaming pudding of horror, sex, vice and moronic fantasy."[69]

Fredric Wertham played a significant role in this campaign.[70] He wrote a letter to the editor of the *Times* declaring, "The evidence that reading of crime comic books is one of the contributing causes to the rising number of violent delinquencies by children is overwhelming." Even worse, Wertham emphasized, was that comics "teach race hatred and nation hatred (yes, including the British) to children and are thereby contributing to the hostilities of the world." He closed with a call for the British government to ban the importation of problematic comic books from the United States.[71] In correspondence with Peter Mauger, he railed against American politicians who were either too weak or too corrupt to regulate the comic book industry. Echoing his letter to the *Times*, Wertham further insisted that Mauger ignore accusations that the British movement was anti-American. The doctor dismissed any connection between the anti–comic book campaign and anti-Americanism as "utter nonsense" and assured Mauger, "I have ascertained from careful studies over the years that 75% of American mothers share my views on this matter[.] So actually anybody who helps to protect children against this type of corruption is a real friend of the American people—as opposed to a ruthless industry and a handful of venial psychiatrists, educators and child 'experts.'"[72] Wertham also corresponded with Gwilym Lloyd George, the British home secretary, a powerful potential ally.[73]

Through an unlikely union among the Church of England, communists, teachers, and Fredric Wertham, the British Parliament passed the Children and Young Persons (Harmful Publications) Bill in 1955. The British campaign had succeeded in a way that its American predecessor had failed. Wertham's dream of a comic book industry legislated into submission came to pass in Britain a year after the American anti–comic book campaign sputtered out. The bill was the first successful effort to legislate comic books at the national level. It also marked a victory against American cultural and economic power, despite the scrupulous elimination of any anti-American language from the bill. The legislation went beyond outlawing the domestic publication or sale of materials that might harm young minds. It banned the importation of not only any printed matter that violated the bill but even materials used to reproduce such matter, including printing plates or photographic film.[74] This could only have been a reference to violent American comic books, which were reproduced in Britain using these materials and were now legally barred.

FIGHTING BACK

Between 1945 and 1955, the American comic book industry expanded in lockstep with American national power and ambition. In the same period, Cold War imperatives drove the American government to seek a competitive advantage over the Soviet Union through a cultural offensive using middlebrow and elite art, including modernist painting and jazz music. But government agencies did not possess a monopoly on cultural transfers, and in the wake of World War II, unsanctioned products like comic books flooded Europe. These posed a four-pronged challenge to American policy makers: (1) comic books worked against the image of America as the cradle of free individual expression; (2) crime, horror, and jungle titles depicted America as culturally primitive; (3) comic books chipped away at the goodwill generated by higher-brow exhibitions; and (4) comic books provided European communists and others opposed to the growth of American authority with a fertile source of ideological ammunition.

Unsanctioned, uninvited American comic books triggered a sweeping, transnational protest. The global anti–comic book campaign was more than a reflexive response to American power. It was a political response to a cultural challenge. Comic books were different than other American products like films and cars. They were unsolicited by-products of American economic aid and military assistance and proved impossible to regulate through conventional means. No quota system or protectionist measure could keep comics out of Europe. The relentless transmission of uncensored comic books threatened the ability of European leaders to induct citizens into the national reconstruction efforts necessitated by the spiritual and physical damage sustained during World War II. The specter of American interference in domestic cultural affairs fueled major political debates in Britain and France. Wertham further corresponded with outraged activists in numerous other European countries, including Austria, Belgium, Holland, Germany, and Sweden. Communists, centrists, and nationalists united against the menace of unchecked American force. The resulting campaign provided Europeans with a means of protesting against American hegemony without unduly antagonizing the wealthiest and most powerful member of the Western alliance.

CHAPTER SIX
THE FREE WORLD SPEAKS

SPREADING THE DISEASE

In December 1951, the *Queen Mary* ocean liner departed New York City for Southampton, England. It carried, in addition to British prime minister Winston Churchill, twenty-six tons of comic books and other printed materials destined for American soldiers stationed in Europe.[1] On a single ship, tons of comic books full of everything from silly stories and letters from children to frightful images of women being assaulted and murdered were on their way to some of America's most crucial Cold War allies, where they would be sold, loaned, shared, and read repeatedly until they crumbled. The comic book constituted a masterpiece of American production techniques. By combining assembly-line art production with enormous print runs, publishers could sell sixty-four pages of color printing for a dime. The finished product weighed practically nothing and could be carried virtually anywhere and consumed by nearly anyone. The *Queen Mary* and other similar ships were disease vectors. They transmitted American comics across the oceans, depositing them among populations quite unused to their form and contents.

Perhaps the ship carried stacks of the premiere issue of *Murderous*

Gangsters. It offers a variety of brutal pleasures, including a gangster firing a machine gun into a crowd of innocents, a crooked, homicidal union boss, and a blonde woman dismissed as a "peroxided cow" before being beaten.[2] Maybe the ship carried a recent issue of *Complete Love*, in which a bright young woman drops out of high school after her mother dies from a lack of medical care and her father drinks himself to death.[3] The issue of *Two-Fisted Tales* on sale in December 1951 included "Corpse on the Imjin," the sympathetic story of a dead North Korean soldier and exactly the sort of EC tale that so worried army intelligence and the FBI.[4] These comics and countless others were packed with cruelties.

American policy makers and propagandists adapted a two-pronged approach to the threat of commercial comic books abroad, simultaneously attacking and co-opting them. Even as domestic policy makers lent their support to the anti–comic book campaign, federal agencies used their own brands of propaganda comics in support of foreign policy. This decision was motivated by both the popularity of the comic book form and policy makers' race-based assumptions about literacy in Asia, Africa, and Latin America. American comic books indisputably enjoyed enormous popularity worldwide. The increasing importance of the decolonizing world, coupled with the institutional belief that non-White peoples were particularly receptive to comic book propaganda, led policy makers at the State Department and other agencies to dispatch millions of comic books to Latin America, Asia, and Africa. Officials appropriated the medium, a source of domestic and international strife, to counteract the very problem it caused: the portrayal of American culture as violent, racist, and imperial. American officials, however, remained wary of the power of the comic book and generally sought to keep it away from White audiences in Europe, who already saw comic books as symbolic of the worst in American culture.

Propaganda comic books became part of the system of American empire: a component of the nation's international control of information in service of the Cold War.[5] The comic book form proved eminently adaptable to the program of expanding American influence. The USIA and its predecessor agencies, along with the State

Department and even the CIA, used comic books directly in pursuit of victory in the cultural and strategic fields of the Cold War. They were utilized in efforts as diverse as Operation Mongoose—a CIA-led program to overthrow Fidel Castro—and the USIA's long-term effort to promote cooperation between American diplomats and private corporations. The comic book brought together commerce, policy making, and propaganda to promote victory over totalitarianism. What connected all the government's comic book propaganda efforts was an unshakable belief in the fundamental comprehensibility of the comic book form and its unique appeal to non-White audiences.[6]

THE COMIC BOOK REENLISTS

The decision to use comic books for international propaganda emerged from a combination of World War II–era experiments and the demands of the Cold War. The Cold War was, at its core, a battle over ideology, with America and the Soviet Union offering competing blueprints for human progress. In the United States, the core tenets of democracy intertwined with nationalism and a commitment to waging the Cold War on a global scale. This hybrid ideology affirmed that all Americans shared a responsibility to advance the nation's beliefs and interests around the globe.[7] Central to this project was the export of selected, state-sanctioned examples of America's cultural achievements. Through glossy publications and traveling exhibitions of "elite" works of American music and visual culture, policy makers promoted the United States as a modern, sophisticated society that cherished the contributions of contemporary artists, designers, and composers.[8]

While commercial comic books undercut this project by portraying a shadowy, crude society, in the process they revealed a distinctive power of the capitalist marketplace, in which mass culture did not have to be a conservative or stabilizing force.[9] In this way, paradoxically, these "primitive" products revealed some of America's cultural strengths. Comics were free from many of the stigmas attached to other forms of American imperial culture: they were affordable and physically modest, egalitarian, and entertaining.

Wartime agencies had recognized these strengths. Although those propaganda programs ended with the Japanese surrender in 1945, institutional memories of their success lingered and seemed increasingly relevant as the Cold War hardened. By 1950, when President Harry S. Truman described the conflict as a "struggle, above all else, for the minds of men," American propagandists were revisiting the idea of tailored, targeted comic books.[10] Properly controlled, the medium seemed to hold significant promise as a means of reaching peoples deemed vital to America's newfound global mission. Co-opted as a component of America's international propaganda offensive, comic books would transform from a threat into a valued means of achieving what President Dwight D. Eisenhower termed America's ultimate Cold War goal: "to get the world, by peaceful means, to believe the truth."[11]

As American strategists revisited the comic book medium, they first needed to decide whether to follow the WWB's lead and use customized commercial titles or build on the OIAA's experience using specifically designed, overtly propagandistic comic books. They chose the OIAA's method, which offered a number of advantages. By making their own comic books, government agencies would not need to cooperate with unsavory publishers or an industry that increasingly saw the American government, alongside Fredric Wertham, as a threat to its existence. Instead, agencies could contract new firms like Commercial Comics to produce targeted, "tamed" comic books, full of approved artwork and text and free from any taint of the crime, horror, or romance titles that so enraged Wertham and other crusaders.

Propagandists next had to solve three significant problems. First, was the form itself: could comic books, by their very nature, promote the best aspects of American society? As a member of the State Department's Office of International Information argued in 1949, "The presentation to foreign audiences of the principles, policies and purposes of the people of the United States should be in forms that illustrate in themselves our highest standards." The comic book form, he argued, was inherently too unsophisticated and too lowbrow, regardless of the messages it was employed to transmit.[12] This privately communicated concern echoed Wertham's very public critique of comic books, which viewed them as fundamentally problematic.[13]

For such propagandists, the comic book's very shape connoted the worst of American society. The medium itself could not fail to remind readers of America's violence, racism, and disposable culture. This was of particular concern in Western Europe, where, one State Department official lamented, "most people, rightly or not, consider themselves our equals, if not our betters." There, it was feared, comic book propaganda could fuel attacks on the United States from tastemakers, left-wing intellectuals, and nationalists.[14] As a result, when the United States Information Exchange (USIE) initiated a program to send American periodicals to strategically important areas of the world, it classified commercial comics as "undesirable," stressing that they "can accomplish little in the way of promoting an understanding of the United States."[15]

The second and one of the largest problems facing propagandists were the copious racist and sexualized images in so-called adventure or jungle comics. Jungle-themed titles were a White supremacist fever dream, full of primitive men, mostly naked women, and primates that sometimes displayed more intelligence than non-White human characters. They cast serious doubt on America's stated commitment to freedom and equality and the image of a racially tolerant, culturally sensitive United States.[16] Many jungle comics took place in unnamed African countries and typically included female protagonists. Characters like Tiger Girl, Sheena, and Princess Daakar were voluptuous, powerful White women who lived among—and in many cases ruled over—Black people. Typical narratives depicted these non-White characters as simultaneously infantile and belligerent and unable to defend their societies without the aid of an authoritative, nearly nude White woman. They carried a dated imperial image of Africa and Asia to a global audience at a time when potential American allies throughout the decolonizing and nonaligned worlds sought self-determination and a path to modernity. Jungle stories also often portrayed American men and women as greedy racists, intent on swindling or killing any number of Africans or Asians in pursuit of fabulous but unearned wealth.

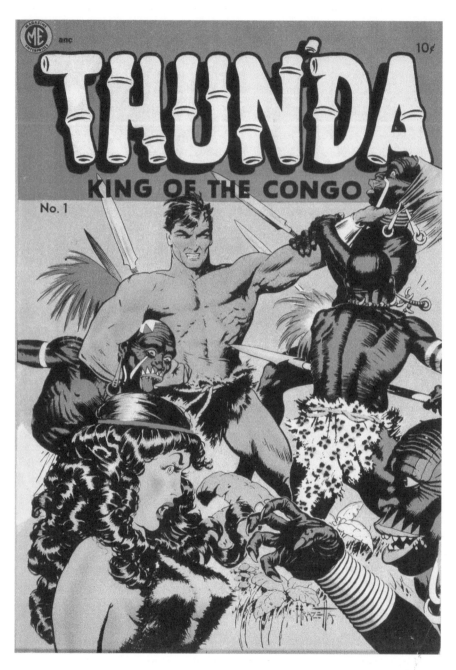

FIGURE 6.1 Images like this one from a 1952 issue of *Thun'da* were common in postwar comics and suggested to global audiences that the United States remained a deeply racist and violent country despite government pronouncements to the contrary.

Tiger Girl, who appeared in Fiction House's *Fight Comics*, typified the jungle comic heroine. Clothed in a tiger-striped bikini, and sometimes nothing at all, she maintained peace through violence with the aid of her Sikh servant Abdolah and a group of trained tigers. In an early postwar adventure, Tiger Girl repeatedly whips a cruel, dark-skinned tribal chief before swimming naked in a river. The offending chieftain then murders one of Tiger Girl's beloved tigers. While she and Abdolah mourn their dead friend, the chief's tribe attacks, leading to a bloody battle in which Africans are stabbed, whipped, and devoured by tigers. Ultimately, the evil tribal chief is run through with a spear, and his stereotypically rendered followers "flee for their lives" in utter terror.[17]

Another narrative, illustrated by Black artist Matt Baker, begins with Tiger Girl smashing the head of an African chieftain garbed in a loincloth and headdress and boasting a large bone through his nose. The story traces a voluptuous American woman and her partner's attempt to enslave the members of Tiger Girl's village by hiding a radio transmitter in a religious statue, then using it to issue orders and plunder the community. The American woman treats her African henchmen as slaves, and they in turn address her as "Missy B'wana." Her partner, an American radio operator, mocks Abdolah, motioning to his equipment and sneering, "Radio! Guess you wouldn't understand about that, big boy!"[18] The story ends in an explosion of violence, with the American woman burning to death at the hands of Tiger Girl and her partner killed by a leopard. As in crime comic books, justice came in the final few panels. But as J. Edgar Hoover warned, young consumers "never read the end."[19]

Adventure-themed comics presented a third problem for propagandists. They applied the racism, imperial tendencies, and violence of jungle comics to Cold War scenarios, replacing chieftains and animals with fanatical communists and non-White nationalists. Typical adventure narratives from the late 1940s and early 1950s included a brawny American hero, sensual and dangerous Asian women, and a multitude of non-White villains, often working on Moscow's behalf. A representative issue of *Wings Comics* from 1946 boasts a torrent of racial stereotypes. Its first story, starring Captain

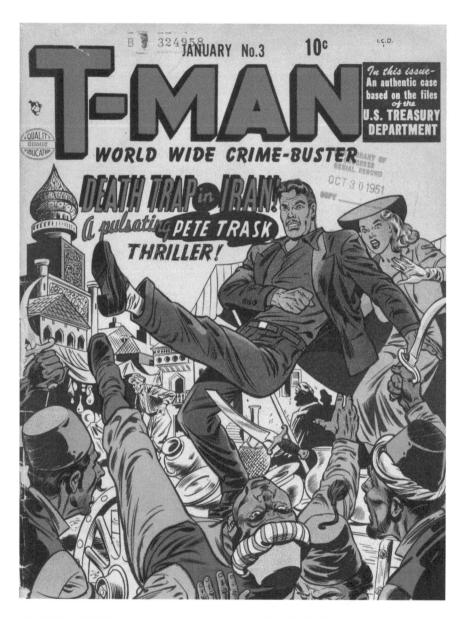

FIGURE 6.2 US Treasury agent Pete Trask spreading ill will throughout the decolonizing world, in this case in Iran in 1952. The next year, the CIA supported a successful plot to overthrow the democratically elected prime minister of Iran.

Wings, includes sexually ravenous Asian women, murderous Sikhs, and buffoonish Chinese men speaking in dialect, all of whom are dependent on a White American pilot. A story about Jane Martin, a curvaceous American nurse and pilot, contains graphic images of a White woman being stabbed in the throat by a sombrero-wearing Mexican crook and numerous close-ups of Jane's legs and cleavage. A story featuring "Suicide Smith" includes another voluptuous Asian woman, who smiles as Smith burns two Latin American men to death in an airplane.

In a 1952 issue of *T-Man* that perhaps unconsciously addressed a contemporary policy challenge—the perceived danger posed by the progressive prime minister of Iran, Mohammad Mossadegh—Treasury agent Pete Trask investigates communist and nationalist influence in Iran's oil industry. Disrupting a meeting between American, British, and Iranian officials, a White character hurls a young pig at an Iranian, shouting, "Here, rag-head! Take this little fellow home and barbecue him for breakfast!" In another scene, a White character beats several Iranians, calling them "dogs." Later, an American woman is disrobed by a blast of air, revealing her underwear and garters. The woman, referred to only by names like "Pet" and "Kitten," ultimately helps Trask defeat a communist espionage ring threatening the Iranian government. In the process, Trask punches a British diplomat, refers to an unnamed Iranian as "Fatty," and tells an outraged Iranian official to "take it up with Washington—see how far you get!"[20] Such stories presented international audiences with images of American power that complicated government efforts to portray the United States as a paragon of enlightened culture and domestic tolerance. They additionally drew unwelcome connections between America's domestic history of racial segregation and violence and American attitudes toward non-Whites in the decolonizing world.

OF SAUDI ARABIANS AND EXISTENTIALISTS

Despite their embarrassing content, commercial comic books were wildly popular. Unlike other cultural forms co-opted by policy makers, such as jazz or modern art, comic books appealed to a large and diverse global audience. Tens of millions of consumers, both at home and abroad, might not be able to identify a Jackson Pollock painting or a Dizzy Gillespie solo, but they surely knew the essential traits of a commercial comic book: it would be American, easy to read, full of lurid advertisements, and likely packed with violence. Comics were also very cheap to produce, distribute, and buy and could be shared among a large group of readers.

Comic books were private media as well. They were not displayed in museums, and libraries wanted nothing to do with such ephemeral entertainment. In contrast to jazz or modern dance, comic book narratives could not be performed in public either. It was as though the form itself marked the medium as private, beyond the control of any federal agency. Some American propagandists and policy makers felt such discomfort over the potential use of comics that they proved unwilling to use even the phrase "comic book" in either internal or external communications. In letters, cables, and memoranda, they tartly corrected any use of the term "comic book," instead suggesting substitutes like "graphic technique," "picture technique," "picture sequence books," "booklet," or "pamphlet."[21] One correspondent was reminded, "'comic' books [is] the wrong name, and liable to misinformation."[22] This uneasiness over the very term *comic book* indicates the sheer power of the form at midcentury and the combination of fear and excitement it raised for federal propagandists. The very traits that made comic books dangerous also made them irresistible to the men and women working to win hearts and minds internationally.

The form was able to meet the complex needs of propagandists tasked with attacking communism and building support for American-style capitalism. At the same time, care had to be taken to ensure that comic book propaganda did not alienate existing or potential allies. The sheer complexity of the task facing propagandists, which required the creation of "material attractive equally to Saudi Arabians and existentialists," led federal officials back to the basic combination of words and images that had proved popular, successful, and adaptable during World War II.[23] Propagandists believed that comic books, with their minimal text and accompanying pictures, were uniquely comprehensible to consumers, regardless of age or level of education. What to critics like Wertham was a dangerous trait—"Comic-book readers are handicapped in vocabulary building because in comics all the emphasis is on the visual image and not on the proper word"—became, in the hands of propagandists, a positive attribute.[24] Essentially, images made propaganda more palatable. As Bartow Underhill of the Private Enterprise Commission (PEC) wrote after reviewing the use of comic book propaganda, "I find that every class of reader, from the top to the bottom, can be reached through the medium of pictures."[25]

Underhill found support for the use of comic book propaganda among the small number of academics who embraced comics as powerful educational tools. Wertham, who attacked their findings as "an all-time low in American science," dismissed these scholars as either dupes or paid apologists for the comic book industry.[26] Still, beginning in the late 1940s, members of the State Department reached out to scholars researching comic book reception, eager to better understand the form's promise as a propaganda delivery system. In April 1950, sociologist Harvey Zorbaugh of New York University hosted a conference titled "The Comics as a Mass Medium of Communication." The attendees included Underhill, and though the PEC noted that "not much [was] accomplished," he remained in contact with Zorbaugh afterward.[27]

Comic books also benefited by being different than the sorts of propaganda used by the Axis powers during World War II, which marked them as something new in formerly occupied territories. The American Embassy in Paris emphasized this, reminding the PEC, "Europeans in general say that they are fed up with the regular propaganda of posters and pamphlets. They are too reminiscent of the Nazis."[28] Comic books' portability and the ease with which they could be hidden or consumed in private also seemed to ensure that they were less subject to censorship or control by hostile governments or groups than other forms of propaganda like radio or film. Comic books were, in the words of the PEC, a "take-it-or-leave-it propaganda"—less strident than a poster or broadcast and able to be consumed at one's own choosing.[29]

Indeed, the comic book's lowbrow form lent it credibility as a means of propaganda. Despite its bold dialogue and brash colors, the comic book seemed a subtle form of communication, capable of moving unnoticed among people in all sorts of environments. Comics could be carried and consumed anywhere, then left behind to be picked up, carried, and consumed again. This meant they could engage readers personally, rather than on a more sweeping, patriotic level.

The most significant factor, though, behind the government's embrace of comic book propaganda was the shifting dynamics of the Cold War and the increasing importance of the decolonizing world.[30] As room for maneuver—both strategically and culturally—disappeared in Europe, American policy makers shifted focus toward Africa, Asia, and Latin America.[31] There, the superpowers competed to offer a more alluring version of modernity to potential client states. In this conflict, culture, technology, and images of an imagined future all played significant roles. The United States could not lure prospective allies simply through sheer strength of arms, and it could not rely on the same kinds of propaganda that it used in Western Europe. This was a new sort of battle for hearts and minds, waged on largely unfamiliar terrain.

American policy makers and propagandists understood that any comic books deployed in the developing world would have to be highly customized and tailored to a specific task. Despite the form's wide applicability, members of the USIE believed that it was equally important to establish where comic book propaganda would not be used. In 1949, Bartow Underhill explained to Malcolm Ater, the head of Commercial Comics, the difference between propaganda destined for Latin America and aimed at Western Europe. Materials used in Latin America, Underhill explained, could "stand a certain amount of emotionalism," while narratives in Western Europe had to "demonstrate rather than preach."[32] John Begg, the head of PEC-endorsed comic book propaganda, stressed, "The cartoon technique

would be good if limited to Latin America and similar areas."[33] Other
members of the PEC affirmed, "The 'comic book' technique—with or
without taste standards—can be a highly effective medium in Latin
America and parts at least of the Far East . . . though pretty certainly
not in most of Europe."[34]

By generally restricting the use of comic books to areas outside
of Europe and to audiences deemed comparatively unsophisticated,
the United States would be less likely to be seen as a cultural plague-
carrier. Propagandists acknowledged this fear of the comic book
form as early as 1949: "The American-born 'comic strip' technique
is one of the most criticized media of entertainment in almost all
sophisticated foreign circles. The criticism, to be sure, is generally
leveled at the contents (crime, war-mongering, sex). It is also aimed
at the form, however: inartistic design, puerile statement of thought,
lack of appeal to the intellect and thereby debasing influence on the
mind. Such criticism stems not only from 'high-brow' academic circles, but also from the intelligent trade-unionist, the businessman,
etc." It was argued that the use of comic book propaganda be limited
to "illiterate" or "semi-literate areas" and kept away from regions
like Western Europe, where elites might attack the United States for
spreading cartoons among the masses.[35]

State Department officials disagreed over whether to emphasize
"cultural diplomacy" or "informational diplomacy." Cultural diplomacy, argued its supporters, would highlight the most desirable and
advanced attributes of American society through cultural exchanges
and the open dissemination of artwork and literature. By appealing
to international elites, cultural diplomacy would win influential
allies abroad, whose pro-American attitudes would, over time, make
their way down to average citizens. Advocates for informational
diplomacy argued that outright propaganda would sway more hearts
and minds, and in less time, than highbrow art and literature. The
Cold War was a constantly shifting battle, and propaganda needed to
be speedily produced and distributed.[36]

Ultimately, President Eisenhower permitted the State Department
to retain authority over cultural diplomacy and granted the USIA
governance over propaganda. Soon, glossy, expensively produced

propaganda comics boasting high-quality artwork and high-minded text were openly distributed abroad as attractive symbols of egalitarian, inclusive American culture. Such titles, with their high production values and positive yet not boastful contents, could be branded as products of the American government or American corporations and used virtually anywhere in overt propaganda campaigns. Other comics could be produced quickly, packed with virulently anticommunist text and language, and distributed without attribution, enabling the American government to reap their benefits without any tangible link to their production. These comics could be customized to suit local needs and contexts and printed internationally to ensure timely distribution. Targeted, covert comic books would circulate through discreet, "highly ingenious" methods. These included furnishing comic books at labor union meetings and stuffing comic books into customers' bags at food markets.[37]

By the early 1950s, the decolonizing world, and Latin America, in particular, became the primary target for American comic book propaganda. In this sense, little had changed since the OIAA's pioneering efforts during World War II. During both conflicts, propaganda comic books highlighted America's cultural and strategic contributions to the hemisphere and the dangers posed by encroaching totalitarian philosophies. Comics in both conflicts held up American society as an ideal while being careful to avoid generating "skepticism" and "envy" and "the temptation to oversell American points of view in too strictly American idiom."[38] Propaganda comics, then, promoted the benefits of American power but only through words and images designed not to inflame locals wary of Yankee imperialism. During World War II, propaganda comics were doubtless aided by the sheer hatefulness of Nazism and its contempt for so-called non-Aryans. Cold War propaganda comics offered similar arguments against a very different sort of enemy. Communism, unlike fascism, offered an alternative, potentially better future to men and women living in the political, cultural, and military shadow of the United States. It was a more insidious and challenging opponent. As part of the larger effort to halt the spread of communism, the United States stepped up its comic book propaganda efforts in countries from Mexico to Argentina.

CRACKING THE IRON CURTAIN

In 1948, the USIA's Private Enterprise Commission (PEC) launched the first postwar comic book propaganda campaign. Headed by John Begg, the PEC functioned as an intermediary between organizations like US corporations, charities, and publishers and policy makers and propagandists. Begg framed the battle between capitalism and communism as, above all, "a struggle for men's minds."[39] In addition to encouraging periodicals like *Time* and *Life* to send unsold editions overseas, the commission collaborated with King Features Syndicate to place "information themes" in comic strips intended for export.[40] The PEC also cooperated with private industry on a variety of comic books.

At least initially, some PEC members dismissed comic books as "highly undesirable" and showed "no enthusiasm" for the medium. But after meeting with several publishers, including Macfadden, whose representatives noted the "commie fear of comic book technique," the project moved forward.[41] Members of the PEC met with organizations including Coca-Cola, General Electric, Kellogg's, and the United Auto Workers, trying to enlist financial and political support for comic book propaganda. But as we saw in chapter 3, the government's effort to reestablish and expand the pulp empire did not gather momentum until the arrival of Malcolm Ater.

Ater's Commercial Comics became the largest producer of state-sponsored propaganda comic books. His relationship with the federal government began in 1949, when the State Department's Press and Publications Division sought to publicize the biographies of several prominent Americans—among them Abraham Lincoln—whose lives might teach readers about key American values. Setting the template for future propaganda titles, the division offered its editorial assistance but requested that Ater deliver a complete package "with design, drawing, captioning, engraving, and printing all provided." The division also provided a set of guidelines regarding artwork and content that typified the tone and appearance of many future government comic books. Drawings and text were to be "in the best possible taste" while remaining "understandable to persons

of rudimentary education who know little about the United States."
For reasons of cost and clarity, the division requested artwork
primarily in black and white, with colors reserved for the cover. To
capitalize on the comprehensibility of the comic book form, Ater was
asked to keep the quantity of text to a minimum and to ensure that
readers could absorb key points through images.[42] Although Ater did
not receive the final contract for this biographical comic book series
due to reasons of cost, the hardening Cold War ensured he was soon
at work on other titles.[43]

The government's use of propaganda comic books accelerated in
1950. On April 20, President Truman gave a speech to the American
Society of Newspaper Editors in which he argued for a global effort
aimed at disproving communist propaganda targeting the United
States. He termed this project the Campaign of Truth. Congress
appropriated funds for the campaign in September, marking the beginning of a new phase in the cultural Cold War and the use of comic
books as propaganda tools.[44] In November, John Dunning of the Press
and Publications Division alerted Ater to the increasing importance
of propaganda and noted the division's plan to make "substantial use
of the cartoons and comic books."[45]

Comics, cartoons, and pamphlets made up a small but significant
part of the larger American propaganda effort. Federal agencies
used a great number of printed materials, including books, original
and reprinted magazines, technical and scientific newsletters, and
photographs. Much of this material was made available to embassies
and outposts around the world, which were often free to choose or
modify selections.

By 1953, the USIA made around five anticommunist cartoons
per week available to American propagandists worldwide.[46] These
included a four-panel, wordless strip called *Little Moe*, which traces
the grim day-to-day life of a beleaguered citizen of an unnamed communist country. A typical example shows Moe shivering in his small
hovel. An overweight party functionary barges in and orders Moe to
hang a picture of a leading communist over his fireplace. In the next
panel, Moe's dog, pleading to come in from the cold, enters the hovel.
In the final panel, the dog sees the grim image above the fireplace

and immediately begins pleading with Moe to let him back outside. In another, Moe spies a communist official, clad in an overcoat, earmuffs, and hat, about to commit suicide by leaping into a frozen river. Moe runs over to the official, presumably to stop him. But Moe instead only asks to have the man's warm clothing. He waves cheerfully to the official as the man drowns.[47] Purely visual comics like *Little Moe* could be used virtually anywhere; there was no need for any translation or adaptation. But *Little Moe* was populated entirely by White characters, which may well have limited its usefulness.

Overall propaganda efforts received additional boosts in 1950. The first followed the presentation by President Truman's advisers of a radical new plan for waging the Cold War. Known as NSC-68, the top secret proposal called for massively increased spending on national security and an emphasis on military, as opposed to diplomatic, containment of international communism.[48] In reframing the Cold War as a zero-sum game waged between communism and democratic capitalism, NSC-68 carried significant implications for America's international propaganda efforts. NSC-68 officially identified propaganda as one of the four means of shaping perceptions of the United States—military, economic, diplomatic, and psychological. Two months later, the invasion of South Korea by communist North Korea seemed to justify the measures recommended by NSC-68.

In the wake of NSC-68, the Campaign of Truth, and the outbreak of war in Korea, Cold War propaganda agencies stepped up the use of comic book propaganda. The USIE deemed comic books a vital weapon in the new conflict. Images, it stressed, along with "the printed word reduced to its simplest form are the most important ways of reaching the great Far Eastern audience. The need is for printed materials produced in great volume, and tailored to the particular race and culture involved." In 1951, as an example, the director of the agency's Far East Regional Production Center (RPC) cited *When the Communists Came*, a comic book that described the results of a communist takeover in a Chinese village. The production center churned out six hundred thousand copies of the title in eight languages—a number most publishers of crime or romance comics would be thrilled to see. He cautioned that this fledgling effort rep-

resented nothing more than a "mere scratch on the vast wall of ignorance, misunderstanding and self-distortion that separates America
from the peoples inhabiting the strife-torn and poverty-stricken
countries of the Far East." More pro-American and anticommunist
comic books would be needed.[49]

That same year, the RPC produced two hundred thousand copies
of *Cracks in the Iron Curtain*, a number so significant that a member
of the Press and Publications Division circled it in an internal document and added an enormous exclamation point. Copies went to the
agency office in Manila and to all diplomatic missions and consular
posts throughout Asia. The comic was a very dark and cynical take
on life behind the Iron Curtain. One panel depicts a man asleep in
bed. His wife opens the door to two hulking secret policemen, their
noses bright red from drink, and screams, "Take him away! He was
cursing our great leader Stalin in his sleep!" In another, two military
officers dine in a fancy restaurant. One of the officers spies a lonely
man at a nearby table and whispers to his comrade, "It's Commissar
Piatkov. He just signed the death sentence for the last of his friends
and feels lonely now. . . ."

Absent the sheer silliness that leavened the *Little Moe* strips, *Cracks
in the Iron Curtain* depicts communism as a system led by crooks
similar to the mob bosses in commercial crime comic books. One
such boss, when confronted by a disheveled and hungry old laborer,
exclaims, "So you complain about the food in the worker's cafeteria?
Who do you think you are, anyway? A Commissar?" Another, while
dining on an enormous bowl of caviar, laughingly declares that this
sort of communism is much too good for proletarians.[50] The images
of betrayal in *Cracks in the Iron Curtain* were staples of crime comics
too, and its heartless communist bosses and military men resemble
characters in them. In the commercial comic book telling of the life of
gangster Louis "Lepke" Buchalter, the killer laughs as one of his hench-
man beats up a teenaged paperboy, flicking a dollar at the bully and
chuckling, "Thanks for the show."[51] He maintains his power through
the relentless use of terror, much like the unfortunate Comrade Piatkov of *Cracks in the Iron Curtain*. In another issue of *Crime Does Not Pay*,
murderer Vic Everhart (the Kill-Crazy Scoundrel) laughs at patriotic

Americans doing their part to win World War II. Condemning them as chumps, he embarks on a wartime crime spree, sustaining himself on the stolen earnings of average citizens and killing an innocent soldier. Just like the communist boss laughing at his hungry worker, Everhart views anyone weaker than himself with contempt.[52]

THE FREE WORLD SPEAKS

Faced with the growing demand for propaganda titles, Commercial Comics duly delivered *The Free World Speaks*, a resounding attack on global communism. In 1951 and 1952, the International Information Agency printed over one million copies of it in thirteen languages, including Arabic, French, Korean, Turkish, and Vietnamese.[53] The comics were distributed through USIA offices around the world.

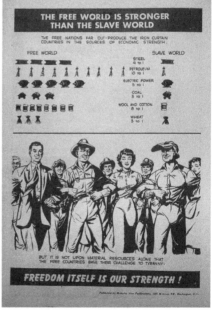

FIGURE 6.3 Federal propaganda titles like *The Free World Speaks* fought against images of the United States formed by commercial comic books. In 1951 and 1952, the government issued over one million copies of *The Free World Speaks* in more than a dozen languages.

Using apocalyptic language and bold imagery, *The Free World Speaks* contrasted the policies of the United States with those of the Soviet Union. It depicted Soviet leader Joseph Stalin as a malignant octopus intent on conquering the world for communism. The most vivid example of Soviet deceit and aggression, argued *The Free World Speaks*, was the invasion of noncommunist South Korea by communist North Korea. The State Department informed Ater that it had received more requests for copies of *The Free World Speaks* than for any other publication and assured Ater that "a repeat performance would be generally welcome."[54]

Other comic books about the war in Korea soon followed and were distributed in multiple languages both inside and outside of South Korea. These included *Korea My Home* and *The Korea Story*, full-color titles that decried communist aggression in Asia. They depicted communists as wholly at fault for the war in Korea and as barbarians who invaded the South "without cause and without warning." *The Korea Story* also stressed that Western nations were not alone in condemning communist actions in Korea. It reminded readers that a variety of leaders in the decolonizing world, including Jawaharlal Nehru of India, Liaquat Ali Khan of Pakistan, and Carlos Romulo of the Philippines, condemned communist aggression in Korea.[55] The title thus promoted two goals: attacking the Soviet Union and its clients and emphasizing a connection between the United States and decolonizing nations. It encouraged readers to see American and the United Nations' intervention in Korea as an effort on behalf of all free peoples.

International reception to *The Free World Speaks* and the subsequent wave of propaganda comics proved to be very positive, and the State Department was soon busy planning future titles.[56] The USIA also began to use the comic book medium under the auspices of the PEC. In 1951, it requested that the Coca-Cola Company fund the production and distribution throughout Latin America of a comic book entitled *Eight Great Americans*, which it described as "suggestive of what can be done for semi-literate people."[57] A representative of Coca-Cola agreed, noting, "Anything more advanced would have no interest for the great majority, and would therefore fail to accomplish a sales promotion or propaganda objective."[58]

FIGURE 6.4 With titles like *Korea My Home*, federal propagandists sought to convince a worldwide audience that the Korean War was wholly the fault of a monolithic communist movement headquartered in Moscow and poised to overwhelm Asia.

The USIA's outreach to Coca-Cola exemplified the growing connection between propaganda and private corporations. Companies like Commercial Comics were already responsible for the creation and production of propaganda comic books, and now federal agencies hoped other companies would help distribute the finished products—which amounted to a covert approach to propaganda.[59] This approach offered significant benefits to the USIA, including reduced costs and a veneer of popular legitimacy.

The relationship, however, was not one-sided but symbiotic. Through their participation in propaganda efforts, corporations received support from the government. In the case of *Eight Great Americans*, Coca-Cola affiliated itself with a comic book boasting exceptionally high production values and the capability of reaching even "semi-literate" consumers. It presumably also received increased visibility in the markets of the decolonizing world. This was undoubtedly of interest to the company's managers, as Coca-Cola and propaganda comic books shared a common problem: they were so unambiguously American and so associated with assembly-line culture that their very presence triggered opposition in postwar Europe. By working together outside the region in which both Coke and comics were derided as lowbrow and imperial, the USIA and the Coca-Cola Company both benefited.

Eight Great Americans epitomized the benefits of comic book propaganda to cultural diplomacy. It was cheap, comprehensible, highly portable, easy to translate, and presented the United States as an inclusive nation dedicated to racial and gender equality and progress. It was initially translated into four languages for distribution across South Asia. Although *Eight Great Americans* shared a common form with commercial comic books, State Department officials ensured that it could not easily be mistaken for an issue of *Crime Does Not Pay* or *Murder, Inc.* It was printed on much heavier, whiter paper stock than a typical comic book, and its interior pages were rendered in sober black and white, rather than lurid primary colors. It contains no advertisements, no violence, and no colloquial language. It opens with an appeal to a global audience, emphasizing the importance of immigrants to the history of the United States. The biographies that

FIGURE 6.5 *Eight Great Americans*, a state-sanctioned propaganda comic book, presented women and people of color as pivotal figures in the history of the United States.

follow include ones of George Washington Carver, Jane Addams, and Walt Whitman, signifying the importance of non-White Americans, women, and cultural creators within American society. It also highlighted the contributions of non-elite Americans, suggesting that American-style capitalism offered opportunities to people ignored under other systems and ideologies. This marked a significant departure from the OIAA's comic books, which had focused on the biographies of White male politicians and military leaders.

The artwork and tone of *Eight Great Americans* is somber, incorporating heroic images of Americans waging war against tyranny and inequality. Although some government-sanctioned propaganda comics were unattributed, *Eight Great Americans* bears the label "Distributed by the Office of International Information of the United States Department of State." *Eight Great Americans* was of high enough quality that the State Department was willing to associate with it.

Indeed, it was distributed even in Europe, since its combination of painterly artwork, glossy paper, and high-minded contents made it safe for distribution in White nations otherwise vehemently opposed to the importation and influence of commercial American comic books.

A very different sort of propaganda comic book was utilized by the USIA in South Asia, however, as early as 1951, while communists there waged war against French forces. That year, it produced millions of copies of a series of anticommunist comics. With names like *Communism and the Family*, *Communism and the Farmer*, and *Communism and Religion*, the comic books appeared in at least seven languages, including Cebuano, Sinhalese, Tamil, and Vietnamese. The black-and-white comics accused communists of disrespecting traditional family structures and values.[60] The titles were printed on lightweight paper and were much less elaborate than *Eight Great Americans* or *The Free World Speaks*. Perhaps as a result of these lower production values, and because the United States had no formal role in the fighting yet, the anticommunist titles were not attributed to any American agency. Such unattributed titles typically required unconventional distribution methods through religious institutions, stores, and as inserts within other, more mundane publications. The contrast between these comics and *Eight Great Americans* exemplified the flexibility of the comic book form and its ability to be employed both overtly as cultural diplomacy and covertly as informational propaganda.[61]

MURDER, INC.

Late in life, Lyndon Johnson told a reporter that he had, upon becoming president, been horrified to learn of the CIA's numerous plans for the violent destabilization of countries in Latin America. The United States had, he exclaimed, "been operating a damned Murder Inc. in the Caribbean."[62] Propaganda comic books were a part of this effort to sow chaos and discontent throughout the region. But they were also used to build support for American aid efforts and to promote American-style capitalism.

As the USIA continued to direct large quantities of comic book propaganda to Latin American audiences, propaganda titles were often coupled to specific policy initiatives, such as the Alliance for Progress and a CIA-backed effort to overthrow Fidel Castro's communist government in Cuba. These programs used comics both as attributed, American cultural outreach and as unattributed, covertly distributed informational propaganda. As with earlier efforts, these campaigns were influenced by American understandings of race and the power of the comic book form.

Operation Mongoose began in late 1961, following the failure of the Bay of Pigs invasion. In its wake, President John F. Kennedy authorized a CIA operation, headed by Major General Edward Lansdale, to stimulate revolution in Cuba and institute a government friendly to the United States.[63] Both President Kennedy and his brother Attorney General Robert Kennedy considered Castro's overthrow to be politically and strategically vital. Robert Kennedy told CIA director John McCone to treat Cuba as "the top priority in the U.S. Government—all else is secondary—no time, no money, effort, or manpower is to be spared."[64] As a result, Operation Mongoose grew into the largest CIA-run operation to date, involving four hundred agents, multiple agencies, sabotage operations, and an array of anti-Castro propaganda.[65] Propaganda strategies included radio broadcasts directed at Cuba and the use of propaganda comics throughout the hemisphere as part of a plan "to utilize all media in mobilizing public opinion in the other countries of Latin America."[66] The USIA was responsible for this aspect of the operation.

Lansdale decreed that USIA comic books would be "gray," or nonofficial, unattributed propaganda material. As such, the USIA handled distribution in much of Latin America, presumably through its well-established, "highly ingenious" methods, while the CIA was responsible for smuggling them into Cuba itself.[67] In July 1962, the USIA reported that it currently had in production or had already distributed five million copies of six anti-Castro comic books. Each addressed a unique topic, including Castro's assault on religion, his control over Cuban media, communist land reform, and communist efforts to indoctrinate children.[68]

El despertar (The awakening), tells the story of two young friends

FIGURE 6.7 Lightweight, compact, and easy to conceal, the federal government made extensive use of titles like *El despertar* in its anticommunist campaigns throughout Latin America and the Caribbean.

who fought together to overthrow Cuban dictator Fulgencio Batista. Their friendship soon crumbles, though, as one man becomes an aggressive communist, prioritizing Castro and revolution over his friends and family. The other, feeling that his family and community have been betrayed by the revolution, which reneged on its promise of land reform, ultimately decides to flee. He tells his fiancée, "There is a saying: the greatest weapon of communism is to promise land, but possession of land is their greatest fear! We were promised land but never received it. I am leaving but I will return one day to live and work in a truly free Cuba." The final panel depicts the pair escaping into the mountains as the cycle of revolution begins again because "the regime of Fidel Castro is a totalitarian dictatorship!"[69] Shaken by the events of the Cuban Missile Crisis, President Kennedy put a stop to Operation Mongoose in December 1962.[70] It was not the last time, however, that his administration turned to comic books to support a specific diplomatic and strategic policy.

The Alliance for Progress began under the Kennedy administration and was billed as a Marshall Plan for the nations of Latin America. Its primary goal was the fostering of democracy in an area dominated by nondemocratic leaders and thought to be susceptible to communist subversion. The program sought to modernize both the social and economic structures of the participating nations.[71] One of American policy makers' primary concerns was that Latin American nations remain free from communist influence. To this end, they deployed a combination of pro-American and anti-Castro comic books.

The USIA launched its "Latin American cartoon book program" in 1961. During the first two years of the program, the USIA produced and distributed over nineteen million propaganda comic books throughout Latin America. They were roughly divided into two types: anti-Castro narratives and stories in support of the Alliance for Progress. Anti-Castro titles were intended to depict "the manner in which communism by its very nature breeds want and hunger in every country it blights." Some of them were the same as titles used in Operation Mongoose (with modifications for local conditions), such as El despertar, La puñalada (The stab), a critique of religious repression in Cuba, and *La mordaza* (The gag), which condemned the communist takeover of mass media. Comics intended to promote the Alliance for Progress were designed to encourage community development and self-help among a variety of demographics, including college students and farmers. One title aimed at farmers, *Hacia una vida mejor* (Toward a better life), set a record after US diplomatic outposts in Latin America ordered over one and a half million copies in its first print run. In 1964, the agency ramped up its effort, channeling over eighteen million comic books into the region. Numbers increased again in 1965 and included five new titles. Such quantities were eerily reminiscent of the domestic postwar comic book craze, during which publishers sold tens of millions of comics every month.[72]

The USIA was as proud of its "highly ingenious" comic book distribution methods as its production numbers. One post issued comic books through schools, billing them as textbooks and reading aids. Comics were given to religious officials for distribution in churches and to labor leaders to pass out at meetings. The USIA even found that its comics could be sold at newsstands alongside commercial titles, even though they displayed no cover price and were not intended for sale. Local newspapers also serialized USIA comic books or packaged them as supplements.[73] In Brazil, Portuguese-language propaganda comic books were folded into copies of mystery magazines and given away to military personnel and students.[74] These methods made clear that the agency still viewed the medium as simultaneously useful and troublesome. Comic books had demonstrated their utility as instruments of American cultural diplomacy, but propagandists still hesitated to distribute them openly. They preferred more clandestine means of dissemination to disassociate the United States from comic book propaganda.

As widespread as they were, propaganda comics did not necessarily convey a single message, as consumers were able to create multiple meanings from their contents. Policy makers hoped that propaganda comics would strike consumers not only as anti-colonial narratives symbolic of the most egalitarian aspects of American society but also as an antidote to the embarrassing wave of uncensored commercial comic books. Doubtless, some consumers did receive such messages. The medium, however, was never really distinct from its earlier, commercial incarnation. Indeed, the propaganda comic book relied on the popularity and lowbrow reputation enjoyed by uncensored commercial titles. Thus, consumers could view propaganda comics as classless media—bold, accessible symbols of a democratic rather than imperial America.

Comic books undoubtedly were a part of America's imperial system, but their appearance and history, along with the controversies they triggered domestically and internationally, provided a useful veneer of authenticity. Popular culture is dynamic. The comic book, which was once a challenging product of marginalized artists, writers, and publishers, was transformed through Cold War imperatives into something quite different. Once appropriated by government propagandists, the comic book traded on its reputation while offering global consumers a controlled and positive image of American society. In short, an unconstrained, violent and racist form was co-opted into a means of fighting communism and promoting an American-style path to the future.[75]

THE FADE OUT

There was no official end to the practice of sending propaganda comic books abroad. The effort, however, had peaked by the mid-1960s. With the end of Operation Mongoose, the eventual failure of the Alliance for Progress, and America's increasing commitment to the war in Vietnam, propaganda comics surely seemed a less compelling means of shaping opinion and policy. The optics of America's war in Vietnam limited the effectiveness of the comic book as a means of promoting American values and policies, particularly in the decolonizing world. American visual propaganda was soon competing with images of Asian children doused with napalm and TV broadcasts of entire Vietnamese villages set ablaze by American soldiers. It was as if the violence, brutality, and racism of uncensored crime and horror comics had been made real. Against these images, printed propaganda had little force.

In the early 1960s, however, a new strain of commercial comic book emerged. It combined the adult themes of postwar comic books with the simple patriotism, bright colors, and superheroes of World War II–era titles. Published by Marvel Comics, they presented the United States in a vastly different light than crime and horror titles. In them, relatable men and women often received superpowers from exposure to atomic radiation. Unlike the simple, uncomplicated, and unsuccessful atomic-powered superheroes that briefly appeared after World War II, Marvel characters were complex, angry, and not always grateful for their newfound abilities. Their adventures performed cultural work at home and abroad that in an earlier decade might have been done by propaganda.

CHAPTER SEVEN
THOR BATTLES THE VIETCONG

THAT RAT BURNED, ALL RIGHT

Martin Goodman, the head of Timely Publications, was a tough and savvy businessman. The son of Russian immigrants, he'd hacked out a place for himself in New York City's competitive publishing industry. Goodman's specialty was magazines. He was not an innovator but skillfully followed trends in the industry. When in 1939 a salesman friend tipped him to the remarkable sales of comic books, Goodman listened. As an experiment, he decided to publish a comic book of his own. In August 1939, immediately before Nazi Germany invaded Poland, the first issue of *Marvel Comics* landed at newsstands. Within its sixty-four pages, Goodman crammed stories designed to reach the widest possible audience. The flurry of new characters included the Sub-Mariner, the belligerent leader of an undersea race; Ka-Zar, a Tarzan knockoff; the Masked Raider, a clone of the Lone Ranger; the Angel, a blond crime fighter; and the Human Torch, an android perpetually engulfed in flames. On the issue's cover, a grinning Human Torch melts his way through a metal wall. Below him, a terrified man fires a gun and gapes as the flames melt the bullet. Initially, Goodman printed eighty thousand copies of his comic book. When they sold out in a week, he ordered a second run of eight hundred thousand copies. This, too, sold out. These were big numbers for a new comic title. At the time, the very popular *Action Comics* sold about a million copies per issue. Suddenly, Timely Publications was in the comic book business.[1]

Like many early superhero comics, the first issue of *Marvel Comics* contained both violent and racist imagery. Ka-Zar's story includes vicious, stereotypical depictions of African men with simian faces. The Human Torch kills a crook by melting his car, shouting, "That rat burned all right!" On the very first page of the Angel's story, one man is beaten to death, another is killed with a gun, and three more are roughed up. Later, the Angel confronts the story's villain, Mike Malone. The narration breathlessly announces that the hero "literally mashes him [Mike Malone] into a pulp." The Sub-Mariner murders two innocent deep-sea divers by crushing their helmets between his hands.[2] In subsequent issues of *Marvel Mystery Comics* (Goodman changed the name after the first issue), the killing and destruction take place in what seems to be New York City. Unlike Superman, who lived in the fictional city of Metropolis, or Batman, the defender of Gotham City, Timely's characters existed in a real and familiar world. During a long-running battle between the Human Torch and the Sub-Mariner, the undersea prince wrecks several notable landmarks, including the Empire State Building, the Bronx Zoo, and the George Washington Bridge. The decision to root fantastic superheroes within a very real context became a tradition at Timely. It made characters more plausible and empathetic—they worked and struggled in a world recognizable to readers.

Although Timely was one of very few major comic book publishers that did not cooperate with the WWB during World War II, the company did wage war against the Axis on its own terms. A year before the Japanese attack on Pearl Harbor, Timely's newest patriotic hero took the war to Germany. Created by Joe Simon and Jack Kirby, Captain America is the alter ego of a weak young man named Steve Rogers. Out of patriotic duty, Rogers volunteers to take an experimental serum designed to transform him into an enormously strong "super soldier." The serum works, but just moments after Rogers

completes his transformation, the serum's inventor, Professor Rein-
stein, is shot by a Nazi spy. He dies before committing the serum's
formula to paper, leaving Rogers as America's lone super soldier. In
December 1940, he made his debut in the first issue of *Captain America*, which bore one of the most striking cover images of all time. On
it, Captain America lunges across a room to smash Adolf Hitler in
the face. Kirby marks the point of impact with a bright, white circle
that draws the viewer's eye to Hitler's head, twisted in agony from
the blow. The Nazi falls backward, as his bodyguards unleash a storm
of bullets at Captain America. The hero deflects one bullet with his
shield and lunges between the others. It remains a powerful antifascist image and a statement of Goodman's hostility toward Nazism.

The first issue of *Captain America* sold about one million copies, a
very respectable number. And as the comic book industry expanded
during World War II, *Captain America* continued to sell about half a
million copies per issue.[3] The war boosted Timely's sales numbers
overall, along with those of the industry in general. Comics not only
grew their juvenile readership but also generated a new and growing
adult audience made up of both civilians and members of the armed
forces.[4] In 1943, an editor at Famous Funnies wrote the WWB to
alert its members that, "whereas the audience we reached was once
primarily childish, our books now have their greatest percentage of
sale in the Army and Navy bases, both in and out of the country."[5]
Wartime market research suggested that nearly half of all soldiers
and sailors bought and read comic books.[6] Timely's many patriotic
superhero titles benefited from this demographic expansion, and
Goodman's comic book stable thrived.

MIGHTY MARVEL

In the wake of the war, Goodman kept chasing the latest trends,
unleashing a torrent of new titles like romance, crime, and horror
comic books. Although he employed talented artists and writers, including Mickey Spillane and Patricia Highsmith, Timely's output was
fairly uninspired, and it faced stiff competition on the newsstand. By
1950, roughly three hundred comic book titles of all genres struggled

to attract readers.[7] One year earlier, faced with declining sales, Goodman laid off a number of his artists. Business got even worse in the wake of Dr. Fredric Wertham's anti-comic book campaign, the publication of *Seduction of the Innocent*, and the 1954 Senate hearings on the comic book industry. By the time the comics code went into effect in 1955, the industry had been shattered. Many comic book publishers went out of business, and the survivors scrambled to revamp their product lines. By the mid-1950s, the number of titles for sale plummeted by 50 percent. In 1956, things got worse when Goodman lost his longtime distributor. His new distributor limited his output to just eight titles per month. This triggered a second round of layoffs at Timely. Business did not significantly improve until 1961, when artist Jack Kirby and writer Stan Lee birthed a new series of superhero titles. As if signaling the break between Timely's derivative postwar products and this fresh wave of superheroes, the company changed its name to Marvel.

Kirby, Lee, and the rest of the staff at Marvel had to not only assemble a compelling new generation of superheroes but also ensure that their creations complied with the extremely restrictive censorship code maintained by the CMAA. Lee, in particular, sought a more mature audience for the new superhero titles, but making comic books appealing to adults was not as straightforward as it had been before the CMAA. The most obvious means of attracting adults—adding sex, violence, romance, and dark scenarios—were all off-limits and risked drawing unwanted attention from the federal government. The challenge facing Marvel then was to craft superheroes appealing not only to younger readers but also to adults through a combination of more sophisticated narratives, emotional conflicts, and realistic settings—all while slipping past the censors. Remarkably, Kirby, Lee, and their colleagues succeeded. They built an entire world that featured bright colors, costumes, and banter that kept younger readers entertained, while realistic settings, relatively complex characters, and quality artwork attracted older readers. The dialogue in early Marvel comic books was clearly geared toward adults too, indicating that the creators saw their own work not as entertainment for kids but as something richer and more nuanced.

Because of their unique combination of pathos and orthodox pro-American politics, the first wave of Marvel superheroes straddled the cultural space between overt propaganda comic books and commercial titles. To be clear, the federal government was not involved in the creation of these characters; indeed, Timely Comics did not even cooperate with the WWB during World War II. What Marvel achieved, though, was a unique and powerful combination of sophistication and emotion that effectively masked their more overt pro–Cold War perspectives. A consumer could read a Marvel comic book and focus on the very human heroes within or the stridently anticommunist narratives. The results were entertaining either way.

There are remarkable similarities in language and image between commercial Marvel comic books and World War II–era propaganda comics produced in conjunction with the WWB. Both types, separated by almost twenty years and created under very different circumstances, stress the need for patriotism, participation, and sacrifice. Both use similar images of war and suffering to emphasize why it is so important to fight totalitarianism. What makes the first generation of Marvel superhero comics unique is that they cloaked this pro-American, anticommunist language and imagery beneath very compelling characters and stories. These qualities served a function similar to that of advertising in World War II–era propaganda titles: both worked to obscure the more conventional, conservative messages beneath. At the same time, Marvel superheroes, just like their wartime predecessors from other publishers, were zealously patriotic and anticommunist. In this sense, the first wave of Marvel superhero comic books was a sort of hybrid between commercial and propaganda titles.

These Marvel characters totally reshaped the popular understanding of American commercial comic books, both at home and abroad. The artwork and writing behind the Fantastic Four, the Hulk, and Spider-Man transformed comic book heroes from corny do-gooders into complex, endearing symbols of American technological and moral achievement. Over time, they would also change the post-code medium from juvenile entertainment into something far more complicated and financially valuable. Comic books became the source of

American myths, a foundation for the most lucrative revolution in American film since World War II. In the wake of Marvel, comics occupied a unique place in global popular culture: neither lowbrow nor sophisticated, but a blend of both. Marvel comics were, and remain, an example of an "American kitsch myth."[8]

Before the implementation of the CMAA and its censorship code in 1955, American commercial comic books circulated around the world as part of the nation's Cold War project. Wherever an American soldier was stationed, comic books soon followed. These comics remained in place long after the soldier returned home, reaching multiple readers before disintegrating. The CMAA's code, indicated by a large, white stamp on the cover of all approved comic books, changed this situation. For the first time, American commercial comic books reached global audiences with a seal of approval from a supervisory agency. The CMAA stamp suggested to adult observers that the contents of a particular comic were harmless. It implied not only that Americans saw no problem with the crude images of non-White characters in Marvel comic books but also that these representations were innocuous to young readers. This was one of Wertham's primary objections to the CMAA: it legitimized any contents, regardless of how they might represent American beliefs or policies domestically and internationally. The CMAA, then, did not eliminate the dangers posed to American global standing by the commercial comic book. Indeed, it complicated global understandings of the medium by suggesting that, after 1955, comic books were essentially benign.

Marvel billed its new superhero comics as edgy and contemporary. But superhero stories, no matter how atypical, are largely conservative. At their core, superheroes aim to enforce justice—typically a synonym for law and order. Tony Stark is a rakish millionaire with a cutting sense of humor, but he is also an integral part of the American military-industrial complex. He is bitterly anticommunist and voices no discomfort with America's imperial adventures. The Fantastic Four, despite their infighting, personal crises, and melancholy, put all these humanizing traits aside to maintain domestic law and order. So, too, does Thor, a Norse god so reflexively pro-American that he volunteers to fight the North Vietnamese. Compared to earlier crime and horror titles, Marvel comic books included virtually no violence or sexual imagery. Heroes generally punched their way out of predicaments or solved problems with technology, and women were neither the perpetrators nor victims of extreme brutality.

PATRIOTISM AND PARANOIA

The first of Marvel's new superhero titles was the *Fantastic Four*, which premiered with a cover date of November 1961, though it likely went on sale in August or September.[9] This was just as the East German leadership, with the consent of the Soviet Union, began construction on the Berlin Wall. It was an extremely tense point in the Cold War, with many West Germans and Americans calling for President Kennedy to take action. Kennedy, though, feared precipitating a nuclear war that would destroy not only Germany but also the United States and the Soviet Union. Ultimately, he concluded that a wall was "a hell of a lot better than a war." And in a sense the decision to seal East Germany off from the West reduced the pressure on Kennedy. Yes, the wall was—and remained—a painful symbol of Soviet strength in Eastern Europe and a monument to political and cultural repression. Its presence, however, largely eliminated the refugee crisis, during which huge chunks of the East German professional classes fled to the West. The wall reduced tensions around this issue, simplifying relations between the superpowers (although the West's refusal to risk war over the wall certainly generated ill will and frustration among portions of the NATO alliance).[10]

The story of the Fantastic Four is drenched in patriotism, paranoia, and the faith in military technology that helped to define American popular culture between 1945 and the height of the war in Vietnam. The four are Dr. Reed Richards, an eminent scientist; Benjamin Grimm, a renowned pilot; Susan Storm, the fiancée of Richards; and Johnny Storm, her teenaged brother. Richards is determined to beat the Soviet Union to space and working feverishly on a rocket of his own design. When he realizes that cosmic conditions are just right for spaceflight, he decides to launch the rocket ahead of

FIGURE 7.1 Unlike earlier heroes created by exposure to radiation, the Thing weeps over his newfound form and powers.

schedule, without the consent of the US government. Although only Richards and Grimm are required to fly the rocket, the Storm siblings insist on joining the mission. On the way to the launchpad, Grimm warns the group that Richards has not adequately studied the effects of radioactive "cosmic rays" on humans. He worries that the four will be injured or even killed by the rays but is convinced to fly the rocket when Susan Storm accuses him of cowardice, shouting, "Ben, we've got to take that chance, unless we want the commies to beat us to it!"

The four sneak aboard the experimental rocket and launch themselves into space. The rocket's shielding proves an inadequate defense against cosmic rays, which cause the crew to lose consciousness. On autopilot, the craft returns to earth, where the four stumble out, unsure of what has happened. Incredibly, Susan Storm soon disappears, terrifying herself and the other members of the group. She eventually reappears but cannot explain what has just happened. Ben Grimm, outraged that Richards has risked all their lives, begins screaming at the scientist. But as he does, his body changes shape, transforming into an enormous animated heap of orange rocks. Now possessing superhuman strength, Grimm tears a tree out of the ground and tries to kill Richards. Recoiling, Richards realizes that his body has become plastic: he can stretch and lengthen himself in any direction. Richards wraps himself around Grimm, screaming, "You've had this coming for a long time, Ben!" Horrified by the scene, Johnny Storm screams, "You've both turned into monsters," as his body bursts into flames.[11]

What makes the origin of the Fantastic Four so compelling is that its members are terrified by their transformations and initially have no real interest in being superheroes. Rather than exulting in their newfound powers, the four are repelled by the changes wrought to their bodies by cosmic radiation. The members argue with each other and wrestle with feelings of self-loathing. Intriguingly, they also eschew the use of alter egos. Although each member of the four takes a new name (Richards becomes Mr. Fantastic, Grimm becomes the Thing, Susan Storm becomes the Invisible Girl, and her brother becomes the Human Torch), they live publicly under their true names. At the same time, there is an inescapable optimism to the Fantastic Four. They inhabit a city (initially called Central City but soon changed to New York City) full of gleaming buildings, massive high-tech machines, and incredible inventions conceived by Jack Kirby. As with Iron Man, the four place enormous faith in the powers of science and technology to solve problems both practical and fantastic. This faith includes confidence in the federal government and the defense industry as well as a cavalier attitude toward nuclear weapons.

In the fourth issue of the series, the Fantastic Four face off against a revived Sub-Mariner, who unleashes Giganto, a vast sea creature, in New York City. To stop Giganto, the Thing sprints from one military depot to the next until he finds a nuclear bomb. Strapping the bomb to his back, the Thing leaps into Giganto's open mouth and slogs through his digestive system. With scant seconds to spare, the Thing drops the bomb inside Giganto and jumps to safety out of his jaw. The monster, which has been standing in the middle of Manhattan, is destroyed by the atomic bomb, but there is no damage to the surrounding city, the Thing, or the rest of the Fantastic Four. Such treatment of atomic weapons is reminiscent of earlier, pre-code comic books like *Atomic War* and *Atom-Age Combat*. In them, the bomb was a uniquely American technology. Created in the United

States, it was capable of inflicting massive damage on the nation's enemies but unable to shatter American society or democracy.[12] The first wave of Marvel superhero comic books took a similar approach, providing Tony Stark with pocket-size nuclear weapons and enabling heroes previously mutated by radiation to use nuclear weapons with impunity.

Using a nuclear weapon to destroy a sea monster in the middle of Manhattan is not terribly different than Donald Duck detonating an atomic bomb in Duckburg.[13] In *Donald Duck's Atom Bomb*, dating from 1947, the bomb is also played for laughs, rather than horror. The essential difference between the two narratives is that *Donald Duck's Atom Bomb* is clearly a humorous title (albeit in very poor taste).[14] *Fantastic Four* is a superhero comic book incorporating fairly sophisticated characters. Yet the story treats atomic weapons as a joke—a means of splattering marine innards across the borough without poisoning anyone.

In another early issue from 1963, the four team up with Nick Fury, then employed by the CIA. Fury is on the trail of the Hate-Monger, who wields a "hate ray" capable of bringing out the deep-seated prejudices and rage in anyone caught in its beam. Clothed in a hooded, purple outfit and surrounded by a team of storm troopers, the Hate-Monger arrives in Manhattan with Fury close behind. Fury explains to the Fantastic Four that the Hate-Monger and his hoods have disrupted an agency plan to remake San Gusto, a fictional South American republic, in the image of United States. Fury brazenly admits, "Well, Uncle Sammy has been pouring billions into San Gusto to make it a show-place of democracy! But suddenly, everything's gone nuts down there! A revolution started, and it looks like the government's gonna collapse! If that happens, it could upset the balance of power in South America! So it mustn't happen, dig?"[15] In this remarkable monologue, Fury summarizes American foreign policy toward newly formed nations in the decolonizing world: if a country was in danger of becoming communist, the American president had an obligation to unleash the CIA and trigger a regime change. No country could be permitted an anti-American government because even one hostile nation would cause all the others in the region

FIGURE 7.2 In a scene from 1963 that echoes actual CIA interventions throughout the decolonizing world, Nick Fury discusses the absurdity of permitting a Latin American nation to go communist after the United States has spent billions turning it into "a show-place of democracy."

to fall. Fury is describing the "domino theory" of international relations, and as this issue of the Fantastic Four went on sale, the US government was embarking on a path that would follow this theory to its ultimate, terrible conclusion in Vietnam.

After absorbing Fury's speech, the Fantastic Four and Fury chase the Hate-Monger back to San Gusto. There, they quash the revolution and remove the Hate-Monger's purple hood. They are aghast to learn that he is, in fact, Adolf Hitler. It is a fantastic, impossible twist ending to a tale of CIA subversion in the South America. The narrative takes it as a given that the citizens of San Gusto want an American-style democracy, rather than an alternative form of government. Indeed, the entire battle takes place between American forces (the CIA and Fantastic Four) and the Hate-Monger's men, without any participation from the country's citizens. It is an eerie echo of the proxy wars fought across the global south during the Cold War. In 1963, this was not yet a discredited philosophy, and the comic book presents the CIA and the concept of American intervention in a very positive light, both beneficial and unbeatable.

The difference between earlier comics that fetishized American military technology and Marvel titles again lies in the perpetrators and targets of technologized violence. In the pre-code title *Atomic War*, the American military uses large numbers of atomic weapons to reduce much of the Soviet Union, Eastern Europe, and Asia to a smoldering, radiating ruin. But it does not show average communist citizens dying from flash burns or radiation poisoning; images of casualties are generally restricted to members of the communist bloc's armed forces. But when Tony Stark weaponizes the transistor and carries it to Vietnam in *Tales of Suspense*, he directs its terrifying power at small groups of Vietcong guerrillas. He does not aim his inventions at vast, faraway cities but at nearby individuals. His adventures, like those of other Marvel heroes, deal in a sort of asymmetrical personal violence. The force of the American military-industrial complex, in the form of Iron Man, is brought to bear on peasants fighting a war of national liberation. The question, then, is whether these depictions of overwhelming American military technology deployed against poorly armed opponents caused the sort of damage, internationally, as earlier pre-code comic books were feared to. It is reasonable to suggest that the sort of technological hubris and intimate violence in the first wave of Marvel comics struck some overseas readers as troubling.

INTO THE BLAZE OF BATTLE

Where modern technology proved unable to solve problems, Marvel's writers and artists often substituted brute force. Perhaps the greatest exemplar of this approach was Thor, the Norse god of thunder, who became a superhero in the pages of *Journey into Mystery*. Despite being a thousand-year-old deity, Thor is also an eager cold warrior and anticommunist. Indeed, in an early appearance, he travels to Vietnam to try and defeat the North Vietnamese single-handed. Unlike Iron Man, who relies on ingenuity and technology, Thor uses Mjolnir, his magic hammer. That which cannot be finessed by American technology may be bludgeoned into submission with his ancient tool. In "Into the Blaze of Battle," Thor chases his archenemy and brother, Loki, to South Vietnam. While flying over the country, Thor is brought down by antiaircraft fire, then knocked out by a gigantic mortar blast. When he wakes, Thor finds himself in the hut of a friendly South Vietnamese family. His initial thought, "They think of me as an omen from their God," is soon confirmed when a young peasant tells Thor, "Buddha has answered our prayers! He sent thee to destroy the guerrillas."

Back on Loki's trail, Thor spots a flight of helicopters. He laments the look of fear on every villager's face and worries that the small number of helicopters is not enough to destroy the numerous and "cunning" communists. Heading into the jungle, Thor transforms into his human alter ego, the thin and disabled Dr. Don Blake, and is ambushed by communist guerrillas who bring him to their jungle base. There, Blake finds himself imprisoned along with the kindly family that rescued him. The family is horrified to learn that their jailer, the communist officer in charge of the base, is their long-lost son and brother. When the family pleads with him for mercy, he screams, "You do not matter! Nobody matters! Only the communist cause is important! People mean nothing! Human lives mean nothing!" He executes his entire family, save for his younger sister, who manages to escape. Thor reassumes his godly form, chasing after the sister and swinging his hammer "with the crushing, smashing force of a nuclear holocaust." He injures or kills virtually every Vietcong soldier on the base and warns the jailer, "No place on earth will hide you from me! For I shall return, and when I do, the hammer of Thor shall be heard in every village—every home—in every heart throughout this tortured land!" After Thor and the sister escape, the brother, horrified by his embrace of communism, commits suicide. His last words offer a grave rebuke: "It was communism that made me what I am—that shaped me into a brutal, unthinking instrument of destruction! To communism, then—may it vanish from the face of the earth and the memory of mankind!"[16]

The representation of guerrillas, communists, and American power in "Into the Blaze of Battle" is quite different from some of EC's earlier, pre-code military narratives, like "Contact," from the second issue of *Frontline Combat*. The story opens in Korea in 1951 as an American army unit tries to clear an area of Chinese opposition.

FIGURE 7.3 In this issue of *Journey into Mystery* from 1965, Thor, the Norse god of thunder, reflexively joins the United States in its battle against communism.

One member of the unit, Durkee, disparages the fighting skill of Chinese soldiers and derisively refers to them as "gooks." Weems, a much smaller and quieter member of the unit, uncharacteristically loses his temper, screaming, "Always using that dumb word, 'gook!' You make it sound like you're a big-shot American superman! You're no superman!" At that moment, the Americans are overrun by a mass of Chinese soldiers. In such close quarters, the men fight hand-to-hand using fists, nails, bayonets, and anything else that falls to hand. It is a savage, intimate struggle sprawling across an entire page. The Americans, for all their overwhelming technical superiority, are no better off than the Chinese. The violence is symmetrical: Durkee cries out for help, and Weems responds by crushing the skull of the Chinese soldier trying to stab Durkee. Nearby, two Americans fall to the ground, stabbed by Chinese bayonets. Unaccustomed to such fighting, all but two members of the American unit are killed; Weems and his sergeant retreat and hide. Soon, a massive collection of American bombers arrives overhead. The two Americans cheer as the aircraft drop bombs on the Chinese forces, wiping them out. Nearly hysterical, the sergeant tells Weems, "Americans aren't supermen! An American is a man just like an Asiatic is a man! But we can produce!" The two know that only the brute force of American industry has saved them. When forced to fight hand-to-hand against Chinese opponents, they cannot win.[17]

Marvel's early superhero stories treated Asians rather differently, hewing to the Cold War consensus idea of Asians as ruthless communists intent on conquest through subversion and other "un-American" means. In another early appearance, Thor confronts a different Asian communist villain, the Radioactive Man, which incorporates the same racial tropes as "Into the Blaze of Battle." Its Chinese characters are universally devious and homicidal, and non-White people are equated with communism. The story opens in India, where Indian troops are fighting Chinese invaders. This reflected a very real contemporary crisis, the Sino-Indian War of 1962. The conflict took place at the same time as the Cuban Missile Crisis, which captivated the attention of the superpowers and much of the remaining world as well. It was not until the end of the crisis that the United States turned its consciousness to India's fight against China. Here, Thor journeys to the war zone to help the Indians. As in Vietnam, he, a god, reflexively enters a Cold War conflict on the side of the United States and the West.

Enraged by Thor's intervention, the Chinese communist leadership demands that the nation's scientists invent a way to defeat him. One nuclear specialist, Chen Wu, volunteers for the task. Mao Zedong accepts his offer but warns that failure will result in Chen Wu's death. Chen Wu, however, is even more cunning than the communist leaders of China. He develops a system that enables his body to safely absorb a massive amount of radiation, which turns him into a living, radioactive weapon. His plan is to first defeat Thor and then conquer the world. Deposited in New York City by a Chinese submarine, Chen Wu issues a challenge to Thor and stomps through the city, leaving a trail of radioactive waste in his wake. Thor eventually defeats him by using his hammer to create a tornado that carries Chen Wu back to China, where he vanishes in an atomic explosion.[18]

In its lighthearted and spectacularly unrealistic portrayal of atomic power, this and other Marvel narratives share similarities with earlier, state-sanctioned propaganda comics like *The H-Bomb and You* and *Bert the Turtle Says "Duck and Cover."* Both Thor stories emphasize the themes of obligation and participation, illustrated by Thor's reflexive participation in the Cold War and his enthusiastic support for American policies, allies, and goals. In *The H-Bomb and You*, children learn that their survival depends on their involvement in the Cold War. The comic book portrays the United States as a nation under siege by hostile, nuclear-armed forces and suggests that all Americans have a role to play in achieving victory. Doubt is poisonous, "the kind of talk an enemy would have you believe."[19] Between participation and American technology, victory is possible. This is the same sort of message woven into early Thor comic books: even a Norse god cannot ignore the conflict between East and West.

These stories also use the same sorts of racial imagery found in World War II–era comic books like *US Marines in Action* and *All-Star Comics*. America's opponents are defined as "others" on the basis of their race, inherent brutality, and intrinsic, warlike nature. Asian characters appear as crudely rendered stereotypes with exaggerated teeth and simian features. Like the WWB titles, which used the low-brow identity of comic books to obscure the propaganda within, the new Marvel titles took similar advantage of the comic form. Their bright colors, unique characters, and sparkling language distracted from the simple fact that they were quintessentially American. The characters went abroad to fight and kept the home front free from infiltrators, criminals, and tyrants. In spite of their overt darkness, these characters were also effortlessly, subtly patriotic.

HUMANITY WEAPONIZED

The "Marvel method" was met with considerable success. Writer Stan Lee found himself in demand as a speaker on college campuses, to the point that the company hired an employee to coordinate communication with schools around the country, "Dazzling" Debby Ackerman.[20] College students wrote letters to Marvel praising their comic books and asking questions about their new characters. Marvel responded by creating a fan club called the Merry Marvel Marching Society (MMMS). The membership kit included a button "designed to look great when worn next to your Phi Beta Kappa key." Soon, MMMS clubs sprung up at schools, including Oxford, Cambridge, and Princeton, and the society claimed fifty thousand members. By 1966, *Esquire* magazine featured the Marvel universe in its annual college issue, and Marvel comics started to include advertisements for adult products.[21] It was clear that Marvel artists and writers had succeeded in creating a comic book world that appealed to a wide range of ages—even within the constraints of the CMAA.

Such cultural unanimity was appropriate to the times in a ghastly way: all humanity was threatened by nuclear annihilation too. It was the era of the Cuban Missile Crisis, which remains one of the most terrifying events in history. The crisis began when Soviet premier Nikita Khrushchev ordered Soviet nuclear missiles sent to Cuba. He imagined that these weapons, just ninety miles from the United States, might offset America's otherwise overwhelming nuclear arsenal. Unfortunately for the Soviets, an American spy plane flying a routine mission over Cuba discovered the missiles as their bases were being assembled. The revelation triggered panic and outrage among American leadership. Fueled by this anger and fear, over the course of thirteen days in October 1962, the United States and the Soviet Union wrestled with the prospect of a nuclear holocaust.

From the vantage point of the twenty-first century, it seems outrageous, if not perfectly insane, that the two superpowers came so close to destroying the planet. But the stakes of the Cold War, coupled with the size of each side's nuclear arsenals, made nuclear war a very real possibility. The apocalyptic tales of planetary suicide printed in comic books like *Captain Marvel Adventures*, *Weird Science*, and *Weird Fantasy* seemed likely to come true. Mercifully, President John F. Kennedy managed to sideline his most hawkish military and civilian advisers. Khrushchev, too, realized that he was in danger of losing control of the situation and that an accident, a misinterpreted order, or a jittery local commander might start an omnicidal war from which there could be no recovery. He and Kennedy reached a secret deal to remove the missiles in Cuba in exchange for the removal of American missiles in Turkey, averting a holocaust.[22] But Americans now understood how very vulnerable they were. Capitalist technology and modernist thinking, it was clear, could not solve all the problems of the Cold War. Some issues hinged on human emotions, restraint, and dumb luck.

Yet in early 1963, in the pages of *Tales of Suspense*, there is no trace of the cultural and political aftershocks of the missile crisis, no challenge to America's embrace of technology and modernism as the means of liberating the decolonizing world. All is well with million-aire bachelor Tony Stark. An inventor and munitions manufacturer, Stark is also a superhero: Iron Man. In one issue, he rattles off his obligations, nearly all of which relate to national defense and the Cold War: "Think of the time I must spend managing my munitions plants around the world. Then, there's my scientific research! Sometimes I work on medical problems. Other times it might be a space problem. And of course, I'm always trying to help the US defense effort." Then, in an internal monologue, Stark details his additional obligations as Iron Man: "If Iron Man isn't battling gangsters, he's fighting America's enemies from within and without."[23] His monologue stretches across two pages, and laced among his pronouncements are images of Stark perfecting an atomic cannon and building a military satellite. He is a happy cold warrior: content in his work and comfortable in his conviction that White America offers a suitable model for other societies. Stark is also the epitome of glamour and a dedicated anticommunist, fighting aggression abroad and subversion at home: a comic book combination of James Bond and Howard Hughes.

Iron Man first appeared in *Tales of Suspense* 39, which went on sale in December 1962. From the outset, both the superhero and his alter ego were inseparable from the American military-industrial complex. Created by artist Jack Kirby and writer Stan Lee, his first story takes place almost entirely in Vietnam. It opens, though, in a secret laboratory "somewhere in the U.S. defense perimeter" built for Stark. In front of an audience of generals, he demonstrates the power of his new invention, a "tiny transistor" that can increase the force of any device. Stark exults in showing that a small magnet, coupled to the transistor, can tear the armored door off a bank vault. He asks a general, "Now do you believe that the transistors are capable of solving your problem in Vietnam?" Elated, the general assures Stark that he is ready to believe anything. The action then shifts to a small village in South Vietnam that is being terrorized by a "Red guerrilla tyrant" named Wong Chu.

In a nearby jungle, Stark is on patrol with a small group of American soldiers who are testing his new transistor. Stark cheers as the soldiers destroy a band of communist guerillas. Suddenly, Stark trips an explosive booby trap that kills everyone else in the group and leaves him severely wounded. A piece of shrapnel lodges in Stark's heart, giving him just days to live. He is soon taken prisoner by Wong Chu's troops and brought to the communists' jungle base. There, Wong Chu recognizes the inventor and falsely promises him access to a doctor if he will build a new weapon for the communists. On the verge of death, Stark agrees but vows to himself, "My last act will be to defeat this grinning, smirking, red terrorist." Wong Chu then brings Stark to a room full of scrap metal, old electronics, and tools and provides him with an elderly South Vietnamese scientist. Soon, Stark and the fiercely anticommunist scientist begin designing an iron suit that will keep Stark alive and enable him to destroy Wong Chu's base.

With Stark teetering between life and death, the Vietnamese scientist straps him into the iron suit. It transforms the slim, dapper Stark into a great movable pile of gray metal. The suit has enormous metal boots and gloves and a mask that obscures his face with a blank, expressionless sheet of iron. Stark has become something akin to the weapons he designs: a triumph of technology and know-how over weakness. He is humanity weaponized in the service of the Cold War. Powered by Stark's transistors, which he has somehow crafted from the junk in his prison, the suit not only keeps him alive but also grants him "unbelievable" strength. He escapes from prison by cloaking himself in an overcoat and a fedora. When night falls, Stark finds Wong Chu beating up a villager and challenges him to single combat as Iron Man. "Then, before the startled eyes of the red hordes, two electronically powered arms seize Wong Chu, lifting him as easily as they would a toy!" Although Wong Chu escapes, Iron Man ultimately kills him before disappearing into the jungle.[24]

Stark's escape offers a window into popular American perceptions

FIGURE 7.4 Seen here in his first appearance in 1962, Iron Man distilled the American military-industrial system into a single human-mechanical hybrid.

of race, militarism, and anticommunism in the mid-twentieth century: using materials discarded by the communist Vietnamese, he engineers his own escape from a technologically primitive and savage society. The idea that a Vietnamese scientist might have been able to achieve similar results given access to similar materials is, in context, laughable. It is Stark's uniquely American genius that enables him to build his iron suit. Stark cheerfully and profitably builds weapons intended to kill communists because he has been asked to do so by his government. He does not permit himself any curiosity as to why communists oppose American interests abroad or why they might not welcome Western intervention in their countries.

In the pages of *Tales of Suspense*, it was as if the enormous postwar wave of violent, sexual comic books had never existed. In this comic book United States, gender roles reverted to World War II–era norms. Stark surrounded himself with attractive women, all of whom disappeared the instant Iron Man was needed. Due in large part to the CMAA, women no longer laughed at cops or shot their way out of abusive relationships. Authority figures were reliable and honest, rather than greedy and two-faced. This extended even to members of the CIA and the American military. In comparison with the America within *Crime Does Not Pay*, the world inhabited by these new Marvel heroes was practically sterile: there were no psychotic killers, no sex-crazed women, and certainly no crooked politicians to poison outside views of American society. It was, quite literally, a bright, White world, with buildings and costumes rendered in bold colors, and protagonists rendered exclusively in white. It was as if the world of *Crime Does Not Pay* had been bleached and stripped of all ethnicity, individuality, and personality. And this was just what the Cold War demanded: a cohesive America full of relatable and eminently likeable heroes.

SPIDER-MAN GOES TO THE PSYCHIATRIST

The initial wave of Marvel heroes, including the Fantastic Four, Iron Man, Thor, the Hulk, and Spider-Man, were all heavily influenced by the Cold War. They emerged from the constraints of a restrictive censorship code and a unique historical setting brimming with racial tensions, anticommunism, faith in American-style democracy, and a growing awareness of the nuclear arms race. Indeed, with the exception of Thor and Iron Man, Marvel's first wave of superheroes owed their abilities to atomic energy. The atomic-powered characters created by Jack Kirby, Steve Ditko, and Stan Lee differed from those in the 1940s, like Atoman or the Atomic Man, who were virtually identical to contemporaries like Superman or Captain Marvel. Marvel's new atomic-powered characters—the Hulk and Spider-Man, in particular—were something new. Bathed in gamma rays during the test of an experimental nuclear weapon, the Hulk was bright green, enormous, and conventionally ugly. Bitten by a radioactive arachnid, Spider-Man gained great strength and agility but remained a scrawny teenager who lived with his aunt in Queens—an unfashionable outer-borough nerd. This was the Marvel difference: with great power came great responsibility, and a lot of personal suffering.[25] The thirteenth issue of *Amazing Spider-Man* wrestled with this pain, asking readers, "Ever see a comic mag super-hero take his troubles to a psychiatrist? You will now!" Spider-Man visits a psychiatrist to try and understand whether he is a positive or destructive force. After speaking for just a moment, though, the hero realizes that he alone can deal with his problems and doubts.[26]

Earlier atomic-powered heroes benefited from exposure to atomic energy and suffered no ill effects. To readers in 1945 or 1961, this was a step too far. It was so unrealistic, so wildly implausible as to fracture the compact between comic book creators and readers, by which both producers and consumers suspended their disbelief and accepted the reality within the pages of a given title. This formula foundered soon after World War II, with the advent of atomic weapons. In the early atomic age, it was simply too much to ask that readers accept a cheerful, radioactive hero like the Atomic Thunderbolt. Hiroshima and Nagasaki left no doubt that the Atomic Thunderbolt would die a lingering, painful death after ingesting uranium-235. Similarly, it was unreasonable to expect postwar readers to continue buying *Captain Marvel Adventures* month after month. If he was vulnerable to atomic weapons, then he was no longer of use as a superhero. And if he was invulnerable to the atom, he should collect and destroy every nuclear weapon on earth to ensure the survival of humanity. By 1946, Americans understood that radiation exposure yielded not a muscular physique and a mass of golden blond hair but catastrophic bleeding, horrific burns, and organ failure. The recent terrors of the Cuban Missile Crisis only reinforced the gruesome realities of atomic energy.

Still, by 1961, American consumers had spent more than fifteen years living under the threat of nuclear war. Some comic book readers had spent their entire lives in the atomic age. It was Americans of this age—in their teens or early twenties by the early 1960s—that put Marvel on the pop culture map. Nuclear weapons doubtless still exerted significant influence on American culture and thought, but the threat of an atomic holocaust, while ever-present, was no longer new.

Despite their more nuanced (if still wildly unrealistic) approach to atomic energy, Marvel's first wave of superheroes worked hard at reinforcing an image of the United States as unambiguously good and its communist enemies as perfectly evil. Many of these communists were non-Whites living in the decolonizing world. This had the effect of creating a binary view of race in early Marvel superhero comics: superheroes were White, and communists were non-White; Americans were democratic, and non-White foreigners were totalitarian; heroes were psychologically complex, and villains were part of an unthinking mass.

The sympathetic outsiders in the early Marvel universe were those disfigured by their superpowers. The Thing, from the Fantastic Four, is ashamed of his appearance and ventures outside only when covered by a trench coat, hat, and sunglasses. His girlfriend, Alicia, is blind. Another physically unique character is a member of the X-Men, a team of superpowered mutants sometimes seen as analogues to America's persecuted minorities. Born Hank McCoy, the Beast is a simian mutant possessing superhuman strength, agility, and intelligence. *The X-Men*, though, contains no heroes of color; indeed, the comic book features virtually no non-White characters at all. If the title represented Marvel's commentary on the civil rights movement, it was a very timid one indeed. Facing off against the X-Men is the Brotherhood of Evil Mutants, a rival supergroup. Attempts to frame the friction between the X-Men and the Brotherhood as an analogue of the civil rights debate between nonviolent and armed protesters similarly fall short. The Brotherhood was misunderstood but also fundamentally evil—and, like the X-Men, entirely White.

For all the new concepts Marvel brought to the superhero genre between 1961 and 1965, they generally refused to broach the issues of race or civil rights at home. In this they again resembled the World War II–era narratives sanctioned by the WWB: calls for unity among Americans were acceptable, but more overt arguments for civil rights might agitate consumers or policy makers and were therefore off-limits. The artists and writers at Marvel did not, until much later in the decade, incorporate any major positive characters that were not White. Marvel comics have received much scholarly praise for their dialogue and treatment of real issues. But on race and diplomacy they were hardly radical. The "Marvel method" produced great stories about teen angst and the loneliness of those marked as "different." It handled international issues, however, with all the subtlety of a government propaganda comic like *Bert the Turtle Says "Duck and Cover."*

Certainly, Marvel comics did not meet the criteria laid out by Dr. Fredric Wertham for respectful treatment of non-White characters. In *Seduction of the Innocent*, Wertham linked the topic of race with mass culture and the domestic with the diplomatic. Although the CMAA ostensibly eliminated many of Wertham's complaints about the effects of comic books in the United States, the narratives and images of Marvel's superheroes remained problematic internationally. Although the first wave of Marvel comics was laughably tame compared to pre-code titles like *T-Man* or *Wings Comics*, they still contained many derogatory and condescending representations of non-White characters from throughout the decolonizing world.

Marvel's superhero titles also did not eliminate the dangers posed by the comic book form itself. The very shape and appearance of American commercial comics implied the worst about American society. Although Marvel superhero titles did not represent the United States as primitive or corrupt, as their predecessors had, they did depict American heroes and leaders as extremely violent and provincial. Within the pages of titles like *Journey into Mystery* or *Tales of Suspense*, the United States appeared as a wealthy, powerful, and frightened nation. It was afraid of communist infiltration at home and communist insurgencies abroad. The nation's defense industry and military met these threats with overwhelming force: detonating atomic devices as though they were hand grenades, attacking communist guerrillas with million-dollar weapons, and sending a Norse god to deal with the Vietcong.

A significant exception appeared in Marvel's *Sgt. Fury and His Howling Commandos*, which traced the adventures of a wild group of Americans fighting their way across Europe during World War II. One commando, added to the group in 1963, was a Black soldier named Gabe Jones. Allegedly, Kirby and Lee had to stop their printer from recoloring Jones as a White person.[27] Jones also appeared in contemporary espionage stories alongside Fury and some of the other Howling Commandos. This was a noteworthy and significant addition to the otherwise White world of superhero comic books in the early 1960s.

Nick Fury starred in two different comics that took place about twenty years apart. In addition to waging World War II in *Sgt. Fury and His Howling Commandos*, Fury also appeared in *Strange Tales* as the head of S.H.I.E.L.D., a Cold War peacekeeping force. He wears an eye patch, gnaws constantly at a cigar, and acts like a combination of James Bond and John Wayne. In an early appearance, he is on foot in Manhattan, trying to evade an assassination squad. As the assassins draw closer, Fury enters what appears to be a barbershop but is actually a safe house staffed by agents of S.H.I.E.L.D. One of the agents, Slim, is Black and disguised as the shop's hatcheck attendant. After the agents dispense with the assassination team, Slim is left behind to tidy up, assuring Fury, "Everything will be cleaned away in a few minutes, colonel."[28] Slim did not reappear in the series.

MARVEL BEATS THE REDS

The CMAA and its censorship code had a global impact on American commercial comic books. The overt racism, violence, and raw sexuality that defined postwar American comic books vanished, to be replaced with a very different image of American society. The obvious benefit for American policy makers was that comics embraced the Cold War consensus and ceased to pose any meaningful challenge to domestic or diplomatic policies. Indeed, a new generation of comic book superheroes from Marvel would actively support American military intervention and grow intertwined with the Cold War national security state. At the same time, however, comics grew rather homogenous and comparatively dull. Comic books, never flush with non-White characters, also became "whitewashed." The code banned racist imagery, and as the comic industry had little interest or practice in providing nuanced, sophisticated non-White characters, it responded by eliminating nearly all of them. The comic book universe depicted an America full of costumed heroes but with few regular, non-White citizens.

Between 1961 and 1965, Marvel's extraordinary creativity partially reclaimed the comic book, and the superhero genre in particular, for more adult audiences. It did so by combining traits from earlier, state-sanctioned propaganda comics with more realistic characters and settings. These new characters inhabited a shared universe, and many ostensibly existed in New York City. Foreign and domestic readers, then, received a very different image of American society than what appeared in earlier comics like *Crimes by Women* or *Weird Fantasy*. This new America was no longer a cruel and vicious place. It was a bright, technologically advanced society where superpowered men and women lived among average Americans and shared some of the same problems. The one similarity between the pre-code image of America and Marvel's post-code imaginings was that the country remained populated almost entirely by conventionally attractive White people. As far as parents were concerned, however, what mattered most was that Marvel comics received the bold, white CMAA stamp of approval on the cover of every issue. The comics code tamed the industry, but it was the first generation of Marvel superheroes that reinvented it as harmless yet engaging entertainment that supported America's Cold War policies.

CONCLUSION
THE GHOSTS AMONG US

FROM PULP TO FILM

The history of the comic book is a history of visual culture, commerce, race, and policy. These four fields evoke the four colors used to print comic books: cyan, magenta, yellow, and black. In isolation, each provides an incomplete image—a blur. When combined atop one another, they form a much more detailed, complex, and complete picture. Together they show us how culture and policy making were connected by World War II and the Cold War and how these conflicts built the American comic book into a challenge to, and an opportunity for, US policy makers and propagandists. Now, nearly seventy years after the global anti–comic book campaign, we are all once again living within a pulp empire—different, yet familiar.

The sheer, nearly unavoidable presence of comic book characters in our society speaks to the significance of the medium. Comic book trash has spawned empires: first as a novel and revolutionary instrument of American imperialism, then as a globally popular and unchecked form of culture that complicated US foreign policy making in the decolonizing world and Western Europe, and now as the far more conservative force behind the most valuable entertainment properties in history. Since World War II, the histories of diplomacy, comic books, and race have intertwined, with each influencing and shaping the others. Comics are sticky culture; their impact reverberates and even grows over the decades. In its current form, the pulp empire has overwhelmed the concerns of millions around the world, nearly obliterating historic reactions to this most American form of visual media and the federal government's complex relationship with the comic book. Similarly, Dr. Fredric Wertham is remembered, where he is remembered at all, as a prude and would-be censor. His more useful contributions to the study of comic books and race are much harder to discern in the midst of a popular culture nearly saturated with comic book characters. This is the power of trash, of the American comic book, and of its creators and consumers.

The comic book was popular from the outset, but it took government intervention to build the pulp empire. Publishers sold first tens and then hundreds of millions of issues every year between 1940 and 1955. Their relatively unfiltered images and stories were available to anyone, of any age, for ten cents. Comics were everywhere—in schools, in waiting rooms, in the back seats of cars, beneath children's beds, and wedged between the pages of textbooks. Comics became weapons in the wars against totalitarianism and inseparable from the growth of American strength abroad throughout the mid-twentieth century.

During World War II, comic books became powerful political media and a strategic asset. Recognizing the utility of the comic book, various wartime agencies made extensive use of the form. Beginning in April 1943, the WWB wove outright propaganda into popular culture to fuel a hatred of fascism, encourage racial tolerance in American society, and promote postwar international cooperation.[1] Major comic book publishers submitted story drafts to the WWB and even created new characters and features at its behest. As artist Alex Schomburg recalled, comic book makers were encouraged to indulge in "anything to make the Japs look ugly or the Nazis look like punks."[2] At the same time, the OIAA took a very different approach, designing overtly propagandistic (noncommercial) comic books for non-English-speaking audiences throughout Latin America. These were distributed free of charge and included stories about historical figures, rather than fictional characters. Wherever service members went during World War II, huge quantities of comic books followed, supplied by the military or sent from home, many including state-sanctioned propaganda narratives and images. This relationship between the US government and the comic book industry ensured that comics became as integral to the global image of the nation, its culture, and its goals as any other sort of visual media.

Federal intervention during World War II built the comic book industry into a wildly popular, profitable, and increasingly adult-themed business. Then, in the wake of victory over fascism, the government suddenly left the industry unsupervised. Wood pulp was no longer rationed, comics were cheap, and wartime policies had turned millions of men and women into regular readers. Publishers responded with wave after wave of new genres—crime, horror, romance, jungle, and even atomic—to try and captivate readers of all ages, across dozens of countries. Sales climbed toward a billion copies every year, while the new machinery of the Cold War facilitated the global spread of these unfiltered, graphic titles. Tourists, diplomats, and professionals carried comic books abroad, and soldiers took them to countries hosting a growing archipelago of American military bases. Easily translated and transported, publishers sent these new and shocking comics to countries across Western Europe and the global south, where consumers read, reread, traded, and scattered comic books until they disintegrated. Everywhere these comics traveled, their stories and images led numerous lives, intersected with multiple readers, and shaped popular perceptions of American society. The federal government had relinquished control over a cultural colossus, a creation partly of its own making that suddenly had the power to confound policies vital to victory in the Cold War. What had been a potent, patriotic, and state-sanctioned weapon against one sort of totalitarianism was now a liability in a new and unfamiliar war against another.

Not long after the postwar separation between the federal government and the comic book industry, state policies created and nourished a second wave of propaganda comic books to win allies abroad, in particular among the peoples of the decolonizing world. Policy makers and propagandists believed that by appropriating the characteristics of the medium that made it dangerous—its portability, powerful combination of simple text and images, and enormous popularity—they could transmit pro-American and anticommunist messages to communities considered beyond the reach of more traditional media. They used the controversies around comic books as camouflage for narratives composed or approved by members of the US foreign policy community. What drove these efforts was an unshakable belief in the fundamental comprehensibility of the comic book form and its unique appeal to less educated and non-White audiences. Where jazz, avant-garde art, books, or even American films could not reach, state-sanctioned comic books could, and federal agencies produced millions tailored to the tastes and languages of the decolonizing world. Millions more, carefully modified for what American propagandists believed were more advanced sensibilities, also reached Western Europe.

Spurred on and coordinated by Wertham, activists and local, state, and federal agencies began to fight against the power and influence of the resurgent comic book industry, both in the United States and around the world. While many of these activists focused on the perceived violence in comics and its possible link with juvenile delinquency, Wertham and federal legislators also understood that racism in uncensored comic books posed a particular threat to US foreign policies. Many millions of comics published every month either contained no non-White characters or offered only vicious racial stereotypes. This flood of hateful images complicated efforts to win hearts and minds in the decolonizing world and to convince foreign states that the United States offered a more humane and sophisticated alternative to communism.

The Senate responded to the anti–comic book movement with an investigation of the publishing industry focused on the hazy connection between comic book consumption and real-world behavior. But legislators also heard from members of the foreign service who testified to the damage done to US foreign policies by violent and racist comic books. According to these reports, comics were so dangerous to US interests that communist propagandists could not invent a more useful weapon with which to turn citizens against American-style capitalism. Members of the Senate subcommittee also received a torrent of letters from angry comic book readers, both young and adult. Many of these letters were written by service members and parents and surely suggested to investigators that grown men and women around the world, as well as children, were reading unfiltered American comic books and basing their views of the United States on the stories and images within.

The result was a comics censorship code that shattered the industry. Many companies responsible for the best-known crime- and horror-themed titles simply disappeared. Others, like EC, frustrated by the code, switched to publishing magazines. Unable to provide the sorts of content demanded by adult audiences, surviving comic book publishers essentially transformed the medium into what its critics had always claimed it was: entertainment for children. Wertham attacked the comics censorship code as a capitulation, a lazy effort to solve a serious political and cultural problem with the minimum possible effort. But the code, along with the anti–comic book campaign and federal investigation of the comic book industry, undoubtedly served as a powerful warning to the publishers that survived these assaults on the medium. Certainly, the new wave of superhero titles published by Marvel in the early 1960s supported US Cold War policies.

Today, comic books are once again everywhere. They have transcended their very form to become something more diffuse and significant: the defining international symbols of American mass culture in the early twenty-first century. Comics themselves are now secondary to the products they spawn, like video games, movies, TV shows, towels, clothing, Halloween costumes, and countless more. A search on Amazon for "Iron Man" returns tens of thousands of results, the vast majority of which are not comic books. A cultural phenomenon this pervasive, and this long-lived, is important. It matters as an example of a uniquely American creation that conquered the world and as a powerful medium inseparable from vital matters of race and foreign policy. Comic books were significant weapons in the twentieth-century wars against totalitarianism, even as they supposedly menaced readers in the United States and around the world. A form of visual culture so compelling, so feared, so unfiltered, and so wildly popular is a wonderful and formidable means of reinterpreting the past.

The matter of race was inseparable from the evolution of the comic book and its relationship to policy. So many of the decisions, conflicts, and images illuminated in this book were driven by federal concerns over the subject: fear that Americans did not sufficiently hate Japanese and Germans during World War II; fear that racism would lead to violence on the home front; fear that non-White people were not able to understand propaganda woven into books, artwork, and music; fear that without a way to reach non-White people in the decolonizing world, the United States would lose the Cold War. Race drove the government to use the comic book, and race pushed the government to suffocate it as well.

From the beginning, the American comic book industry was a refuge for racial, political, ethnic, and sexual outsiders. It was a business in which a communist made a fortune, a Black artist helped define White female sexuality, and an editor went to prison for murder. Significantly, until 1955 no censorship office restricted these men and women. Subject to the most minimal of filters, they poured out images of the racism, violence, sadness, and optimism pervading postwar American society. Their work would become the foundation of modern American myths and the basis of the most lucrative entertainment franchises in history. It was a sordid, totally American industry that entertained many millions of people around the world.

As a historian, it is also a rare delight to discover a cultural form that gave voice to so many marginalized groups of Americans. Pre-code comic books offer artwork and text composed by African Americans, women, Jewish Americans, Asian Americans, and other people pushed to the sides during the American century. Better yet, these comic books were relatively uncensored: they are a window into the frustrations, fears, and hopes of men and women whose opinions were not valued by contemporary society.

For nearly twenty years, commercial comic books carried some of the clearest and least-filtered images of American society, its bigotry, its frustrations, and its swagger. Using comics for propaganda was a bold and creative policy decision. The comics produced by or in conjunction with federal agencies were designed to draw attention to the most positive aspects of American culture. But the history omitted from their narratives tells an even richer story.

As embarrassing as commercial and propaganda comic books may have been, in different ways, they boasted one positive attribute: they were fun. Yes, commercial comics caused no end of headaches for the State Department and provided limitless material for Eastern bloc propagandists. But there was no denying the simple pleasure of flipping the pages of a comic and enjoying the artwork within. Thanks to America's array of military bases and outposts, it was an indulgence available to a Brazilian toddler, an American teenager, or a Ghanaian engineer. Comic books spoke to everyone, everywhere. Soviet-style propaganda was resolutely serious, and American comic books operated as a constant reminder of that joylessness. Winning hearts and minds could not always be about chess, literature, or modern dance. Millions of perfectly respectable people enjoyed reading a comic book, and the Soviet Union had nothing similar to offer.

More importantly, comic book propaganda seemed to work. Even members of the State Department who bemoaned their use also admitted that comics seemed effective. That various agencies used propaganda comic books for so long also suggests they were satisfied by the results. And why not? Comic books were cheap, comprehensible, and easy to disavow. They made for a wonderful propaganda delivery system.

A FRESH MEANS OF INTERPRETING OUR PAST

In their time, comic books were considered ephemeral objects to read and throw aside. Printed on high-acid paper that fades and disintegrates over time, comic books are fragile things. Nobody imagined they would be a rich resource for future scholars. My father still tells the story of Mr. Bieber, an Austrian man who owned a used bookstore in Jersey City. Although, my father had to put up with anti-Semitism and grime at Mr. Bieber's store, he viewed these as minor problems because Mr. Bieber sold old issues of *Wonder Woman* and *Mighty Mouse*. And the bookseller did so because he believed in their importance. Mr. Bieber also acquired a huge collection of his own. When he died in the late 1950s, Mrs. Bieber tried to donate her husband's trove—likely one of the largest private comic book collections in the country—to the Smithsonian. The Smithsonian passed, having concluded that comic books were unimportant. Who knows how many millions of comics have disappeared, like those that belonged to Mr. Bieber?

Still, twentieth-century comics exist as ghosts among us. The excitement, the trauma, the rage generated by the swirl of uncensored American comic books—they are not dead. Contemporary global perceptions of the United States are an assembly of old and new; they emerge from memory as much as experience. And the cultural impressions left by billions of uncensored comic books continue to do cultural work both at home and abroad. The twentieth-century commercial comic book is still a sticky cultural object: powerful, compelling trash that attracts, repels, and fascinates us. Characters conceived to fight World War II and the Cold War now dominate American and global popular visual culture. And now, as during these earlier times, they operate with the implied consent of the US government. Characters in these billion-dollar movies represent the United States worldwide, and the films work to shape international understandings of the nation's fears, policy goals, and self-image. At the same time, these characters and movies offer clues as to how the United States views the rest of the world. While now supplied on film instead of pulp, comic book narratives remain imperial, political media.

These are the phantoms swirling around us still, shaping our popular culture in ways we cannot always single out because their prevalence feels so familiar. We live within the pulp empire and are accustomed to the almost oppressive presence of comic books in our popular culture. Even harder to identify are the reverberations of the thousands of men and women who produced a billion comic books a year during the industry's heyday. We occupy a world shaped by the remarkable characters they created, some of which survive into the present day. The ghosts of the industry are everywhere. They affect all of us who participate in American popular culture. This is the legacy of men and women who were not reasonably rewarded in life but in death are the unsung kings and queens of Hollywood.

It was not always this way. In the wake of World War II, Joe Simon and Jack Kirby, the cocreators of Captain America, bought houses in the same suburb on Long Island, New York. The two kept odd work hours, and their new neighbors began muttering about how Simon and Kirby earned their money: the men had to be either mobsters or bookies, as they never seemed to go outside during the daytime and worked at night. They decided to let their neighbors believe that they were bookies, as "it was more prestigious than being known as comic book artists."[3]

In the late 1940s, working in the comic book industry was a shameful thing, even for artists as skilled, accomplished, and successful as Simon and Kirby. Those on the margins of the industry and American society were much less fortunate. They were the men and women immortalized by Hank Williams during the late 1940s: the people that did not benefit from the great postwar boom. They were the poor kids like Elvis Presley, who grew up reading borrowed copies of Captain Marvel Jr. and based his stage persona on his comic book hero. They were men like the World War II veteran of combat and atomic testing at Bikini Atoll who, upon returning to a very different United States, told a reporter, "The only thing I have in common with my son is the comic books."[4] These men and women, too, are ghosts in our cultural machine.

Today, comic books offer us an entirely new means of interpreting both the mid-twentieth century and our current popular culture. Comic books provide fresh insights into American diplomacy, cultural imperialism, and self-image. We can now embrace the American comic for what it is: a wonderful and powerful means to better understand the connections among policy, race, and culture.

THE END OF THE BEGINNING

There is no clean ending to this narrative, because it isn't over. On a much smaller scale, the US government continues to use comic books for propaganda, overtly and (presumably) covertly. But our understanding of the comic book as a cultural object has undergone profound changes since the Cold War. A copy of *Our Gang Comics* from 1944, with its vicious racism, unabashed patriotism, and remarkable violence, would be unrecognizable to an American adolescent brought up reading Japanese manga or modern graphic novels. To truly comprehend and use the power of the twentieth-century comic book, we must continue unpacking the relationship between the medium and the American government. In the course of researching this book, I discovered many documents that refer to CIA comic books. Some were likely used in the early 1960s, primarily in Latin America. Others seem to have been used in preparation for America's 1984 invasion of Grenada and the Nicaraguan Revolution. So far, my efforts to compel the agency to make these documents and comics public have been unsuccessful. We will gain access to these materials someday, and they will enrich our understanding of how and why the American government appropriated something as pedestrian as the comic book to gain an advantage in the Cold War. I am so confident of this because more and more students, scholars, and consumers now acknowledge the importance of comic books and their significance to any study of popular culture, race, gender, diplomacy, or policy making in the twentieth and twenty-first centuries.

Early on, I spent many months trying to track down Malcolm Ater's surviving family. I scoured newspapers, searching for Ater's obituary and some mention of his wife and children. I found obituaries for many men named Malcolm Ater, and I sent letters to their survivors. After nearly a year, I received a response from a man who said he was the son of the Malcolm Ater who had owned Commercial Comics. He very kindly permitted me to interview him along with his elderly mother. While we spoke, Mrs. Ater told me that her husband had worked hand in hand with a variety of federal agencies,

FIGURE C.1 Much about the creation and distribution of this comic book, produced by Commercial Comics and entitled *Grenada: Rescued from Rape and Slavery*, remains a mystery to be solved.

including the FCDA, the State Department, and, apparently, the CIA. She and her son then told me an incredible tale.

They said the CIA contacted Malcolm Ater in the early 1980s to make an anticommunist comic book about the new Marxist government on the Caribbean island of Grenada. They were sure that it was not the first time the agency reached out to him for assistance. Indeed, Ater and the CIA had an established routine. Whenever the agency needed a run of special comic books, Ater would drive to Dupont Circle in Washington, DC, and stand on the sidewalk until a car driven by CIA employees pulled up. Once Ater entered the car, it drove in endless loops around Dupont Circle. The employees told Ater what sort of comic book they wanted, what languages to use, and when it was needed. They then handed him a large bag of cash and let him out. Once the comic was finished, Ater would return to Dupont Circle. In the car again, he would hand over proofs for agency approval. After he received the go-ahead, he would print the comic book and deliver the copies to the CIA.

The most thrilling part of this story is that it reads like something out of a comic. But tracing its actual history through comic books, documents, and the memories of others involved in its creation would be even more satisfying. Let's do these things, and many more, together.

ACKNOWLEDGMENTS

At the age of twenty-five, I was run over by a truck. The impact tore off my left leg and knee and crushed my right leg. The driver of the truck fled, leaving me alone in the middle of a quiet, rural road. I was conscious and knew I was going to die. There was no other way. But a few minutes later, a man and woman, Fred and Lori, found me and in that incredible, impossible moment set me on a path where, suddenly, life became an option. I underwent months of hospitalization and dozens of surgeries before spending years relearning to walk with robotic limbs and canes. Throughout that time, I thought over and over of my new path. This work exists in part because of all the support I've received from family, friends, doctors, mentors, and miraculous strangers. I thought about all these people while writing this book, thanking them silently as I sat and wrote. They helped me along my brighter path, pushed me to accomplish the beautiful things I once only imagined while lying in a hospital bed: walking, earning a doctorate in history, building a family, making peace with my disability, and writing this book. I struggle to describe my gratitude.

This book is inseparable from my disability. It opened me to an incredible, previously unseen world, a place of challenges and quiet struggle but also of power, warmth, and support. It fueled my interest in the people behind great global shifts and movements. My disability drove me to dig deeper, beneath archival documents and interviews, into source materials created by some of the least powerful people in American society and to marvel at the changes and conflicts shaped by their artwork and writing. Their stories provided me with the focus and sense of joy necessary to write this book. From them—from us—I learned that there is always a path forward. This book is my evidence.

I am supremely grateful to my parents, Joyce and Jerry Hirsch, and my sisters, Alison Hirsch and Aroussiak Gabrelian. My father, Jerry Hirsch, taught me early on that old comic books were wonderful, dangerous, and full of mystery. He showed me that looking backward offers a way forward. My mother taught me the self-reliance and self-respect I've depended on as a disabled person, for which I am endlessly thankful. My sisters are incredible role models and always on my side, and their love and accomplishments push me ahead. My Auntie Diane kept me company every weekend, month after month, while I was hospitalized. I thought of her so often while writing, traveling, and savoring the adventures wrapped up with this book. I lack the means to thank her appropriately for all the love and encouragement she's given me. And Laura Lee, I'm so happy we got lost. Simply put, this book would not exist without you and your smile. Somehow, you turned the writing process from an agony into a source of joy and pride. My young son Milo is a delight beyond language. He kept me company for countless hours while I worked on this book, helped me work out my frustrations with round after round of our Totoro game, and has shown me an effortless, graceful love that I did not know existed but am so grateful to know.

I am indebted to the people and institutions that provided financial support for this book. Their advocacy made it possible for me to travel, research, and write without fear. A generous grant from the Robert B. Silvers Foundation enabled me to finish the project and include the full-color images peppering its pages. Seth Garfield and the staff of the Institute for Historical Studies in the Department of History at the University of Texas at Austin provided me with funding, direction, and a home. Robert Chesney and UT's Robert S. Strauss Center for International Security and Law also funded my work, extending my wonderful time in Austin. The Caroline and Erwin Swann Foundation and the John W. Kluge Center both provided me with terrific fellowships-in-residence at the Library of Congress. Marilyn Young, Michael Nash, and their staff supported me through a fellowship at the Center for the United States and the Cold War at

New York University's Tamiment Library. The editorial staff at the *Pacific Historical Review* helped hone my first article, which members of the American Historical Association subsequently awarded a Jackson Prize, along with financial assistance. Donors to the History Associates at the University of California, Santa Barbara, provided some of the earliest support for my research and writing. Particular thanks are due to the National Science Foundation's Integrative Graduate Education and Research Traineeship program, which provided exceptionally generous, long-term support for my research and writing, and Susan Shirk at the University of California, San Diego, who ably mentored me through this program.

Many outstanding historians contributed to this book. Marty Sherwin encouraged me from the outset, and his support never flagged. I received similarly vital, long-term encouragement from Fred Logevall. Frank Couvares has been a mentor and a friend through the years spent writing this book and beyond. Emily Rosenberg supported me with her time and advice, particularly in the early stages of this project. I've also benefited from Jason Parker's warm and positive counsel. At UCSB, scholars Salim Yaqub, Laura Kalman, Paul Spickard, Toshi Hasegawa, Linda Adler-Kassner, Alice O'Connor, Lisa Jacobson, John Majewski, Kate McDonald, Patrick McCray, and Don Lubach all helped me hone and improve my project. I am so appreciative of the time, support, and direction they provided me. Special thanks are due to George Lipsitz, who opened up whole new ways to think and write and gave generously of his time and advice. I learned so much from him. Members of the Center for Cold War Studies at UCSB, the George Washington University, and the London School of Economics provided camaraderie and advice. This book additionally benefited from feedback provided by Seth Garfield, Jeremi Suri, Mark Lawrence, Judy Coffin, and Megan Raby of the University of Texas at Austin.

Writing is a lonely activity, and I'm appreciative of the friends and colleagues who supported me and helped to hone this book. I am particularly grateful to Jay Ruttenberg, of the *Lowbrow Reader*, for his time, edits, and suggestions. They were a major influence on the shape of my work. Pornsak Pichetshote, an exceptional writer of comic books, provided me with connections in the industry, along with vital encouragement and advice. Paul Baltimore gave me support and affection as only a brother can. Eric Pliner supported me in so many ways, across so many years, that it is difficult to know how to express my gratitude. In his wonderful way, Craig Staub made sure I always kept working and moving forward. Comic book scholars Michael Uslan, Ian Lewis Gordon, Carol Tilley, Leonard Rifas, and Bart Beaty pushed me to find answers to questions not yet investigated. Historians Toshi Aono, Megan Bowman, Julia Brock, Tim Daniels, Sarah Griffith, John Hammond, Ken Hough, John Munro, Nicole Pacino, Roger Pryor, and Rachel Winslow all read portions of my manuscript and provided invaluable feedback, along with their friendship. Matt Russell helped me translate my work into the realm of digital history and encouraged me to be bold. Lauren Sinclair showed me unexpected joys and insights on my brighter path. Mayumi Kodani, Al Silva, and Aaron Sokoll provided laughter, nourishment, and support over many years. Mary Toothman and Phil Murphy gave so much to me for so long that I struggle to be more specific about the immensity of their love. Jax Maloney's kindness, laughter, and gentle generosity did much to keep me on my path. To these people, and all those in my heart and mind, I am so thankful.

The first time I entered the National Archives to conduct research for this project, I had a panic attack. I am grateful to the archivists and librarians that helped me persevere. Special thanks are due to Georgia Higley and her staff in the Manuscript Reading Room and Martha Kennedy and her team in the Popular and Applied Graphic Art division at the Library of Congress, Judy Adkins at the Center for Legislative Archives, Richie Graham and John Wiese at the University of Nebraska–Lincoln, Cindy Jackson at the Virginia Commonwealth University Comic Arts Collection, David Langbart and his staff at the National Archives, Randy Scott at the Michigan State University Comic Art Collection, Elizabeth Wilkinson at the Georgetown University Special Collections Research Center, and the staff at the Davidson Library of the University of California, Santa Barbara. They helped me uncover the raw materials for this book and enabled the thrill of discovery so relished by historians. Particular thanks are due to Malcolm Ater Jr., who opened his home and his father's archival materials to me and permitted me to interview him and his mother while this book was in its early stages. I appreciate his trust.

This book exists in part because of the legal and medical support I received from a group of incredible people scattered across the United States. Their expertise, time, and advocacy helped me heal and enabled me to earn the fellowships that permitted me to conduct essential research. I am particularly grateful, then, to Dr. Reuben Weininger, Mark Bronstein, Ralph Nobbe, Emily Cotton, and everyone at Austin Prosthetic Center for keeping me mentally and physically balanced and able to venture into the world. For a physically disabled person, something as simple as getting to campus—let alone to some far-flung archive—can be a complex and terrifying process. These men and women alleviated some of that terror and, in doing so, helped keep me on my new path.

Finally, I am so thankful for my supremely supportive editor at the University of Chicago Press, Tim Mennel, his exceptional editorial associate, Susannah Engstrom, and my skilled copy editor, Elizabeth Ellingboe. They are thorough, careful, and patient, and the final shape of this book owes much to their care.

NOTES

INTRODUCTION

1. *Crime Must Pay the Penalty* 1 (Ace, 1948)—issue is listed as number 33 on the cover.

2. *The Killers* 2 (Magazine Enterprises, 1948).

3. *T-Man Comics* 3 (Quality, 1952).

4. "Atomic Bomb with Troop Exercises in HD," YouTube, accessed Feb. 13, 2018, https://www.youtube.com/watch?v=4kG9kD8bPnA. Images of soldiers reading comic books in a trench before an atomic test begin at 3:30.

5. Melani McAlister, *Epic Encounters: Culture, Media, and U.S. Interests in the Middle East since 1945* (Berkeley: University of California Press, 2005), 5. McAlister terms this process the "active production" of values—the practice of generating significance from a text.

6. Stuart Hall, "Notes on Deconstructing 'the Popular,'" in *Cultural Theory and Popular Culture: A Reader*, ed. John Storey (Harlow, UK: Pearson, 1998), 443.

7. E. J. Penny, "Are Comics Bad for Children?," *Rotarian*, May 1940, 2; "Are the Comics Harmful Reading for Children?," *Coronet*, Aug. 1944, 179; and "Are Comics Fascist? Are They Good for Children?," *Time*, Oct. 22, 1945, 66–67.

8. "Comic Book Out Next Sunday," *Los Angeles Times*, July 28, 1940, 1; "Comic Books Held Beneficial for Children by Psychologist," *Los Angeles Times*, Feb. 23, 1941, 2; "Art Parade Reviewed," *Los Angeles Times*, March 31, 1940, C8; and "Educators Uphold Children's Comics," *New York Times*, Feb. 2, 1944, 18.

9. "Educators Uphold Children's Comics," 18.

10. Catherine Mackenzie, "The Second Baby vs. the First," *New York Times Sunday Magazine*, March 2, 1941, 22.

11. Sterling North, "A National Disgrace," *Chicago Daily News*, May 8, 1940, 21.

12. "Educators Uphold Children's Comics," 18.

13. "The Cartoon Book Program in Latin America," May 22, 1963, box 4, folder 3, Ernest A. Keller Papers, Georgetown University Special Collections, Washington, DC (hereafter cited as Keller Papers).

14. "A *Life* Round Table on Modern Art," *Life*, Oct. 11, 1948, 81.

15. The wonderful phrase "economics and poetics of the dime novel" appears in Michael Denning's cultural and theoretical history of dime novels and working-class culture in America during the late nineteenth century. Michael Denning, *Mechanic Accents: Dime Novels and Working-Class Culture in America* (New York:

Verso, 1998), 2. Bradford W. Wright, *Comic Book Nation: The Transformation of Youth Culture in America* (Baltimore: Johns Hopkins University Press, 2001), 7. This minimal oversight ensured that the voices, experiences, and fears of the men and women who wrote and drew comic books permeated the finished products. This is different, though, than arguing that readers absorbed these perspectives and fears as intended.

16. As Denis Kitchen and Paul Buhle note, comics were produced both in factory-style sweatshops and also by artists working in assembly-line fashion at home or in rented rooms, a method similar to the "putting-out" system formerly employed in the garment industry. Denis Kitchen and Paul Buhle, *The Art of Harvey Kurtzman: The Mad Genius of Comics* (New York: Harry N. Abrams, 2009), 60.

17. David Hajdu, *The Ten-Cent Plague: The Great Comic-Book Scare and How It Changed America* (New York: Picador, 2008), 22. For more on the early comic industry in New York City, see Gerard Jones, *Men of Tomorrow: Geeks, Gangsters and the Birth of the Comic Book* (New York: Basic Books, 2004).

18. Edd Ashe to Jerry Bails, n.d., Dr. Jerry G. Bails Archive, Michigan State University Comic Art Collection, East Lansing, MI.

19. Jim Amash and Eric Nolen-Weathington, eds., *Matt Baker: The Art of Glamour* (Raleigh, NC: TwoMorrows, 2012), 39.

20. Bob Andelman, *Will Eisner: A Spirited Life* (Milwaukie, OR: M Press, 2005), 70.

21. Hajdu, *The Ten-Cent Plague*, 58; Jones, *Men of Tomorrow*, 193. The FBI opened a file on Gleason in the early 1940s, and in 1944 they identified him as "a key figure in Communist activities in the New York area." Untitled FBI document, May 10, 1944, p. 2, FBI file for Leverett Gleason (hereafter cited as Gleason FBI file).

22. Hajdu, *The Ten-Cent Plague*, 58–68.

23. *Amazing Mystery Funnies* 3 (Centaur, 1938).

24. *Mystery Men Comics* 14 (Fox, 1940); *Mystery Men Comics* 15 (Fox, 1940).

25. *Silver Streak Comics* 9 (Lev Gleason, 1941)

26. Jones, *Men of Tomorrow*, 77–86.

27. *Action Comics* 1 (DC, 1938); *Action Comics* 2 (DC, 1938). For the sake of clarity, in the endnotes comic books published by National, All-American, and DC are all described as having been published by Detective Comics (DC), as the company composed of National, All-American, and other imprints, is best known today as DC.

28. Wright, *Comic Book Nation*, 7.

29. Jones, *Men of Tomorrow*, 88–89, 148.

30. *Crimes by Women* 10 (Fox, 1949).

31. Emily S. Rosenberg, "Consuming Women: Images of Americanization in the 'American Century,'" *Diplomatic History* 3 (Summer 1999): 489.

32. "Press Keeps Envoy of Pakistan Busy," *Los Angeles Times*, June 18, 1952, 25; "Pakistan Envoy Qualifies as Guest of Honor," *Los Angeles Times*, June 19, 1952, 3.

33. "Use Made of U.S.I.E. Material in French Press," March 1, 1950, box 2387, Records of the Department of State, Record Group 59, National Archives, College Park, MD (hereafter cited as RG 59, NA).

34. Hajdu, *The Ten-Cent Plague*, 291. For a detailed description of the comics code, see Amy Kiste Nyberg, *Seal of Approval: The History of the Comics Code* (Jack-

son: University Press of Mississippi, 1998), 104–28, and Hajdu, *The Ten-Cent Plague*, 290–95.

35. *Newsdealer*, July 1955, 3–7, box 167, Records of the U.S. Senate Subcommittee on Juvenile Delinquency, Record Group 46, National Archives, Washington, DC (hereafter cited as RG 46, NA).

36. In 1949, Arthur Schlesinger Jr. published *The Vital Center*, arguing that America needed a combination of liberalism and state intervention at home, coupled with American leadership abroad, to navigate a path between communism and fascism. Americans had to reject extremism and embrace the politics of consensus to solve the pressing political, national security, and economic challenges of the time. Arthur Schlesinger Jr., *The Vital Center: The Politics of Freedom* (Boston: Houghton Mifflin, 1949). For a consensus—or orthodox—explanation of the origins of the Cold War and America's obligation to contain the Soviet Union, see Arthur Schlesinger Jr., "Origins of the Cold War," *Foreign Affairs* 46 (Oct. 1967).

37. Ariel Dorfman and Armand Mattelart, *How to Read Donald Duck: Imperialist Ideology in the Disney Comic* (New York: International General, 1975), preface.

CHAPTER ONE

1. I draw a distinction between comic book characters and narratives inspired by the patriotism and jingoism of individual comic book artists and writers, on the one hand, and the comic book propaganda created and endorsed by the Writers' War Board (WWB), on the other. For works on patriotic comic books created without the input of wartime agencies, see Ian Gordon, *Comic Strips and Consumer Culture, 1890–1945* (Washington, DC: Smithsonian Institution Press, 1998); Christopher Murray, *Champions of the Oppressed: Superhero Comics, Popular Culture, and Propaganda in America During World War II* (New York: Hampton Press, 2011); and Bradford W. Wright, *Comic Book Nation: The Transformation of Youth Culture in America* (Baltimore: Johns Hopkins University Press, 2001).

2. See Thomas Howell, "The Writers' War Board: U.S. Domestic Propaganda in World War II," *Historian* 59 (1997): 800. See also John Morton Blum, *V Was for Victory: Politics and American Culture During World War II* (New York: Harvest, 1977), 21–45.

3. "Comic on Germany," Nov. 17, 1944, box 11, Papers of the Writers' War Board, Manuscripts Division, Library of Congress, Washington, DC (hereafter cited as WWB Papers).

4. National Comics began as National Allied Publications in 1935 and has been known by a variety of names, including its current one, Detective Comics (DC). During its early years, National also had affiliates, like All-American Comics, which owned some of the characters and titles discussed in this chapter, including *All-Star Comics*. National absorbed All-American in 1945 after publisher M. C. Gaines sold his shares for five hundred thousand dollars. For the sake of consistency, I refer to all these entities as simply National or National Comics. See Grant Geissman, *Feldstein: The Mad Life and Fantastic Art of Al Feldstein* (New York: IDW, 2013), 62–63; and Carol Tilley, "Superman Says, 'Read!' National Comics and Reading Promotion," *Children's Literature in Education* 44 (2013): 252.

5. Howell, "The Writers' War Board," 803–4.

6. "Comics Committee Progress Report," May 15, 1944, box 11, WWB Papers.

7. Fawcett Publications cooperated with the navy on stories intended to glamorize the service.

8. Gordon, *Comic Strips and Consumer Culture*, 139.

9. William E. Blake Jr., "A View of History: True Comics, 1941–1945," unpublished paper presented to Popular Culture Association on April 19, 1980, pp. 10–11, box 1, Dr. William E. Blake Collection of True Comics, Comic Art Collection, Virginia Commonwealth University, Richmond, VA (hereafter cited as VCU Comic Arts Collection). Blake's paper focuses on *True Comics*, which rejected traditional superhero tales in favor of narratives based on real people and events. While Blake does not discuss comic books produced in cooperation with wartime agencies, he notes the confused and jarring juxtaposition of the appeals for unity and racism in comic books.

10. Thomas Borstelmann, *The Cold War and the Color Line: American Race Relations in the Global Arena* (Cambridge, MA: Harvard University Press, 2001), 34.

11. Borstelmann, *The Cold War and the Color Line*, 39

12. Emily Rosenberg, *Spreading the American Dream: American Economic and Cultural Expansion, 1890–1945* (New York: Hill and Wang, 1982), 206–7.

13. For a summary of the agency's various locations and personnel, see Office of Inter-American Affairs, *History of the Office of the Coordinator of Inter-American Affairs: Historical Reports on War Administration* (Washington, DC: Government Printing Office, 1947), 260.

14. For letters to the editor that describe the popularity of comic books among servicemen, see *Boy Comics* 30 (Lev Gleason, 1946), Michigan State University Comic Art Collection, East Lansing, MI (hereafter cited as MSU Comic Art Collection).

15. *Aviation Cadets* 1 (Street & Smith, 1943), box 1, VCU Comic Arts Collection; C. C. Beck to Russell Crouse, Aug. 7, 1943; Stanley Kauffman to Crouse, Aug. 19, 1943; and Selma Hirsch to Kauffman, Aug. 25, 1943, all in box 11, WWB Papers.

16. See Marya Mannes, "Junior Has a Craving," *New Republic*, Feb. 17, 1947, 22; and a 1949 radio discussion, "How Do the Comics Affect Your Child," in which Paul Witty of Northwestern University cites the same number. "How Do the Comics Affect Your Child," box 109, folder 12, Fredric Wertham Papers, Library of Congress, Washington, DC (hereafter cited as Wertham Papers).

17. Bob Andelman, *Will Eisner: A Spirited Life* (Milwaukie, OR: M Press, 2005), 83–85.

18. Nancy Bernhard, *U.S. Television News and Cold War Propaganda, 1947–1960* (New York: Cambridge University Press, 2003), 17–21; Blum, *V Was for Victory*, 21–45; Susan A. Brewer, *Why America Fights: Patriotism and War Propaganda from the Philippines to Iraq* (New York: Oxford University Press, 2009), 88–104; Howell, "The Writers' War Board," 795; Alan M. Winkler, *The Politics of Propaganda: The Office of War Information, 1942–1945* (New Haven, CT: Yale University Press, 1978), 2–5.

19. Morgenthau also made appearances in comic books during World War II. See *Picture Stories from the Bible* 1 (DC, 1942), box 2, and *War Victory Comics* 1 (Harvey, 1942), box 4, both in VCU Comic Arts Collection. Additionally, Chester Bowles, the head of the Office of Price Administration, appeared in patriotic comic book adver-

tisements. Even President Franklin D. Roosevelt appeared in both advertisements and fictional stories.

20. Howell, "The Writers' War Board," 795–800.

21. In 1942, the OWI absorbed the Office of Facts and Figures. For a history of the OWI and its predecessor agencies, see Winkler, *The Politics of Propaganda*, and Brewer, *Why America Fights*, 94–99.

22. Rex Stout to Selma Hirsch, March 5, 1942, box 6, WWB Papers, cited in Howell, "The Writers' War Board," 796.

23. Clifton Fadiman to Lorraine Beim, Nov. 4, 1944; "Extract From Minutes of July 7," n.d., 1944; "Comics Committee," Aug. 9, 1943; Charles W. Wessell to Frederica Barach, July 24, 1943; "Comics Committee Progress Report," all in box 11, WWB Papers. Paul Gallico was a sportswriter and novelist, perhaps best remembered today for his novel *The Poseidon Adventure*, published in 1969.

24. "Comics Committee—Joint Project with Race Hatred Committee," July 7, 1944, box 11, WWB Papers. At least eight comic book publishers cooperated with the board to some degree, whether soliciting instructions from the board, permitting board members to critique and edit scripts, proposing ideas for new stories to the board, or maintaining communication with the board and in particular the Comics Committee.

25. "Review of Comic Magazines," Irmengarde Eberle to Writer's War Board, March 30, 1943, box 11, WWB Papers; Mike Benton, *Superhero Comics of the Golden Age: The Illustrated History* (Dallas: Taylor Publishing, 1992), 45.

26. Wright, *Comic Book Nation*, 36; Jean-Paul Gabilliet, *Of Comics and Men: A Cultural History of American Comic Books* (Jackson, MS: University Press of Mississippi, 2010), 22–23.

27. In 1942, George Hecht, publisher of fact-based titles like *True Comics* and *Real Heroes*, issued a similar comic book specifically aimed at adults, *Comics Digest*. The cover of the first issue emphasized that it was "for the millions of adults who read comic books." On the first page, Hecht reiterated, "Nearly everybody reads the comics—old and young alike! They are America's best-loved kind of reading." *Comics Digest* 1 (1942), box 2, VCU Comic Arts Collection. On the popularity of comic books among adults, see E. R. Ross to Rex Stout, June 21, 1943; William DeGrouchy to Stout, June 29, 1943; and "Extract from Minutes of July 7," n.d., all in box 11, WWB Papers. For additional government documents on the popularity of comic books, see *Readership of Comics Magazines Among 1021 Girls and Boys in Providence, R.I. and Buffalo, N.Y.*, box 211, RG 46, NA.

28. "Review of Comic Magazines," March 30, 1943; unknown to Barach, April 21, 1943; and Ross to Stout, June 21, 1943, all in box 11, WWB Papers. DeGrouchy, editor at publisher Street & Smith, gushed, "There is so much that can be done with the 'comic' magazines and their tremendous circulation among the youth of our country, and the large new audience of adults both in the defense industries and in our armed forces." DeGrouchy to Stout, Aug. 29, 1943, in box 11, WWB Papers.

29. Mannes, "Junior Has a Craving," 22; "How Do the Comics Affect Your Child"; "Superman's Dilemma," *Time*, April 13, 1942, 78; and Gabilliet, *Of Comics and Men*, 29.

30. M. C. Gaines to Fadiman, Aug. 25, 1944, box 11, WWB Papers; *Boy Comics* 30 (Lev Gleason, 1946). Another issue from the same year included another service member's demand–a threat, really—for sexy female characters: "*Wings Comics* can be found each month on the table of the Flight 'I' Ready Room on the flight line. We all like the magazine—and like the display of feminine pulchritude found in Jane Martin. If she leaves, *Wings Comics* must leave the Ready Room. Such beauty is a help to morale, and I know it helps our flying." *Wings Comics* 38 (Fiction House, 1943); *Wings Comics* 35 (Fiction House, 1943).

31. See David Kennedy, *Over Here: The First World War and American Society* (New York: Oxford University Press, 1980), 45–92.

32. Barach to George Marcoux, July 15, 1943, box 11, WWB Papers.

33. Blum, *V Was for Victory*, 39.

34. See John Fiske, *Understanding Popular Culture* (New York: Routledge, 2010), chap. 1. See also Theodor W. Adorno and Max Horkheimer, "The Culture Industry," in *Dialectic of Enlightenment* (Stanford, CA: Stanford University Press, 2007).

35. Barach to Paul Gallico, Dec. 30, 1944, box 11, WWB Papers.

36. "Comics Committee Progress Report."

37. Unknown to Barach, n.d.; Irmengarde Eberle to Barach, March 30, 1943, both in box 11, WWB Papers.

38. *War Heroes* 9 (Dell, 1944), box 4, VCU Comic Arts Collection.

39. Bruce Lenthall, "Outside the Panel—Race in America's Popular Imagination: Comic Strips Before and After World War II," *Journal of American Studies* 32 (1998): 57.

40. *Young Allies* 1 (Marvel, 1941), MSU Comic Art Collection. For the sake of clarity, in the endnotes comic books published by Timely and Marvel are all described as having been published by Marvel, as the company once known as Timely is known today as Marvel.

41. Barach to Eugene Tillinger, Dec. 2, 1944; Barach to Gaines, Dec. 13, 1944; and Barach to Sheldon Mayer, Nov. 13, 1944, all in box 11, WWB Papers.

42. Fadiman to Gaines, June 30, 1944, box 11, WWB Papers.

43. *All-Star Comics* 24 (DC, 1945).

44. Howell notes that in 1944, the WWB, at the behest of the Treasury Department, embraced Secretary of the Treasury Morgenthau's draconian postwar plan to destroy Germany's industry and reduce the country to an agrarian existence. Howell, "The Writers' War Board," 802.

45. *All-Star Comics* 24 (DC, 1945).

46. Howell, "The Writers' War Board," 802.

47. Gallico to WWB Advisory Council, Feb. 13, 1945; Dinah Gelbin to Barach, Feb. 13, 1945, both in box 11, WWB Papers. Gaines and Barach believed the issue demanded even wider distribution, and the WWB helped Gaines draft an appeal for an allotment of additional paper. The head of the OWI's Book and Magazine Bureau rejected the appeal and chided Barach for becoming involved, suggesting that "it is better to remain on the editorial and policy side of the fence." See Barach to Gaines, Dec. 2, 1944; Oscar Schisgall to Barach, Dec. 7, 1944; and Barach to Gaines, Dec. 13, 1944, all in box 11, WWB Papers.

48. John W. Dower, *War without Mercy: Race and Power in the Pacific War* (New York: Pantheon, 1993), 9, and Robert G. Lee, *Orientals: Asian Americans in Popular Culture* (Philadelphia: Temple University Press, 1999), 146–47. Lee argues that a combination of political, economic, and cultural factors contributed to this flexible definition of Asians in American popular culture.

49. Dower, *War without Mercy*, 8–9.

50. Robert Lee argues that during the nineteenth century and the first half of the twentieth century, racial tropes defined Asians as pollutants, coolies, deviants, or the Yellow Peril—all of which marked them as unable to assimilate into American society. He also suggests that popular culture—rather than science or the law—was "the ultimate arbiter of whiteness." Certainly, both standard and WWB-sanctioned wartime comics embraced the most vicious elements of these tropes, portraying the Japanese as a profound threat not only to democracy but also to the very fabric of white, American society. Lee, *Orientals*, 142–44.

51. Lee, *Orientals*, 106–9, 144.

52. *Silver Streak Comics* 7 (Lev Gleason, 1941), in Greg Sadowski, ed., *Supermen: The First Wave of Comic Book Heroes, 1936–1941* (Seattle: Fantagraphics, 2009), 138–53.

53. Within the pages of comic books, the Claw terrified even Adolf Hitler. When the two meet in the first issue of *Captain Battle Jr.*, Hitler's cowardice upsets the Claw, who shaves the Nazi's head and mustache as punishment. While Hitler appears simpering and unthreatening, the Claw is terrifying and intelligent. Confronted with Hitler's unwillingness to attack the United States, the Claw exclaims, "The cowardly piece of scum! I will torture him to death for this!" *Captain Battle Jr.* 1 (Lev Gleason, 1943).

54. *Our Gang Comics* 11 (Dell, 1944); *Our Gang Comics* 12 (Dell, 1944), MSU Comic Art Collection. Walt Kelly, the political cartoonist and creator of Pogo Possum, drew stories for *Our Gang Comics*, including these issues.

55. Unknown to Barach, April 1944; Milton Kramer to Barach, April 6, 1943, both in box 11, WWB Papers. In addition to serving on the board, Kramer wrote comic books. For more on Kramer, see "Suggestion re: Comic Strip Writers," Feb. 20, 1943, box 11, WWB Papers.

56. Henry Gemmill, "War Experts Cool toward the Comics: They Read Them All," *Wall Street Journal*, Nov. 2, 1942, 1.

57. Quoted in Dower, *War without Mercy*, 38–40.

58. Richard Rhodes, *The Making of the Atomic Bomb* (New York: Simon and Schuster, 1988), 596–97.

59. The covers of issues two and three of *The United States Marines* read, "Authentic U.S. Marine Corps Picture Stories," and the inside covers describe the publication as "Published in cooperation with the U.S. Marine Corps."

60. *The United States Marines* 2 (Magazine Enterprises, 1944); *The United States Marines* 3 (Magazine Enterprises, 1944), both in box 6, VCU Comic Arts Collection.

61. Barach to Gallico, Dec. 30, 1944; cover letter from Fadiman, Sept. 8, 1944; and Barach to Fadiman, Oct. 5, 1944, all in box 11, WWB Papers.

62. Fadiman to Mayer, Sept. 21, 1944, box 11, WWB Papers. Fadiman's use of the word "wench" to describe a Japanese woman may have arisen from the long-

standing stereotype of the geisha. For a history of the origins of the geisha in American art and culture, see Mari Yoshihara, *Embracing the East: White Women and American Orientalism* (New York: Oxford University Press, 2003), chap. 2.

63. Lee, *Orientals*, 51–60.

64. Philip P. Choy, Lorraine Dong, and Marlon K. Hom, *Coming Man: 19th Century American Perceptions of the Chinese* (Seattle: University of Washington Press, 1995), 19–20.

65. Dower, *War without Mercy*, 164–70.

66. "Review of Comic Magazines," March 30, 1943, box 11, WWB papers.

67. Barach to Gallico, Dec. 3, 1944, box 11, WWB papers. Despite Barach's condemnation, "The Four Musketeers" premiered in the May 1944 issue of *Air Ace*. Intriguingly, the cover touts the connection between the series and the WWB. In bright lettering, it advertises "The Four Musketeers" as "The Writers' War Board Comic." *Air Ace* 3 (Street & Smith, 1944).

68. Fadiman to William Lieberson, Oct. 23, 1944, box 11, WWB Papers.

69. *Comic Cavalcade* 9 (DC, 1944).

70. Gaines to Fadiman, Aug.18, 1944; Fadiman to Mayer, Sept. 21, 1944, box 11, WWB Papers. For a history of the East and West Association, see Robert Shaffer, "Pearl S. Buck and the East and West Association: The Trajectory and Fate of 'Critical Internationalism,' 1940–1950," *Peace & Change* 28 (2003): 1–36.

71. *Military Comics* 1 (Quality, 1941); *Military Comics*, 28 (Quality, 1944).

72. Lee, *Orientals*, 58–60.

73. Fadiman to Beim, Nov. 4, 1944; "Extract From Minutes of July 7," n.d., 1944, both in box 11, WWB Papers.

74. Lenthall, "Outside the Panel," 42. Lenthall argues that wartime comic strips, not comic books, described an ideal America, where the brutal realities of race relations were tempered by the hopes and ideals of readers. By contrast, I suggest that the positive depictions of race relations in comic books owed more to the beliefs— both pragmatic and idealistic—of board members, rather than of consumers.

75. Lary May, *The Big Tomorrow: Hollywood and the Politics of the American Way* (Chicago: University of Chicago Press, 2000), 164.

76. "Joint Project with Race Hatred Committee," July 7, 1944; "Covering Letter on 'Why Race Hatred As A Special Subject," July 12, 1944, both in box 11, WWB Papers. Some WWB documents refer to this organization as the Committee to Combat Race Hatred. For an example, see Milton Kramer to Fadiman, May 26, 1944, box 11, WWB Papers.

77. Enoch P. Waters, "Troops on New Guinea Furnish Own Amusement," *Chicago Defender*, June 10, 1944, 7.

78. Harvey Zorbaugh, "The Comics—There They Stand!," *Journal of Educational Sociology* 18, no. 4 (Dec. 1944): 201.

79. Benton, *Superhero Comics of the Golden Age*, 45.

80. *Captain Marvel Jr.*, 22 (Fawcett, 1944).

81. Fadiman to Lieberson, Oct. 23, 1944, box 11, WWB Papers. The WWB did find a contemporary Fawcett comic book plot objectionable. It criticized Fawcett for a script submitted in late 1944 that implied all industrialists and businessmen were

greedy monopolists. The story, "The Cartels of Crime," starred Radar the International Policeman. Radar was cocreated by members of the WWB and Fawcett editor Will Lieberson. With the board's support, Radar promoted international cooperation and the postwar United Nations. A revised version of "The Cartels of Crime" that no longer equated wealth with corruption appeared in Fawcett's *Master Comics* 62 (1945). Lieberson to Fadiman, Oct. 30, 1944; Barach to Gallico, Nov. 1, 1944; and Barach to Lieberson, Nov. 13, 1944, all in box 11, WWB Papers.

82. Steamboat appeared in *Captain Marvel Adventures* 36 (Fawcett, 1944) and 40 (Fawcett, 1944), bracketing "The Necktie Party" in issue 22 of *Captain Marvel Jr.* Steamboat made over fifty appearances in Fawcett comic books, primarily in *Captain Marvel Adventures*, between early 1942 and early 1945. Although the WWB had nothing to do with removing Steamboat, board member Robert Landry sent a thank-you letter to Lieberson after learning of his mid-1945 meeting with the students of Junior High School 120. Robert Landry to Lieberson, May 2, 1945, box 11, WWB Papers.

83. "Negro Villain in Comic Book Killed by Youngsters," *Chicago Defender*, May 5, 1945, 11.

84. The WWB requested material on the 99th Pursuit Squadron from the OWI. Fadiman to Gaines, July 10, 1944; Barach to Ted Poston, July 3, 1944, both in box 11, WWB Papers.

85. Gaines to Fadiman, Aug. 18, 1944, box 11, WWB Papers.

86. *Comic Cavalcade* 9 (DC, 1945).

87. Unknown to Barach, Jan. 22, 1945, box 11, WWB Papers.

88. George Lipsitz, *The Possessive Investment in Whiteness: How White People Profit from Identity Politics* (Philadelphia: Temple University Press, 1998), 3.

89. For a unique discussion of why Americans agreed to fight in World War II, see Robert B. Westbrook, "'I Want a Girl, Just Like the Girl that Married Harry James': American Women and the Problem of Political Obligation in World War II," *American Quarterly* 42 (1990): 587–614. The core argument is that during World War II, Americans were not asked to think of their wartime obligations in political terms. Rather, the US government based its call for sacrifice on two moral arguments: first, the claim that citizens were obliged to defend moral values—democracy, freedom, and equality—that superseded the need to fight for the United States as an individual nation; and, second, that Americans were duty bound, as individuals, to defend the pursuit of private property made possible by liberal democracy. His second point, in particular, supports the arguments in Blum, *V Was For Victory*, esp. 92–105. See also Dana Polan, *Power and Paranoia: History, Narrative, and the American Cinema, 1940–1950* (New York: Columbia University Press, 1986), 1–20.

90. Barach to Gaines, July 21, 1944; Barach memorandum, July 12, 1944; Barach memorandum, Oct. 4, 1944; and Barach to Walter White, July 5, 11, 1944, box 11, WWB Papers. It is unclear whether Walter White responded to Barach's request for assistance. Board records do not include a written response.

91. Barach to Gaines, Sept. 31, 1944, box 11, WWB Papers.

92. Memorandum from Helen Trager of the Bureau for Intercultural Education to Writers' War Board, box 11, WWB Papers. For an overview of the Bureau for Inter-

cultural Education, see Shafali Lal, "1930s Multiculturalism: Rachel Davis DuBois and the Bureau for Intercultural Education," *Radical Teacher* 69 (2004): 18–22.

93. Comic book writers often worked in anonymity, and most stories from the wartime period were not signed. See Greg Metcalf, "'If You Read It, I Wrote It': The Anonymous Career of Comic Book Writer Paul S. Newman," *Journal of Popular Culture* 29 (1995): 147–62.

94. *Wonder Woman* 13 (DC, 1945).

95. *Wings Comics* 38 (Fiction House, 1943).

96. Richard Phillips to Nelson Rockefeller, Nov. 25, 1943, box 1233; Harry Frantz to John Begg, "Text of New Pamphlet," Sept. 12, 1944, both in box 1460, Records of the Department of Press and Publications, RG 229, Office of Inter-American Affairs, National Archives and Records Administration, College Park, MD (hereafter cited as OIAA).

97. Frieda Everett to Harry Frantz, "CIAA Pamphlets and Posters, 1944–45 Fiscal Year," box 1460, OIAA.

98. Richard I. Phillips to Nelson D. Rockefeller, Nov. 25, 1943, box 1233, OIAA.

99. *Paladines de la libertad* (1943), box 1233, OIAA.

100. *Estados Unidos en la guerra* (1944), box 1232, OIAA.

101. Kurtis Friend Naylor to Wallace Harrison, "La Sordida Amenaza," April 24, 1945; Margaret Pumpelly to Wallace Harrison, "Pamphlet—La Sordida Amenaza," May 29, 1945; and Kenneth Campbell to Wallace Harrison, "Pamphlets Printed by Cuban Committee," June 19, 1945, all in box 1232, OIAA.

102. *La sórdida amenaza* (1945), box 1232, OIAA.

103. *Young Allies* 8 (Marvel, 1943).

104. Rosenberg, *Spreading the American Dream*, 212.

CHAPTER TWO

1. Kate Doyle and Peter Kornbluh, "CIA and Assassinations: The Guatemala 1954 Documents," National Security Archive at George Washington University, accessed Aug. 5, 2020, https://nsarchive2.gwu.edu/NSAEBB/NSAEBB4/.

2. Tim Weiner, *Legacy of Ashes: The History of the CIA* (New York: Anchor Books, 2007), 107.

3. Weiner, *Legacy of Ashes*, 112–13.

4. Weiner, *Legacy of Ashes*, 119.

5. Doyle and Kornbluh, "CIA and Assassinations."

6. *Racket Squad in Action* 1 (Charlton, 1952).

7. *T-Man Comics* 27 (Quality, 1955).

8. *Comic Magazine Publishing Report* no. 129, Oct. 1952, n.n., box 212, RG 46, NA; *Comic Magazine Publishing Report* no. 134, March 1953, n.n., box 212, RG 46, NA; "Fact Sheet on Comic Magazines," n.d., box 167, RG 46, NA.

9. Cited in Carol Tilley, "Seducing the Innocent: Fredric Wertham and the Falsifications that Helped Condemn Comics," *Information & Culture* 47, no. 4 (2012): 409.

10. "The Most Profitable Magazines You Can Handle Are . . . ," n.d., box 167, RG 46, NA.

11. For documents describing the popularity of comic books among adults, see E. R. Ross to Rex Stout, June 21, 1943; William DeGrouchy to Stout, June 29, 1943; and "Extract from Minutes of July 7," n.d., all in box 11, WWB Papers. For additional government documents on the popularity of comic books, see *Readership of Comics Magazines Among 1021 Girls and Boys in Providence, R.I. and Buffalo, N.Y.*, box 211, RG 46, NA. See also Mike Benton, *Crime Comics: The Illustrated History* (Dallas: Taylor Publishing, 1993), 20–21.

12. Tilley, "Seducing the Innocent," 387.

13. "The ABC's of Comic Magazines," 1947, box 167, RG 46, NA; "Comic Book Curbs Asked," *New York Times*, Nov. 18, 1948, 32.

14. "Fugitive from Atom Finds Idyllic Life," *Washington Post*, April 18, 1948, B2. Although exact numbers are difficult to discern during the immediate postwar period, adults read over one-third of the comic books sold during 1942, due in part to the expanding audience among military personnel. See Benton, *Crime Comics*, 21.

15. *Boy Comics* 30 (Lev Gleason, 1946).

16. "The Eastern Color Printing Company: Report of Comic Magazine Production, July 1, 1953–June 30, 1954," box 172, RG 46, NA. The document concerns comic books printed by the Eastern Color Printing Company between July 1, 1953, and June 30, 1954, during which time it produced 124,000 Spanish-language copies and 1,406,735 English-language copies of *Wings Comics*. The cover letter of the document makes clear that Eastern Color Printing also produced *Wings Comics* and many other titles before July 1, 1953. The company restricted its report to the given twelve-month period at the request of the Senate Subcommittee on Juvenile Delinquency, which utilized the information as part of its investigation of the comic book industry.

17. *Wings Comics* 84 (Fiction House, 1947); *Wings Comics* 86 (Fiction House, 1947); *Wings Comics* 105 (Fiction House, 1949).

18. *Wings Comics* 88 (Fiction House, 1947).

19. The "comic book philosophy" panel is from *Lawbreakers Always Lose* 7 (Marvel, 1948); I believe but cannot confirm that the "how to hurt people" panel is from a comic book titled *Top Secrets* 7 (Street & Smith, 1949). Both can be found in Fredric Wertham, *Seduction of the Innocent* (New York: Rinehart, 1954), n.n.

20. Wertham, *Seduction of the Innocent*, n.n.

21. "Police Fight Comic Books," *New York Times*, Aug. 12, 1947, 20.

22. "Comic Book Inspires Boys' Torture Of Pal," *New York Times*, Aug. 19, 1948, 17.

23. Malcolm Kildale to Fredric Wertham, July 19, 1950, box 112, folder 4, Wertham Papers.

24. Elaine Tyler May, *Homeward Bound: American Families in the Cold War Era* (New York: Basic Books, 1988). Peter Filene also suggests that American leaders applied the political concept of containment to the American family. According to policy makers, international security depended on a strong domestic foundation, which relied on sturdy family units. As a result, whatever longings American women still harbored for sexual freedom or employment after World War II had to be contained for the benefit of the family and the nation. Americans thus promoted the modern female consumer as the pinnacle of male achievement—evidence of a successful male provider able to "elevate" his spouse above the need to work outside

the home. Peter Filene, "'Cold War Culture' Doesn't Say It All," in *Rethinking Cold War Culture*, ed. Peter J. Kuznick and James Gilbert (Washington, DC: Smithsonian Institution Press, 2001), 156–74.

25. Anne M. Boylan, "Containment on the Home Front: American Families During the Cold War," *Reviews in American History* 2 (June 1989): 301.

26. Relying on information drawn from teaching experience, Gallup polls and sociological studies on human memory, Peter Filene argues that average Americans paid little attention to the Cold War on a day-to-day basis. They defined their world in more intimate terms, worrying far more about the high cost of living than communist subversion or vague threats beyond America's borders. According to Filene, the Cold War was waged primarily at an elite level, while the majority of Americans retained a more personal view of their surroundings. Filene, "'Cold War Culture,'" 156–74.

27. Joel Williamson, *Elvis Presley: A Southern Life* (Oxford: Oxford University Press, 2015).

28. "'Comics' Blamed in Death," *New York Times*, Sept. 15, 1947, 12.

29. A *New York Times* article from late 1945 described American comic books as "infecting" international consumers hungry for tales of crime, horror, and romance. J. L. Brown, "A Report from France," *New York Times*, Nov. 11, 1945, 104. Contemporary observers noted that 44 percent of men in the army identified as comic book readers. The figure comes from two sources. The first is Marya Mannes, "Junior Has a Craving," *New Republic*, Feb. 17, 1947, 22; the second is the transcript of a 1949 radio discussion, "How Do the Comics Affect Your Child," where Professor Paul Witty of Northwestern University cites the same number, both in box 109, folder 12, Wertham Papers.

30. "Economic Cooperation Administration Office of Administration," box 111, folder 4, Wertham Papers.

31. Gleason's FBI file reports that he served from April 26, 1917, until September 4, 1919. Untitled FBI file dated March 18, 1947, p. 2, Gleason FBI file.

32. Mike Benton, *The Comic Book in America: An Illustrated History* (Dallas: Taylor Publishing, 1989), 36.

33. *Boy Comics* 6 (Lev Gleason, 1942).

34. *Crime Does Not Pay* 25 (Lev Gleason, 1943).

35. *Crime Does Not Pay* 24 (Lev Gleason, 1942).

36. Denis Kitchen, ed., *Blackjacked and Pistol-Whipped: A "Crime Does Not Pay" Primer* (Milwaukee, OR: Dark Horse Books, 2011), 18.

37. Kitchen, *Blackjacked and Pistol-Whipped*, 12.

38. *Crime Does Not Pay* 26 (Lev Gleason, 1943).

39. *Crime Does Not Pay* 62 (Lev Gleason, 1948).

40. *Crime Does Not Pay* 55 (Lev Gleason, 1947).

41. *Crime Does Not Pay* 57 (Lev Gleason, 1947).

42. Kitchen, *Blackjacked and Pistol-Whipped*, 20–21.

43. Lary May, *The Big Tomorrow: Hollywood and the Politics of the American Way* (Chicago: University of Chicago Press, 2000), 164.

44. Several female superheroes did appear during the war, the most famous of which was National's Wonder Woman. Fawcett Publications boasted Mary Marvel,

the twin sister of Captain Marvel. June Tarpé Mills created the character of Miss Fury, who appeared in Timely Comics. See Maurice Horn, *Women in the Comics* (New York: Chelsea House, 1980); Jill Lepore, *The Secret History of Wonder Woman* (New York: Vintage, 2015); Trina Robbins, *The Great Women Super Heroes* (Northampton: Kitchen Sink Press, 1996); and Trina Robbins and Catherine Yronwode, *Women and the Comics* (Columbia: Eclipse Books, 1985).

45. *Wings Comics* 23 (Fiction House, 1942).

46. *Fight Comics* 20 (Fiction House, 1942).

47. *Fight against Crime* 20 (Story, 1954).

48. *Crime SuspenStories* 19 (EC, 1953).

49. *Underworld Crime* 23 (Fawcett, 1952).

50. *Uncanny Tales* 17 (Marvel, 1954).

51. Emily S. Rosenberg, "Consuming Women: Images of Americanization in the 'American Century,'" *Diplomatic History* 3 (Summer 1999): 489.

52. *Crimes by Women* 12 (Fox, 1950).

53. *Crimes by Women* 10 (Fox, 1949).

54. *Fight against Crime* 6 (Story, 1951).

55. J. Edgar Hoover, "How Good A Parent Are You?," *Los Angeles Times*, April 20, 1947, E4.

56. *Eerie* 1 (Avon, 1947).

57. *Crime SuspenStories* 22 (EC, 1954).

58. Frank Jacobs, *The Mad World of William M. Gaines* (Secaucus, NJ: Lyle Stuart, 1972), 80.

59. *Shock SuspenStories* 14 (EC, 1954).

60. Joe Simon and Jim Simon, *The Comic Book Makers* (Lebanon, NJ: Vanguard Productions, 2003), 110–12.

61. "Hank Williams: Filmmaker Interview with Director Morgan Neville," *American Masters*, PBS, accessed Feb. 4, 2018, http://www.pbs.org/wnet/americanmasters/database/williams_h_interview.html.

62. Roger M. Williams, *Sing a Sad Song: The Life of Hank Williams* (Champaign: University of Illinois Press, 1981), 202.

63. *Country Weekly*, Sept. 13, 1998.

64. Richard Leppert and George Lipsitz, "'Everybody's Lonesome for Somebody': Age, the Body, and Experience in the Music of Hank Williams," *Popular Music* 9, no. 3 (Oct. 1990): 260.

65. Peter Guralnick, *Careless Love: The Unmaking of Elvis Presley* (Boston: Little, Brown, 1999), 439, 484.

66. Simon and Simon, *The Comic Book Makers*, 112.

67. Simon and Simon, *The Comic Book Makers*, 112.

68. Subscriptions to *My Secret Life* were available to readers in the United States, Mexico, Spain, and South America.

69. *My Secret Life* 27 (Fox, 1951).

70. *Young Romance* 30 (Prize, 1951).

71. "Digest of Comic Magazine Conference," Dec. 5, 1944, Box 11, WWB Papers.

72. Black Haitians appear as slaves, ghosts, and zombies in "All The King's Men," from *Amazing Ghost Stories* 15 (St. John, 1954).

73. *Love Confessions* 9 (Quality, 1951).

74. "Digest of Comic Magazine Conference," Dec. 5, 1944, box 11, WWB Papers.

75. Bradford W. Wright, *Comic Book Nation: The Transformation of Youth Culture in America* (Baltimore: Johns Hopkins University Press, 2001), 57. Wright notes that no successful superheroes appeared after 1946. The genre would remain relatively dormant until 1961, when Marvel Comics premiered *The Fantastic Four*.

76. David Hajdu, *The Ten-Cent Plague: The Great Comic-Book Scare and How It Changed America* (New York, Picador, 2008), 69.

CHAPTER THREE

1. Eileen Welsome, *The Plutonium Files: America's Secret Medical Experiments in the Cold War* (New York: Delta, 1999), 83–86.

2. Welsome, *The Plutonium Files*, 152–55, 300–301.

3. *Target Comics* 11 (Novelty, 1940).

4. Some atomic-themed comics challenged the Cold War consensus, such as an accord between Republican and Democratic policy makers, forged during the late 1940s and early 1950s, regarding the importance of containing international communism and battling domestic subversion. The consensus also suggested that Americans resolve political and economic debates through reasoned debate, rather than through more violent methods, out of respect for the nation's political traditions and in the interest of projecting a unified front to the Soviet bloc. For a discussion of the creation of the Cold War consensus, see the introduction to Michael J. Hogan, *A Cross of Iron: Harry S. Truman and the Origins of the National Security State, 1945–1954* (New York: Cambridge University Press, 2000).

5. When founded, the company was known as Malcolm Ater Productions, but in 1950 it became Commercial Comics Inc. For a history of Commercial Comics and the creation of the President Truman biography, see Malcolm W. Ater, "Sugar Coated Ballyhoo," unpublished submission to the *Saturday Evening Post*, July 10, 1962, box 1, Private Papers of Malcolm W. Ater, Sheperdstown, WV (hereafter cited as Ater Papers).

6. Tom Christopher, "Malcolm Ater and the Commercial Comics Company," accessed Aug. 1, 2014, http://www.tomchristopher.com/comics2/malcolm-ater-and-the-commercial-comics-company/.

7. *The Story of Harry S. Truman*, n.n. (1948).

8. Christopher, "Malcolm Ater and the Commercial Comics Company."

9. *Louisiana Needs Chep Morrison; Alabama Needs John Patterson for Governor; Alabama Needs George Wallace for the Big Job* (Malcolm Ater, n.d.), Ater Papers.

10. Agencies such as the Office of Press and Publications, USIA, and the Private Enterprise Commission also consulted with comic book publishers, including Fawcett, Marvel, General Comics, Magazine Enterprises, and Lloyd Jacquet Studios. See boxes 6 and 7, Private Enterprise Cooperation Subject Files, Record Group 59, National Archives, College Park, MD (hereafter cited as PEC NA).

11. *If an A-Bomb Falls*, n.n. (Malcolm Ater, 1951).

12. Hogan, *A Cross of Iron*, 210–19.

13. The Federal Civil Defense Administration was formed in January 1951 and merged the responsibilities of the Office of Civil Defense, a wartime agency, and the National Security Resources Board. JoAnne Brown, "'A Is for Atom, B Is for Bomb': Civil Defense in American Public Education, 1948–1963," *Journal of American History* 75, no. 1 (June 1988): 69.

14. Malcolm Ater to Carl Denman, April 14, 1953, folder 26, Ater Papers.

15. Carl Denman to Malcolm Ater, Aug. 16, 1954; Ater to Denman, Nov. 22, 1954, folder 26, Ater Papers. Ater's private papers do not clarify the total number of orders for *The H-Bomb and You* and in most cases do not indicate which state or federal civil defense agencies ultimately paid for copies of the comic book. In addition to an initial order for two hundred thousand copies from a federal agency (possibly the FCDA), Ater's papers record subsequent orders for fifteen thousand copies and forty thousand copies without any attribution to a specific state or federal agency. See J. Paulsen to Ater, July 5, 1955; Paulsen to Ater, Nov. 1, 1955, folder 29, Ater Papers. For additional information regarding orders for *The H-Bomb and You*, see correspondence between Ater and Denman, folder 26, folder 28, folder 29, and folder 30, Ater Papers.

16. *The H-Bomb and You*, n.n. (Malcolm Ater, 1955).

17. Hogan, *A Cross of Iron*, 210–11.

18. Andrew D. Grossman, *Neither Dead nor Red: Civilian Defense and American Political Development during the Early Cold War* (New York: Routledge, 2001), 2–3.

19. *Bert the Turtle Says "Duck and Cover"* (1951). See Brown, "'A Is for Atom, B Is for Bomb,'" 68–90; Richard L. Graham, *Government Issue: Comics for the People, 1940s–2000s* (New York: Abrams ComicArts, 2012), 144–45; and Allan M. Winkler, *Life under a Cloud: American Anxiety about the Atom* (New York: Oxford University Press, 1999), 114–16. Brown and Winkler suggest that three million copies of *Bert the Turtle Says "Duck and Cover"* reached American public schools, while Graham cites a total of twenty million copies.

20. Brown, "'A Is for Atom, B Is for Bomb,'" 69–70.

21. *Bert the Turtle Says "Duck and Cover,"* n.n. (1951).

22. *Journal of Educational Sociology* 18, no. 4 (Dec. 1944); *Journal of Educational Sociology* 22, no. 5 (Jan. 1949); *Journal of Educational Sociology* 23, no. 4 (Dec. 1949).

23. In April 1950, Zorbaugh—a professor at New York University—hosted a conference, "The Comics as a Mass Medium of Communication." Held at NYU, the attendees included Bartow H. Underhill of the State Department. B. H. Underhill to Mr. Begg, "Project No. 114—Comic Book Technique," April 5, 1950; Harvey Zorbaugh to Bartow H. Underhill, April 21, 1950, box 7, PEC NA.

24. Harvey Zorbaugh, "The Comics—There They Stand!," *Journal of Educational Sociology* 18, no. 4 (Dec. 1944): 202.

25. W. W. D. Sones, "The Comics and Instructional Method," *Journal of Educational Sociology* 18, no. 4 (Dec. 1944): 233.

26. Based on Hutchinson's description, the weekly collection *Puck—The Comic Weekly* consisted of reproductions of popular comic strips, rather than reproductions of narratives from comic books. This suggests that the materials used in the classroom were much less explicit than those found in contemporary crime, horror,

romance, and even superhero comic books. Katharine H. Hutchinson, "An Experiment in the Use of Comics as Instructional Material," *Journal of Educational Sociology* 23, no. 4 (Dec. 1949): 236–37.

27. Hutchinson, "An Experiment in the Use of Comics," 237–40.

28. Hutchinson, "An Experiment in the Use of Comics," 240.

29. Hutchinson, "An Experiment in the Use of Comics," 245.

30. Fredric Wertham to Arthur Freund, June 14, 1950, box 111, folder 4, Wertham Papers.

31. Volta Torrey, "Communications Mediums Explain and Illustrate Nuclear Energy," *Journal of Educational Sociology* 22, no. 5 (Jan. 1949): 325–26.

32. The State Planning Committee for School and Community Health Education, "The Blondie Comic Book: A Teaching Aid in Mental Health," Sept. 1953, box 167, RG 46, NA.

33. Torrey, "Communications Mediums," 325–26.

34. *Learn How Dagwood Splits the Atom* (King Features, 1949). For a description of *Man and the Atom*, the 1948 exposition where the government dispensed free copies of *Learn How Dagwood Splits the Atom*, see Paul Boyer, "'Some Sort of Peace': President Truman, the American People, and the Atomic Bomb," in *The Truman Presidency*, ed. Michael J. Lacey (New York: Cambridge University Press, 1989), 188–89; and John R. Dunning, "Atomic Power and the Future," *Journal of Educational Sociology* 22, no. 5 (Jan. 1949): 365.

35. *Learn How Dagwood Splits the Atom* was also included as part of the A. C. Gilbert toy company's "U-238 Atomic Energy Lab." According to company founder A. C. Gilbert, the company was "encouraged by the government, who thought that our set would aid in public understanding of atomic energy and stress its constructive side. We had the great help of some of the country's best nuclear physicists and worked closely with M.I.T. in its development." Sold during the early 1950s, the science kit also included a government pamphlet entitled "Prospecting for Uranium." See A. C. Gilbert, *The Man Who Lives in Paradise* (New York: Rinehart, 1954).

36. *Headline Comics* 16 (Prize, 1945).

37. *The Atomic Thunderbolt* 1 (Regor, 1946).

38. *Atoman* 1 (Spark, 1946).

39. Paul Boyer, *By the Bomb's Early Light: American Thought and Culture at the Dawn of the Cold War* (Chapel Hill: University of North Carolina Press, 1994), 31.

40. "For the Future," *Newsweek*, Aug. 20, 1945, 59–60.

41. Paul Boyer, "Exotic Resonances," in *Hiroshima in History and Memory*, ed. Michael J. Hogan (New York: Cambridge University Press, 1999), 145.

42. J. Robert Oppenheimer, "The New Weapon: The Turn of the Screw," in *One World or None: A Report to the Public on the Full Meaning of the Atomic Bomb*, ed. Dexter Masters and Katharine Way (New York: McGraw-Hill, 1946), 22.

43. *Picture News in Color and Action* 1 (Jan. 1946).

44. "Extract from Minutes of July 7," no year indicated, box 11, WWB Papers. Although there is no year indicated on this document, information from other related documents suggests that it refers to a meeting on July 7, 1943. During the war, Street & Smith promoted President Roosevelt's concept of the "Four Policemen"—the United States, Britain, the Soviet Union, and China—dedicated to

enforcing peace within the international system. Using a group of characters called "the Four Musketeers," Street & Smith's efforts were met with a warm response from the WWB, which proclaimed, "It did our hearts good to know that you are going ahead with this series, since we believe, as you know, in the good that can be done by such popularization of the idea of cooperation between the four great powers." Paul Gallico to William DeGrouchy, April 20, 1944, box 11, WWB Papers.

45. *Air Ace* 7 (Street & Smith, 1947).

46. *Donald Duck's Atom Bomb*, Cheerios Premium Y1 (Disney, 1947).

47. Bruce Hamilton, "The Carl Barks Library: Donald Duck Adventures in Color Comic Albums," accessed Jan. 28, 2020, https://www.brucehamilton.com/GLAD/AAA%20Steve%20Files/Series2Albums/DDA25pages/ddaincolor.htm.

48. Boyer, *By the Bomb's Early Light*, 204.

49. During the 1940s and 1950s, comic books typically appeared on newsstands one or two months earlier than the date indicated on the cover of the comic book. This allowed retailers to display the comic book for many weeks without it appearing outdated. As an example, the copy of *Action Comics* 101 in the Library of Congress bears an "August 2" cover stamp presumably applied by a newsdealer or distributor, suggesting it went on sale about two months earlier than the cover date of October 1946.

50. *Action Comics* 101 (DC, 1946).

51. Jules Feiffer, *The Great Comic Book Heroes* (New York: Bonanza Books, 1965), 24.

52. Fawcett's claim that *Captain Marvel Adventures* was the best-selling comic book in the country after 1945 may have been an exaggeration. The title enjoyed enormous popularity during World War II, but by the end of the conflict, sales of superhero comics began to wane. For more information on comic book circulation numbers in the immediate postwar period, see Bradford W. Wright, *Comic Book Nation: The Transformation of Youth Culture in America* (Baltimore: Johns Hopkins University Press, 2001), 58.

53. *Captain Marvel Adventures* 66 (Fawcett, 1946). "The World's Mightiest Mortal" was one of Fawcett's nicknames for Captain Marvel.

54. Editorials and stories warning of the dangers posed by atomic power appeared in lowbrow, middlebrow, and elite forms of mass culture. But other evidence suggests that at least in the immediate aftermath of World War II, a majority of Americans supported the bombings. In a *Fortune* magazine poll conducted in late 1945, just 5 percent of the respondents opposed America's use of two atomic bombs against Japan. A small but significant number of respondents also felt that the United States should have used more atomic weapons against the Japanese. See "The Fortune Survey," *Fortune*, Dec. 1945, 305.

55. *World War III* 1 (Ace, 1952).

56. *Atomic War* 2 (Ace, 1952).

57. *Atomic War* 1 (Ace, 1952).

58. Interview with Al Feldstein by John Benson, recorded July 16, 1981, published in *The Haunt of Fear*, vol. 2 (West Plains, MO: Russ Cochran, 1985), n.n.

59. *Weird Science* 14 (EC, 1950).

60. *Weird Fantasy* 11 (EC, 1952).

61. John Lear, "Hiroshima, U.S.A—Can Anything Be Done?," *Collier's*, Aug. 5, 1950.

62. *Weird Fantasy* 14 (EC, 1950).

63. William W. Savage Jr., *Comic Books in America: 1945–1954* (Norman: University of Oklahoma Press, 1990), 37.

64. Edward W. Judge and John W. Langdon, *The Cold War: A History through Documents* (Saddle River, NJ: Prentice Hall, 1999), 74–75.

65. C. Wright Mills, *The Causes of World War III* (1958), quoted in David Talbot, *The Devil's Chessboard: Allen Dulles, the CIA, and the Rise of America's Secret Government* (New York: HarperCollins, 2015), 245.

CHAPTER FOUR

1. Fredric Wertham to Harry Slochower, Nov. 1, 1956, box 22, folder 8, Wertham Papers.

2. Wertham to Slochower, Nov. 1, 1956, Wertham Papers.

3. Because Wertham was not called to testify on Koslow's behalf, he reduced his fee for the ten hours of consultations from five hundred dollars to four hundred dollars. Fredric Wertham to Morris Eisenstein, Jan. 20, 1955; "Professional Services Rendered to Samuel Koslow," Feb. 1955, box 22, folder 8, Wertham Papers.

4. "Nights of Horror," n.d., box 16, folder 8, Wertham Papers.

5. Wertham believed the bullwhip came from an advertisement that ran in multiple titles during 1954. He did not manage to connect Koslow's switchblade to a specific comic book advertisement because as he explained to James Fitzpatrick, New York state senator, a friend gave the knife to Koslow. But in the course of his research, he had seen "many such ads." Fredric Wertham to James Fitzpatrick, Jan. 1, 1955; Wertham to Fitzpatrick, Jan. 18, 1955, box 16, folder 8, Wertham Papers.

6. Wertham to Fitzpatrick, Jan. 1, 1955; Wertham to Fitzpatrick, Jan. 18, 1955, box 16, folder 8, Wertham Papers.

7. Wertham closed the letter with a generous offer to Koslow: "If there is anything I can do for you later on, please write me." Wertham to Jack Koslow, Dec. 15, 1954, box 22, folder 8, Wertham Papers.

8. "Youth's Death Puzzles Dad and Police," *Chicago Defender*, April 23, 1949, 5; "Health Talk," *Chicago Defender*, Sept. 18, 1948, 14.

9. "Boy Confesses Fatal Fire," *Chicago American*, June 13, 1954; "Boy, 11, Who Smokes, Drinks, Admits He Set Fire Fatal to 7," *Daily Calumet*, June 16, 1954; "Drunken Boys Comics Blamed for Fatal Fire," *New York Post*, June 14, 1954, box 7, folder 9, Wertham Papers.

10. "Comic Books Held Harmful to Youth," *New York Times*, May 5, 1948, 35; "Urges Comic Book Ban," *New York Times*, Sept. 4, 1948.

11. Surveys entitled "The Comic Book Industry," folder "Questionnaire on Crime Comics, Organized Crime Committee," box 171, RG 46, NA.

12. Gleason's FBI file states that he joined the Communist Party "in or about the year 1938 or 1939." Untitled FBI file dated March 18, 1947, p. 3, Gleason FBI file.

13. Brett Daikin, "Leverett Gleason: Brief Life of a Comics Impresario, 1898–1971," *Harvard Magazine*, May–June 2011, 32–33.

14. Quoted in David Hajdu, *The Ten-Cent Plague: The Great Comic-Book Scare and How It Changed America* (New York: Picador, 2008), 58.

15. It is difficult to piece together details of the business relationship among Gleason, Biro, and Wood. Joe Simon suggests that Lev Gleason financed and published *Crime Does Not Pay*. Biro and Wood, in turn, contracted out to artists and writers for stories, which the pair then sold to Gleason. Biro and Wood received royalties from sales of *Crime Does Not Pay*. Joe Simon and Jim Simon, *The Comic Book Makers* (Lebanon, NJ: Vanguard Productions, 2003), 57.

16. Untitled FBI document, May 10, 1944, p. 2, Gleason FBI file.

17. "Asks House to Act on Barsky Board," *New York Times*, March 7, 1946, 11; "New House Move Hits 'Anti-Fascists,'" *New York Times*, April 5, 1946, 25.

18. Gleason was eventually fined five hundred dollars for contempt of Congress. Edward K. Barsky, the chairman of the JAFRC, received a six-month jail term in addition to a fine. "17 Foes of Franco Voted in Contempt," *New York Times*, April 17, 1946, 29; and "Barsky, 10 Aides Sent to Prison, Fined for Contempt of Congress," *New York Times*, July 17, 1947, 1.

19. Untitled FBI file dated Jan. 30, 1950, p. 8, Gleason FBI file.

20. Louis Budenz, an editor at the *Daily Worker* who later disavowed communism, also identified Gleason as an "active communist in 1944 and 1945" and a "concealed communist." An FBI memorandum from 1950 includes a short biography of Gleason, provided by Budenz. Gleason is identified first and foremost as an "editor and publisher of comic magazines." Office Memorandum, July 27, 1950, p. 4, Gleason FBI file. During an interview conducted by the FBI in 1953, Gleason also admitted to membership in the Communist Party beginning in 1936 or 1937 and continuing for about two years. SAC, New York to Director, FBI, Sept. 25, 1953, p. 2, Gleason FBI file.

21. Thomas Borstelmann, *The Cold War and the Color Line: American Race Relations in the Global Arena* (Cambridge, MA: Harvard University Press, 2001), 70–71.

22. Untitled FBI file dated Jan. 30, 1950, p. 12, Gleason FBI file.

23. Untitled document, May 10, 1944, p. 3, Gleason FBI file.

24. J. Edgar Hoover to SAC, New York, Dec. 13, 1948, Gleason FBI file.

25. Mr. Nichols to Clyde Tolson, Feb. 8, 1949, Gleason FBI file.

26. Hajdu, *The Ten-Cent Plague*, 110.

27. Denis Kitchen and Paul Buhle, *The Art of Harvey Kurtzman: The Mad Genius of Comics* (New York: Harry N. Abrams, 2009), 50.

28. The only significant restrictions on comic book contents were postal regulations and internal editorial policies. National Comics forbade graphic depictions of violence in any of its titles. Dell Comics, which specialized in titles for very young readers, similarly banned violence from its comic books. Other publishers, like Victor Fox, Lev Gleason, and EC, used the boldest imagery possible.

29. Frank Jacobs, *The Mad World of William M. Gaines* (Secaucus, NJ: Lyle Stuart, 1972), 75; Fred von Bernewitz and Grant Geissman, *Tales of Terror: The EC Companion* (Seattle: Fantagraphics, 2000), 10–11. In 1953, the World Color Printing Company produced about four hundred thousand copies per issue of EC's *The Vault of Horror*. A year later, in testimony before Congress, Gaines claimed that EC printed a total of two and a half million comic books per month, of which one and a half million were "guaranteed sale." Roswell Messing Jr. to Herbert W. Beaser,

June 4, 1954, box 170, RG 46, NA; United States Senate Committee on the Judiciary, *Hearings before the Subcommittee to Investigate Juvenile Delinquency*, 83rd Cong., April 1954, 106.

30. James M. McInerney to Director, FBI, April 29, 1952, pp. 1–2, FBI file for William Gaines (hereafter cited as Gaines FBI file). Confidential informants "familiar with Communist activity in NYC" informed the FBI that the owners, publisher, and editors of EC were not familiar to them. Untitled document, Aug. 28, 1952, p. 1, Gaines FBI file.

31. McInerney to Director, FBI, April 29, 1952, pp. 1–2, Gaines FBI file.

32. Kitchen and Buhle, *Art of Harvey Kurtzman*, 3, 56.

33. *Two-Fisted Tales* 25 (EC, 1952).

34. J. Edgar Hoover to Charles B. Murray, Sept. 16, 1952, p. 1, Gaines FBI file.

35. SAC, New York, to Director, FBI, March 10, 1953, p. 1; untitled document, Dec. 30, 1953, p. 1; SAC, New York, to Director, FBI, Jan. 18, 1954, p. 1, all in Gaines FBI file.

36. Mr. A. Jones to Mr. Wick, April 24, 1967, p. 1, Gaines FBI file.

37. Bart Beaty, *Frederic Wertham and the Critique of Mass Culture* (Jackson: University Press of Mississippi, 2006), 17, 82; Thurgood Marshall to Wertham, May 25, 1954, box 2, folder 13, Wertham Papers.

38. Fredric Wertham, "The Comics . . . Very Funny!," *Saturday Review of Literature*, May 29, 1948, 6. Norman Cousins, editor of the *Saturday Review of Literature*, wrote to Wertham in January 1947 to request that the doctor write an article on comic books. Although Wertham was busy with other obligations at the time, his article appeared in the *Saturday Review of Literature* about one year later. Norman Cousins to Wertham, Jan. 5, 1947; Wertham to Cousins, Jan. 28, 1947, both in box 159, folder 10, Wertham Papers.

39. For examples of Wertham's clinical notes, see box 109, folders 12, 15, and 16; box 111, folder 3; and box 121, Wertham Papers. I have not identified specific clinical notes by title because they may include the names of patients.

40. Untitled clinical notes, box 111, folder 3, Wertham Papers.

41. Untitled clinical notes, box 109, folder 12, Wertham Papers.

42. Fredric Wertham, *Seduction of the Innocent* (New York: Rinehart, 1954), 26.

43. Wertham, "The Comics . . . Very Funny!," 27.

44. Wertham, *Seduction of the Innocent*, 311.

45. Wertham, "The Comics . . . Very Funny!," 27.

46. Wertham, "The Comics . . . Very Funny!," 28.

47. Dewitt Wallace to Wertham, Nov. 24, 1948, box 112, folder 6, Wertham Papers.

48. Wertham apparently appeared on *Court of Current Issues* on the DuMont Television Network on July 6, 1948. Other panel members included Al Capp, creator of *Li'l Abner*, and Lev Gleason, publisher of *Crime Does Not Pay*. Irvin Paul Suds to Wertham, June 30, 1948, box 111, folder 5, Wertham Papers.

49. Memorandum to Dr. Wertham RE: Comic Book Artist, March 31, 1949, box 112, folder 3, Wertham Papers.

50. *T-Man Comics* 4 (Quality, 1951); Wertham, *Seduction of the Innocent*, 284.

51. James Gilbert, *A Cycle of Outrage: America's Reaction to the Juvenile Delinquent in the 1950s* (New York: Oxford University Press, 1986), 101.

52. *Howdy Doody* 6 (Dell, 1951), box 113, folder 2, Wertham Papers.

53. Wertham to Rosemary Rau, Feb. 1, 1954, box 124, folder 1, Wertham Papers.

54. Wertham to Editor, *The Times*, July 24, 1952, box 112, folder 6, Wertham Papers.

55. In addition to her work at the Child Study Association of America, Frank was a paid consultant at National Comics and a target of Wertham's ire. Josette Frank to Wertham, Jan. 23, 1948; T. S. Foster to Frank, Jan. 24, 1948, both in box 111, folder 4, Wertham Papers.

56. W. Bruce Thorburn to Senate Special Subcommittee, Sept. 26, 1950; "Report by Hon. Louis Goldstein, Chairman," Sept. 8, 1950, box 171, folder "Questionnaire on Crime Comics, Organized Crime Committee," RG 46, NA.

57. Frederic M. Thrasher, "The Comics and Delinquency: Cause or Scapegoat," *Journal of Educational Sociology*, 23 (Dec. 1949): 195–205. Also see Frances Ilg and Louise Ames, "Comic Book Menace Doubted," *New York World Telegram and Sun*, Nov. 9, 1954, box 109, folder 14, Wertham papers. Dr. Ilg and Professor Ames downplayed Wertham's fears of comic books. The comic book "situation," they argued, was one easily contained by the average family. Children grew out of their fascination with comic books, just as they eventually lost interest in stamp collections, dolls, and other pursuits.

58. For examples of the diversity within the anti–comic book campaign, see Wertham's correspondence with various clergymen, rabbis, law enforcement officers, politicians, children, housewives, soldiers, and even a small number of white supremacists. See box 113, folders 2–5; box 115, folder 1; and box 159, folders 10 and 13, all in Wertham Papers.

59. Wertham, *Seduction of the Innocent*, 15, 32.

60. "Cross-Section U.S.A.—The Jewish Newsletter Ahead of the News," Dec. 21, 1950, box 11, folder 4, Wertham Papers.

61. Marya Mannes, "Junior Has a Craving," *New Republic*, Feb. 17, 1947, 22.

62. David Platt, "100 Million 'Comic Books' Yearly Feed War Propaganda to Children," *Daily Worker*, Dec. 10, 1952, 7; Charles Corwin, "Comic Book Art: School for Sadism," *Daily Worker*, May 13, 1949, 13. Although the *Daily Worker* found little to like about comic books, it offered readers a long-running comic strip entitled *Pinky Rankin*.

63. Albert E. Kahn, "Comics, TV and Your Child," *Masses & Mainstream*, June 1953, 36.

64. In 1948, the *Chicago Defender* also warned that comic books contributed to poor eyesight and poor academic performance. "Health Talk," *Chicago Defender*, Sept. 18, 1948, 14. See also Lillian Scott, "Along Celebrity Row," *Chicago Defender*, April 30, 1949, 8.

65. "Book of the Week," *Jet*, May 20, 1954, 48.

66. "Uses Mouth to Hide Dope Caps," *Chicago Defender*, Oct. 20, 1951, 1.

67. "Are Teen-Agers Growing Up Too Fast?," *Jet*, May 19, 1955, 27.

68. "Tenney Warns Parents on Red Comic Books," *Los Angeles Times*, April 10, 1946, 6. Tenney was the chair of the California Committee on Un-American Activities between 1941 and 1949.

69. J. Edgar Hoover, "How Good A Parent Are You?," *Los Angeles Times*, April 20, 1947.

70. "Legion Will Help Fight Communism in School Rooms," *New York Times*, Oct. 21, 1948, 1.

71. Other cities and regions in California also initiated efforts to ban crime comic books in 1948. "Sacramento's Lady Mayor Studies Comics in Move to Control 'Em," *Los Angeles Times*, Aug. 25, 1948, A2.

72. "Vice in Comic Books Assailed," *Los Angeles Times*, July 29, 1948, 15; Bess M. Wilson, "PTA Moves to Curb Harmful Comic Books, *Los Angeles Times*, Sept. 10, 1948, C1; "Comic Book Fight Told by State PTA," *Los Angeles Times*, Nov. 12, 1948, B4.

73. Harold W. Kennedy to Wertham, Dec. 1, 1948, box 113, folder 5, Wertham Papers.

74. Kennedy to Wertham and Rosemary Kiefer, Oct. 27, 1948; Wertham to Kennedy, Nov. 7, 1948, both in box 113, folder 5, Wertham Papers.

75. John E. Twomey, "The Anti-Comic Book Crusade" (PhD diss., University of Chicago, 1955), 17. Also see "Crime Comics and the Constitution," *Stanford Law Review* 2 (March 1955): 237–60.

76. Winters v. New York, 333 U.S. 507, 68 Sup. Ct. 665 (1948), cited in Twomey, "The Anti-Comic Book Crusade," 17–18. See also Amy Kiste Nyberg, *Seal of Approval: The History of the Comics Code* (Jackson: University Press of Mississippi, 1998), 38–39.

77. Wertham, *Seduction of the Innocent*, 284.

78. Wertham, *Seduction of the Innocent*, 284, 294.

79. Borstelmann, *The Cold War and the Color Line*, 54–55.

80. *Slave Girl* 1 (Avon, 1949); *Slave Girl* 2 (Avon, 1949); *White Princess of the Jungle* 2 (Avon, 1951).

81. Wertham, *Seduction of the Innocent*, 32, 101.

82. "Age 15 -- #A85135," May 12, 1950, box 111, folder 3, Wertham Papers.

83. Hajdu, *The Ten-Cent Plague*, 251.

84. "Comic Book Hearing Is Set," *New York Times*, Feb. 21, 1954, 45; "Senators to Press Delinquency Study," *New York Times*, March 15, 1954, 25; "Comic Book Hearing to Start Tomorrow," *New York Times*, April 20, 1954, 32.

85. C. Wright Mills, "Nothing to Laugh At," *New York Times*, April 25, 1954, BR20. Sterling North's endorsement of *Seduction of the Innocent* appeared in newspaper advertisements for the book. See the *New York Times*, April 26, 1954, 23; Clifton Fadiman to Wertham, Aug. 17, 1954, box 124, folder 3, Wertham Papers. The figure of sixteen thousand sales in six months appears in Carol Tilley's "Seducing the Innocent," in which she notes that Wertham's literary agent actually believed that the doctor's appearance before the subcommittee hampered sales of *Seduction of the Innocent*. See Carol Tilley, "Seducing the Innocent: Fredric Wertham and the Falsifications that Helped Condemn Comics," *Information & Culture* 47, no. 4 (2012): 384.

86. United States Senate Committee on the Judiciary, *Hearings before the Subcommittee to Investigate Juvenile Delinquency*, 83rd Cong., 2nd sess., 1954. In *Seduction of the Innocent*, Wertham drew several comparisons between comic book imagery and Nazism, with most appearing in chapter 4, "The Wrong Twist." One such passage noted, "Comic books read with glee by many children, including very young ones, teach the props of anti-Semitism. There is the book with the story of the 'itch-ray projector,' with illustrations which might be taken directly from Nazi magazines like Streicher's *Stuermer*." Wertham, *Seduction of the Innocent*, 102.

87. *Crime SuspenStories* 22 (EC, 1954)

88. United States Senate Committee on the Judiciary, *Hearings before the Subcommittee to Investigate Juvenile Delinquency*, 83rd Cong., 2nd sess., 1954.

89. For the complete language of the 1954 comics code, see Nyberg, *Seal of Approval*, 166–69.

90. Nyberg, *Seal of Approval*, 123.

91. Wertham to Estes Kefauver, Sept. 21, 1954, box 22, folder 8, Wertham Papers.

92. Wertham, *Seduction of the Innocent*, 351.

CHAPTER FIVE

1. "Crime and Horror Comic Books In Foreign Countries" (incomplete statement for the record), June 4, 1954, box 172, RG 46, NA.

2. "Foreign Opinion Concerning American Comics: Far East," n.d., box 172, RG 46, NA.

3. "Foreign Opinion Concerning American Comics: Near East, South Asia, and Africa," n.d., box 172, RG 46, NA.

4. "Delinquency Fruit of U.S. Education," n.d.; "Iran Papers Report U.S. Hooliganism," n.d.; "U.S. Destroying Latin American Culture," n.d.; and "Europe Satiated with U.S. Vulgarity," n.d., all in box 172, RG 46, NA.

5. United States Senate Committee on the Judiciary, *Hearings before the Subcommittee to Investigate Juvenile Delinquency*, 83rd Cong., 2nd sess., 1954.

6. "Crime and Horror Comic Books in Foreign Countries," June 4, 1954, box 172, RG 46, NA.

7. Chester Bowles, *Ambassador's Report* (New York: Harper & Brothers, 1954), 297; "Foreign Opinion Concerning American Comics: Near East, South Asia, and Africa," n.d., box 172, RG 46, NA.

8. *Captain Marvel Adventures* 140 (Fawcett, 1953).

9. "Jackson Pollock: Is He the Greatest Living Painter in the United States?," *Life*, Aug. 8, 1949, 42; Richard H. King, "The Enigma of Bob Thompson," in *The Hearing Eye: Jazz and Blues Influences in African American Visual Art*, ed. Graham Lock and David Murray (New York: Oxford University Press, 2009).

10. Art patron, collector, and one-time gallery owner Peggy Guggenheim exhibited Jackson Pollock's work in her New York City gallery, Art of This Century, as early as 1943. Richard Pells, *Modernist America: Art, Music, Movies, and the Globalization of American Culture* (New Haven, CT: Yale University Press, 2011), 55.

11. "A *Life* Round Table on Modern Art," *Life*, Oct. 11, 1948, 81.

12. Laura A. Belmonte, *Selling the American Way: U.S. Propaganda and the Cold War* (Philadelphia: University of Pennsylvania Press, 2008), 3–4.

13. For a history of the Marshall Plan, see Michael Hogan, *The Marshall Plan: America, Britain, and the Reconstruction of Western Europe, 1947–1952* (New York: Cambridge University Press, 1989), and Nicolaus Mills, *Winning the Peace: The Marshall Plan and America's Coming of Age as a Superpower* (New York: Wiley, 2008).

14. Cited in Serge Guilbaut, *How New York Stole the Idea of Modern Art: Abstract Expressionism, Freedom, and the Cold War*, trans. Arthur Goldhammer (Chicago: University of Chicago Press, 1983), 128. The French were also unnerved by the 1946

Byrnes-Blum accord, which waived France's wartime debts to the United States in return for certain considerations, one of which compelled the French to screen American films, overriding existing rules that had protected the French film industry. "French Film Head Seeks U.S. Pictures," *New York Times*, Jan. 10, 1946, 29; Guilbaut, *How New York Stole the Idea of Modern Art*, 133–35.

15. Fredric Wertham, *Seduction of the Innocent* (New York: Rinehart), 284.

16. John A. Lent, "The Comics Debate Internationally: Their Genesis, Issues, and Commonalities," in *Pulp Demons: International Dimensions of the Postwar Anti-Comic Book Campaign*, ed. John A. Lent (Madison, NJ: Fairleigh Dickinson University Press, 1999), 27.

17. Richard I. Jobs, "Tarzan under Attack: Youth, Comics, and Cultural Reconstruction in Postwar France," *French Historical Studies* 26, no. 4 (Fall 2003): 688.

18. Cleaves Jones, "Americans in Germany Lead a Strange Life," *Los Angeles Times*, Feb. 26, 1950, B5; Edward A. Morrow, "ECA Underwrites Laughter for Germans; Finances Comic as Well as True Love Tales," *New York Times*, Nov. 6, 1948, 6; Francis J. Bassett, "Comic Books for Germany," *New York Times*, Nov. 11, 1948, 26.

19. United States Senate, *Hearings before the Subcommittee to Investigate Juvenile Delinquency*.

20. Walter L. Hixson, *Parting the Curtain: Propaganda, Culture, and the Cold War, 1945–1961* (New York: St. Martin's Griffin, 1997); Reinhold Wagnleitner, *Coca-Colonization: The Cultural Mission of the United States in Austria after the Second World War* (Chapel Hill: University of North Carolina Press, 1994).

21. Victoria De Grazia, *Irresistible Empire: America's Advance through Twentieth-Century Europe* (Cambridge, MA: Belknap, 2005), 4–5.

22. Guilbaut, *How New York Stole the Idea of Modern Art*, 125.

23. Thomas Borstelmann, *The Cold War and the Color Line: American Race Relations in the Global Arena* (Cambridge, MA: Harvard University Press, 2001), 1.

24. "A Life Round Table on Modern Art," *Life*, Oct. 11, 1949, 79.

25. Despite the seemingly obvious appeal of modern art as a counterpoint to state-sponsored socialist realism, congressional conservatives opposed avant-garde artwork as communist-inspired and anti-American.

26. Belmonte, *Selling the American Way*, 18–19; Taylor Littleton and Maltby Skyes, *Advancing American Art: Painting, Politics, and Cultural Confrontation at Mid-Century* (Tuscaloosa: University of Alabama Press, 1989).

27. Belmonte, *Selling the American Way*, 23, 32–33.

28. Michael J. Hogan, *A Cross of Iron: Harry S. Truman and the Origins of the National Security State, 1945–1954* (New York: Cambridge University Press, 1998).

29. Pells, *Modernist America*, 59.

30. "Export of Culture," *New York Times*, Dec. 4, 1951.

31. Emily Rosenberg, review of *Parting the Curtain: Propaganda, Culture, and the Cold War, 1945–1961*, by Walter Hixson, and *Not like Us: How Europeans Have Loved, Hated, and Transformed American Culture since World War II*, by Richard Pells, *Journal of American History* 84, no. 4 (March 1998): 1576. Outside the United States, the agency was typically referred to as the United States Information Service, as it was thought that the word *agency* connoted intelligence or espionage. For an institu-

tional history of the USIA, see Nicholas J. Cull, *The Cold War and the United States Information Agency* (New York: Cambridge University Press, 2008).

32. Kenneth Osgood, *Total Cold War: Eisenhower's Secret Propaganda Battle at Home and Abroad* (Lawrence: University Press of Kansas, 2006), 89–90.

33. Osgood, *Total Cold War*, 92–98. Under Eisenhower, the USIA produced large amounts of propaganda that could not be attributed directly to the agency or the United States. Indeed, a 1956 report found that a very high percentage of the USIA's output was unattributed propaganda "almost indistinguishable" from similar efforts by the Central Intelligence Agency.

34. Penny M. Von Eschen, *Satchmo Blows Up the World: Jazz Ambassadors Play the Cold War* (Cambridge, MA: Harvard University Press, 2006).

35. Jazz fueled modern visual art—Jackson Pollock's wife, painter Lee Krasner, said her husband listened to jazz "day and night for three days running. . . . He thought it was the only other really creative thing that was happening in this country"—and modern art functioned as a visual representation of jazz's creative freedom. Jazz saxophonist Ornette Coleman believed that "Pollock was in the same state I was in and doing what I was doing" and included an image of Pollock's *White Light* on the cover of his album *Free Jazz*. Pells, *Modernist America*, 55.

36. Richard Kuisel, *Seducing the French: The Dilemma of Americanization* (Berkeley: University of California Press, 1993), 16–17; Guilbaut, *How New York Stole the Idea of Modern Art*, 5.

37. Kuisel, *Seducing the French*, ix, 3.

38. Brian Angus McKenzie, *Remaking France: Americanization, Public Diplomacy, and the Marshall Plan* (New York: Berghahn Books, 2005), 21.

39. France received the largest share of continental assistance under the Marshall Plan, at $2.9 billion. See McKenzie, *Remaking France*, 21.

40. McKenzie, *Remaking France*, 206–7.

41. McKenzie, *Remaking France*, 96.

42. In 1957, *Le Figaro* had a circulation of 486,500 copies, and *Le Monde* had a circulation of 211,500 copies. *Le journal de Mickey* sold 633,000 copies per issue. Jobs, "Tarzan under Attack," 690.

43. J. L. Brown, "A Report from France," *New York Times*, Nov. 11, 1945, 104.

44. Marjorie Fischer, "A Report from Overseas," *New York Times*, Nov. 10, 1946, G3, G59.

45. Pascal Ory, "Mickey Go Home! La désaméricanisation de la bande dessinée (1945–1950)," *Vingtième Siècle* 4 (Oct. 1984): 77–88.

46. "Special Anti-American Communist Publication in France," Nov. 2, 1951, box 2387, RG 59, NA.

47. Jobs, "Tarzan under Attack," 693.

48. Jobs, "Tarzan under Attack," 700. Legman was a self-described folklorist and independent scholar who in 1949 published *Love and Death*, in which he argued that American society simultaneously repressed sexual expression and tolerated graphic displays of violence. In *Love and Death*, Legman attacked violent comic books as harmful to young readers. However, his assertion that violent comic books were a response to repressed sexuality made his work less palatable to the general public

than that of Fredric Wertham. See Gershon Legman, *Love and Death: A Study in Censorship* (New York: Breaking Point, 1949).

49. The French anti–comic book crusaders and policy makers conflated American comic books, with their shocking images and themes, with comparatively benign American comic strips of characters like Mickey Mouse and Tarzan. Some of the most popular French comic publications, like *Le journal de Mickey*, were not comic books in the traditional sense but collections of translated comic strips. See Maurice C. Horn, "American Comics in France: A Cultural Evaluation," in *For Better or Worse: The American Influence in the World*, ed. Allen F. Davis (Westport, CT: Greenwood Press, 1981), 49–60.

50. Jobs persuasively argues that the French anti–comic book campaign was about more than the contents of imported comic books, such as the construction of a new national identity and the status of French culture in a world dominated by the United States, though he does see the debate as strictly a domestic one. Jobs, "Tarzan under Attack," 688.

51. Jobs, "Tarzan under Attack," 701.

52. Jobs, "Tarzan under Attack," 695.

53. The Communist Party actually voted against the final bill, despite its earlier support, because it was insufficiently anti-American. McKenzie, *Remaking France*, 218.

54. Jobs, "Tarzan under Attack," 705.

55. This was inaccurate, as the commission did not have the power to ban publications. It was, however, able to recommend prosecution of offending publishers.

56. Dean Acheson to American Embassy in Paris, July 14, 1950; Paris to Secretary of State, July 17, 1950, box 5951, RG 59, NA.

57. Memorandum, Jan. 4, 1951; "French Legislation to Restrict Amount of Foreign Material In Children's Publications," Jan. 18, 1951, box 5951, RG 59, NA.

58. Bonsal to Secretary of State, Feb. 1, 1951, box 5951, RG 59, NA.

59. Martin Barker, *A Haunt of Fears: The Strange History of the British Horror Comics Campaign* (Jackson: University Press of Mississippi, 1992), 8.

60. Martin Barker, "Getting a Conviction: Or, How the British Horror Comics Campaign Only Just Succeeded," in Lent, *Pulp Demons*, 70–71; Barker, *A Haunt of Fears*, 18, 27.

61. *The Lure of the Comics*, box 112, folder 6, Wertham Papers.

62. Barker, *A Haunt of Fears*, 20–35.

63. Barker, *A Haunt of Fears*, 18.

64. Barker, "Getting a Conviction," 71–72.

65. Barker, *A Haunt of Fears*, 42.

66. The British anti–comic book campaign never received the same level of publicity as its American counterpart. *The Times* documented the growing controversy over violent comic books and the subsequent passage of anti–comic book legislation. It did not, though, run the sort of hysterical, anti–comic book stories and editorials that appeared by the dozens in American newspapers. I have found no evidence that any British newspaper opposed the anti–comic book campaign or the passage of the 1955 Children and Young Persons (Harmful Publications) Bill, but an absence of opposition is not the same as evidence of support. Still, the British public

and policy establishment paid sufficient attention to the anti–comic book campaign to pass that bill.

67. Barker, *A Haunt of Fears*, 49–55.

68. "Crime and Horror Comic Books in Foreign Countries," June 4, 1954, box 172, RG 46, NA.

69. "Copy of Clipping," Oct. 13, 1954, box 119, folder 3, Wertham Papers.

70. Wertham did not, however, accept an invitation from Mauger to visit Britain in support of the effort. See Fredric Wertham to Peter Mauger, Jan. 7, 1955, box 112, folder 6, Wertham Papers.

71. "Editor, The London Times," July 24, 1952, box 112, folder 6, Wertham Papers.

72. Wertham to Mauger, June 22, 1952, box 112, folder 7, Wertham Papers.

73. H. E. Forbes to Wertham, Nov. 16, 1954, box 112, folder 6, Wertham Papers. In his correspondence, Wertham offered to send a copy of *Seduction of the Innocent* to Lloyd George.

74. Children and Young Persons (Harmful Publications) Bill, box 119, folder 3, Wertham Papers.

CHAPTER SIX

1. "Churchill Sailing Put Off to Today," *New York Times*, Dec. 31, 1951, 1.

2. *Murderous Gangsters* 1 (Avon, 1951).

3. *Complete Love* 1 (Avon, 1951).

4. *Two-Fisted Tales* 25 (EC, 1952).

5. Seth Fein, "New Empire into Old: Making Mexican Newsreels the Cold War Way," *Diplomatic History* 28 (Nov. 2004): 704.

6. Wherever possible, I provide printing or distribution dates and locations for propaganda comic books. But many if not all of these titles were produced for a variety of countries at different times and in different places. It is difficult to trace the bureaucratic histories of these comics, as the available archival evidence is incomplete and scattered. The dates and locations cited may not be the very first for a particular title.

7. John Fousek, *To Lead the Free World: American Nationalism and the Cultural Roots of the Cold War* (Chapel Hill: University of North Carolina Press, 2000), 2, 7–8. See also Lyn Gorman and David McLean, *Media and Society into the 21st Century* (Malden, MA: Wiley-Blackwell, 2009), 113–15.

8. Laura A. Belmonte, *Selling the American Way: U.S. Propaganda and the Cold War* (Philadelphia: University of Pennsylvania Press, 2008), 3–4. See also Penny Von Eschen, *Satchmo Blows Up the World: Jazz Ambassadors Play the Cold War* (Cambridge, MA: Harvard University Press, 2006); and Reinhold Wagnleitner, *Coca-Colonization and the Cold War: The Cultural Mission of the United States in Austria after the Second World War* (Chapel Hill: University of North Carolina Press, 1994).

9. Reinhold Wagnleitner, "The Irony of American Culture Abroad: Austria and the Cold War," in *Recasting America: Culture and Politics in the Age of Cold War*, ed. Lary May (Chicago: University of Chicago Press, 1989), 285–303. Wagnleitner notes that American mass culture or "consensus culture" contained a significant con-

tradiction: while it initially encouraged homogeneity and corporatization, it also sparked the creation of critical and alternative types of culture like jazz, avant-garde art, and rock 'n' roll. Nan Enstad also argues that mass culture in the form of pulp fiction and clothing can have a radicalizing effect on consumers. Nan Enstad, *Ladies of Labor, Girls of Adventure: Working Women, Popular Culture, and Labor Politics at the Turn of the Twentieth Century* (New York: Columbia University Press, 1999).

10. Quoted in Walter L. Hixson, *Parting the Red Curtain: Propaganda, Culture, and the Cold War, 1945–1961* (New York: Palgrave Macmillan, 1997), 14.

11. Quoted in Frances Stonor Saunders, *The Cultural Cold War: The CIA and the World of Arts and Letters* (New York: New Press, 1999), 148.

12. Walter Schwinn to Harvey Lehrbas, "Comic Books," April 4, 1949, box 6, PEC NA.

13. Fredric Wertham, *Seduction of the Innocent* (New York: Rinehart, 1954), chap. 11.

14. John L. Dunning to Lloyd A. Free, July 29, 1949, box 6, PEC NA.

15. "Magazine Collection for Foreign Distribution: An Important Auxiliary of the Campaign of Truth," n.d., box 6, PEC NA.

16. Expanded International Information and Education Program, *Hearings before the Senate Foreign Relations Committee*, 81st Cong., 2nd Sess., July 5–7, 1950, 160–61. Cited in Belmonte, *Selling the American Way*, 44.

17. *Fight Comics* 36 (Fiction House, 1945).

18. *Fight Comics* 50 (Fiction House, 1947).

19. J. Edgar Hoover, "How Good a Parent Are You?," *Los Angeles Times*, April 20, 1947, E4.

20. *T-Man Comics* 3 (Quality, 1952).

21. Bartow Underhill to John Begg, "Project no. 114-Comic Book Technique," Feb. 23, 1950, Underhill to Begg, "Proposed Article in Advertising Agent Magazine," March 13, 1950, both in box 7, PEC NA.

22. Underhill to Begg, "Project no. 114-Comic Book Technique," Feb. 23, 1950, box 7, PEC NA.

23. "Use Made of U.S.I.E. Material in French Press," March 1, 1950, box 2387, RG 59, NA.

24. Wertham, *Seduction of the Innocent*, 125.

25. Underhill to Begg, "Comic Books," April 28, 1949, box 6, PEC NA. Emphasis in the original.

26. Wertham, *Seduction of the Innocent*, 220.

27. Underhill to Begg, "Project No. 114—Comic Book Technique," April 5, 1950; Harvey Zorbaugh to Underhill, April 21, 1950, both in box 7, PEC NA.

28. "Report No. 5" by Morrill Cody, American Embassy, Paris, Dec. 26, 1951, p. 9, box 6, PEC NA.

29. "Report No. 5" by Morrill Cody, p. 9.

30. Odd Arne Westad, *The Global Cold War: Third World Interventions and the Making of Our Times* (New York: Cambridge University Press, 2007).

31. Marc Trachtenberg, *A Constructed Peace: The Making of the European Settlement, 1945–1963* (Princeton, NJ: Princeton University Press, 1999); Thomas Borstel-

mann, *The Cold War and the Color Line: American Race Relations in the Global Arena* (Cambridge, MA: Harvard University Press, 2001), 1–5.

32. Underhill to Malcolm W. Ater, Dec. 8, 1949, box 7, PEC NA.

33. Begg to Underhill, "General Comics," May 10, 1949, box 6, PEC NA.

34. John L. Dunning to Lloyd A. Free, July 20, 1949, box 7, PEC NA. Emphasis in the original.

35. Unknown to Walter Schwinn, March 14, 1949, box 6, PEC NA.

36. Frank Ninkovich, *The Diplomacy of Ideas: U.S. Foreign Policy and Cultural Relations, 1938–1950* (New York: Cambridge University Press, 1981). For a discussion of the differences between "cultural diplomacy" and "informational diplomacy," see Emily Rosenberg, *Spreading the American Dream: American Economic and Cultural Expansion, 1890–1945* (New York: Hill and Wang, 1982), 214–16.

37. "The Cartoon Book Program in Latin America," May 22, 1963, box 4, folder 3, Keller Papers.

38. Dunning to Free, July 29, 1949, box 6, PEC NA.

39. "Address by Mr. John M. Begg, Director of Private Enterprise Cooperation," Feb. 27, 1951, box 7, PEC NA.

40. Nicholas J. Cull, *The Cold War and the United States Information Agency* (New York: Cambridge University Press, 2008), 56–57.

41. Underhill to Begg, "Project No. 114—Comic Book Technique," April 5, 1950, box 7, PEC NA.

42. Jack C. McDermott to Ater, Feb. 21, 1949; Ater to McDermott, May 3, 1949, both in box 3, Ater Papers. Ater was also in communication with Bartow H. Underhill of the State Department's Press and Publications Division at this time.

43. McDermott to Ater, May 5, 1949, box 3, Ater Papers. I was not able to find the name of the company that did win this contract or able to read the finished comic.

44. Cull, *The Cold War*, 54–56. For a rigorous and useful review of the USIA, its predecessor agencies, and the relationship between domestic and international Cold War propaganda, see Kenneth Osgood, *Total Cold War: Eisenhower's Secret Propaganda Battle at Home and Abroad* (Lawrence: University Press of Kansas, 2006).

45. Dunning to Ater, Nov. 9, 1950, box 3, Ater Papers.

46. United States International Information Administration, 1954–1955 Mission Prospectus, Paris, France, n.d., box 1, General and Classified Subject Files of the USIA Office, 1946–55, Paris Embassy, Record Group 84, National Archives, College Park, MD (hereafter cited as Paris Embassy).

47. Untitled "Little Moe" Comic Strips, 1953, box 54, Paris Embassy.

48. For an overview of the strategic and political processes behind the creation and acceptance of NSC-68, see John Lewis Gaddis, *Strategies of Containment: A Critical Appraisal of American National Security Policy during the Cold War* (New York: Oxford University Press, 2005), 80--115.

49. "USIE Newsletter," June 1951, box 3, folder 29; E. White to R. Busick, Jan. 16, 1953, box 2, folder 24, both in Keller Papers. For titles and production totals of other comic books produced at the Far East Regional Production Center, see "Projects Originated by RPC," n.d., box 3, folder 28, Keller Papers.

50. *Cracks in the Iron Curtain*, 1951, box 6, USIA Press and Publications, Record Group 306, National Archives, College Park, MD (hereafter cited as Press and Publications NA).

51. *Crime Does Not Pay 55* (Lev Gleason, 1947).

52. *Crime Does Not Pay 59* (Lev Gleason, 1948).

53. "Pamphlets: The Free World Speaks," n.d., box 9, Press and Publications NA.

54. Ater to Jack Iams, Nov. 16, 1951; Iams to Ater, Nov. 21, 1951, box 3, Ater Papers.

55. *Korea My Home* (n.d.); *The Korea Story* (n.d.), box 12, Press and Publications NA.

56. Ater to Iams, Nov. 16, 1951; Iams to Ater, Nov. 2, 1951, box 3, Ater Papers.

57. "Eight Great Americans," July 20, 1953, box 7, PEC NA.

58. "Cooperation with Coca-Cola Export Corporation," Jan. 14, 1951; Carl Stevens to Underhill and M. Philip Copp, July 26, 1951; and "Coca Cola Export Corporation Pamphlets," Aug. 8, 1951, all in box 6, PEC NA.

59. Osgood, *Total Cold War*, 7–8. For a discussion of a postwar controversy over Coca-Cola in France, during which communists attempted to bar its importation, see Richard Kuisel, *Seducing the French: The Dilemma of Americanization* (Berkeley: University of California Press, 1996), 52–69. Reinhold Wagnleitner offers a different perspective on Coca-Cola in postwar Europe, suggesting that the beverage received a relatively warm welcome in Austria, at least in comparison with more elite forms of American culture. See Wagnleitner, *Coca-Colonization*, 277.

60. *Communism and the Family* (1951); *Communism and the Farmer* (1952); and *Communism and Religion* (n.d.), all in box 3, Press and Publications NA.

61. Available evidence does not indicate which methods were used to distribute *Eight Great Americans*.

62. Leo Janos, "The Last Days of the President," *Atlantic*, July 1973.

63. Lansdale had earned a reputation for waging successful anticommunist insurgencies during the 1950s, when he worked with Philippine president Ramon Magsaysay against the Hukbalahap guerillas. However, the CIA deemed his plans for Cuba implausible and considered him "a nut." Presumably, it was his reputation for past successes that led to his position of authority within Operation Mongoose. Aleksandr Fursenko and Timothy Naftali, *One Hell of a Gamble: Khrushchev, Castro, and Kennedy, 1958–1964* (New York: W. W. Norton, 1997), 144–45.

64. Quoted in Fursenko and Naftali, *One Hell of a Gamble*, 150.

65. Phillip Brenner, "Cuba and the Missile Crisis," *Journal of Latin American Studies* 22 (1990): 118–20. For another perspective on Operation Mongoose, see David C. Martin, *Wilderness of Mirrors: Intrigue, Deception, and the Secrets That Destroyed Two of the Cold War's Most Important Agents* (Guilford, CT: Lyons Press, 2003), 126–44.

66. Memorandum from the United States Information Agency Operations Officer for Operation Mongoose (Wilson) to the Chief of Operations, Operation Mongoose (Lansdale), July 20, 1962, *Foreign Relations of the United States, 1961–1963*, vol. 10, 857 (hereafter cited as *FRUS 1961–1963*, vol. 10).

67. "The Cartoon Book Program in Latin America," May 22, 1963, box 4, folder 3, Keller Papers; Memorandum from the Chief of Operations, Operation Mongoose (Lansdale) to the Special Group (Augmented), July 25, 1962, *FRUS 1961–1963*, vol. 10, 879.

68. *FRUS 1961–1963*, vol. 10, 858–59.

69. *El despertar* (n.d.), box 1, Press and Publications NA.

70. Fursenko and Naftali, *One Hell of a Gamble*, 320, 329.

71. Jeffrey F. Taffet, *Foreign Aid as Foreign Policy: The Alliance for Progress in Latin America* (New York: Routledge, 2007). See also Stephen G. Rabe, *The Most Dangerous Area in the World: John F. Kennedy Confronts Communist Revolution in Latin America* (Chapel Hill: University of North Carolina Press, 1999).

72. "The Cartoon Book Program in Latin America," May 22, 1963; "Cartoon Book Program Report," March 19, 1964; and "Cartoon Books and Fotonovelas," n.d., all in box 4, folder 30, Keller Papers.

73. "The Cartoon Book Program in Latin America," Keller Papers.

74. "The Cartoon Book Program in Latin America," Keller Papers; "A Punha-lada," July 1962, box 20, Press and Publications NA.

75. Stuart Hall, "Notes on Deconstructing 'the Popular,'" in *Cultural Theory and Popular Culture: A Reader*, ed. John Storey (Harlow, UK: Pearson, 1998), 227–39.

CHAPTER SEVEN

1. Carl Burgos, Bill Everett, Paul Gustavson, and Ben Thompson, *Marvel Masterworks: Golden Age Marvel Comics* (New York: Marvel Comics, 2011), n.n.

2. *Marvel Comics 1* (Marvel, 1939).

3. Sean Howe, *Marvel Comics: The Untold Story* (New York: HarperCollins, 2012), 24–25.

4. In 1942, George Hecht, publisher of fact-based titles like *True Comics* and *Real Heroes*, issued a similar comic book specifically aimed at adults. Titled *Comics Digest*, the cover of the inaugural issue emphasized that it was "for the millions of adults who read comic books." In an open letter on the first page, Hecht reiterated, "Nearly everybody reads the comics—old and young alike! They are America's best-loved kind of reading." *Comics Digest* 1 (1942), box 2, VCU Comic Arts Collection. For documents describing the popularity of comic books among adults, see E. R. Ross to Rex Stout, June 21, 1943; William DeGrouchy to Stout, June 29, 1943; and "Extract from Minutes of July 7," n.d., all in box 11, WWB Papers. For additional government documents on the popularity of comic books, see *Readership of Comics Magazines Among 1021 Girls and Boys in Providence, R.I. and Buffalo, N.Y.*, box 211, RG 46, NA.

5. "Review of Comic Magazines," March 30, 1943; unknown to Frederica Barach, April 21, 1943; and Ross to Stout, June 21, 1943, all in box 11, WWB Papers.

6. Marya Mannes, "Junior Has a Craving," *New Republic*, Feb. 17, 1947, 22; "How Do the Comics Affect Your Child," box 109, folder 12, Wertham Papers; "Superman's Dilemma," *Time*, April 13, 1942, 78; and Jean-Paul Gabilliet, *Of Comics and Men: A Cultural History of American Comic Books* (Jackson: University Press of Mississippi, 2010), 29.

7. "Fact Sheet on Comic Magazines," n.d., box 167, RG 46, NA.

8. Abraham Reisman, "It's Stan Lee's Universe," *Vulture*, accessed May 5, 2017, http://www.vulture.com/2016/02/stan-lees-universe-c-v-r.html.

9. Kirby, Lee, and the Marvel team must have begun work on the issue many months prior. In it, the members of the Fantastic Four use an experimental rocket

to beat the Soviets into space. The Soviet Union, though, launched the first manned spaceflight months earlier in April 1961 when it sent cosmonaut Yuri Gagarin aloft in his *Vostok* space capsule.

10. Hope M. Harrison, *Driving the Soviets Up the Wall: Soviet-East German Relations, 1953–1961* (Princeton, NJ: Princeton University Press, 2003); Frederick Kemp, *Berlin 1961: Kennedy, Khrushchev, and the Most Dangerous Place on Earth* (Berkeley: University of California Press, 2012); Marc Trachtenberg, *A Constructed Peace: The Making of the European Settlement, 1945–1963* (Princeton, NJ: Princeton University Press, 1999).

11. *Fantastic Four* 1 (Marvel, 1961).

12. *Fantastic Four* 4 (Marvel, 1962).

13. See chapter 3 for a discussion of *Donald Duck's Atom Bomb*.

14. *Donald Duck's Atom Bomb*, Cheerios Premium Y1 (Disney, 1947).

15. *Fantastic Four* 21 (Marvel, 1963).

16. *Journey into Mystery* 117 (Marvel, 1965).

17. *Frontline Combat* 2 (EC, 1951).

18. *Journey into Mystery* 93 (Marvel, 1963).

19. *The H-Bomb and You* (Malcolm Ater, 1955).

20. *Marvel Tales Annual* 1 (Marvel, 1964).

21. Cited in Howe, *Marvel Comics*, 54. Howe has conducted a remarkable amount of research on the history of Marvel and is one of very few scholars or writers to be given access to some of the company's internal records.

22. For excellent histories of the Soviet decision-making leading up to the crisis and of the crisis itself, see Aleksandr Fursenko and Timothy Naftali, *One Hell of a Gamble: Khrushchev, Castro, and Kennedy, 1958–1964* (New York: W. W. Norton, 1997), and Fursenko and Naftali, *Khrushchev's Cold War: The Inside Story of an American Adversary* (New York: W. W. Norton, 2006).

23. *Tales of Suspense* 41 (Marvel, 1963).

24. *Tales of Suspense* 39 (Marvel, 1962).

25. This is a play on the now-famous phrase, "With great power comes great responsibility," that appeared in the first Spider-Man story.

26. *Amazing Spider-Man* 13 (Marvel, 1964).

27. Howe, *Marvel Comics*, 97.

28. *Strange Tales* 136 (Marvel, 1965).

CONCLUSION

1. "Comics Committee Progress Report," May 15, 1944, box 11, WWB Papers. See also Thomas Howell, "The Writers' War Board: U.S. Domestic Propaganda in World War II," *Historian* 59 (1997): 803–4.

2. Mike Benton, *Superhero Comics of the Golden Age: The Illustrated History* (Dallas: Taylor Publishing, 1992), 55.

3. Joe Simon and Jim Simon, *The Comic Book Makers* (Lebanon, NJ: Vanguard Productions, 2003), 72.

4. "Fugitive from Atom Finds Idyllic Life," *Washington Post*, April 18, 1948, B2.

INDEX

Wertham, Fredric (*continued*)
academics/scholars and, 128, 176,
221; and the anti–comic book cru-
sade/campaign, 28, 158; background
and life history, 169; Britain and, 198,
208, 313n70; censorship and, 16, 175,
179, 208, 269, 272; characterizations
of, 16, 158, 269; CMAA and, 189–90,
247, 265; on comic book advertisements, 155, 171, 304n5; on comics as
providing a "map for crime," 84–85;
"The Comics . . . Very Funny," 169,
171–72, 306n38; correspondence,
86, 128, 157, 158, 160, 169, 189f, 208,
304n7, 307n58; Norman Cousins
and, 306n38; on delinquency, 84,
157, 173, 176, 178; expert testimony, 160–61, 172, 184–85; on fascist
superheroes, 177; on foreign policy
issues, 265, 271; Frank and, 307n55;
Bill Gaines and, 185, 191; in historical context, 16; "How did Nietzsche
get into the nursery?," 177; *Howdy
Doody* and, 173, 174f; interviews with
criminals, 153, 155, 183–84; Harold
Kennedy and, 179; Kildale and, 86;
Koslow and, 155, 157, 304n3, 304n5;
legacy, 16, 269; legislation proposed
by, 175; Mauger and, 208, 313n70;
on Nazism, 308n86; photograph of,
156f; on racial issues, 155–57, 160–61,
169, 173, 174f, 175, 178, 180, 183–85,
190, 197, 208, 265, 271; research, 16,
169, 176; Shuster and, 155. See also
Seduction of the Innocent (Wertham)
When the Communists Came, 227–28
whipping, 155, 217. See also bullwhips
White characters: attractiveness, 267; as
victims of violence, 80
Whiteness: popular culture as the ultimate arbiter of, 293n50; the power
of, 66
White Princess of the Jungle, 181
White supremacy, 40, 160, 180–81, 215.
See also racial superiority
whitewashed comic books, 171, 266
whitewashing: romance, 110–13; wartime, 110–12

"Wild Spree of the Laughing Sadist,
The—Herman Duker" (*Crime Does
Not Pay*), 94
Williams, Hank, 106
Wings Comics, 43, 68, 82, 265, 292n30;
circulation, 297n16; covers, 82, 83f;
Eastern Color Printing Company
and, 297n16; readership, 83f
Winters, Murray, 179–80
women: Asian, 216, 218; heroic, 30,
66, 98, 298n44. See also crimes by
women; gender roles; romance;
sexuality
women's liberation, 297n24
Wonder Woman, 36, 66, 270, 298n44
Wonder Woman, 66, 67f, 275
"Wonder Women of History" (*Wonder
Woman*), 66, 67f
Wood, Bob, 24, 89, 97
Woodard, Isaac, 180–81
World War II, 39, 166, 180, 270; aftermath, 3–4, 6–7 (*see also* Cold War);
attack on Pearl Harbor, 40, 50–51, 89;
Blacks and, 39, 62–65, 65f; Chinese
characters and, 56, 57, 59–61, 60f;
contrasted with Cold War, 113;
contributions of non-White people
in, 39, 57; *Estados Unidos en la guerra*
(The United States in the war), 70,
71f, 72; Fawcett Publications and,
140–41; Gleason and, 89, 162; OIAA
and, 74, 113, 224; patriotism during,
7, 8, 29, 42, 114, 133, 228–29, 243–44,
246, 277; racism and, 7, 29, 30, 39, 73,
110–11; reasons Americans agreed to
fight in, 295n89; steps for the Allies
to win, 50; US government's use of
popular culture to win, 10; wartime
whitewashing, 110–12. See also
fascism; Japan during World War II;
Writers' War Board (WWB)
World War III, 119, 143
Writers' War Board (WWB), 7–8, 36,
40–42, 64, 69–70, 73, 118, 132, 157,
185, 214, 244, 257, 264, 289n1, 291n24,
292n44; *Air Ace* and, 57, 136; *Captain
Marvel Jr.* and, 57, 62; China and, 57,
60–61; dissolution, 74, 80; fascism